Adventure Guide

Puerto Vallarta

& Vicinity

Adventure Guide

Puerto Vallarta
& Vicinity

Vivien Lougheed

HUNTER

HUNTER PUBLISHING, INC,
130 Campus Drive, Edison, NJ 08818
732-225-1900; 800-255-0343; fax 732-417-1744
www.hunterpublishing.com

Ulysses Travel Publications
4176 Saint-Denis, Montréal, Québec
Canada H2W 2M5
514-843-9882, ext. 2232; fax 514-843-9448

Windsor Books
The Boundary, Wheatley Road, Garsington
Oxford, OX44 9EJ England
01865-361122; fax 01865-361133

ISBN 10: 1-58843-594-6
ISBN 13: 978-1-58843-594-1

*This and other Hunter guides are available as e-books
in a variety of formats through our online partners, including
Netlibrary.com, Amazon.com and BarnesandNoble.com.*

Cover photo: Hotel Descondido, Puerto Vallarta
© Larry Dunmire/Superstock
Index by: Mary Ellen McGrath

Maps by Kim André, © 2007 Hunter Publishing, Inc.

1   2   3   4

www.hunterpublishing.com

Hunter's full range of guides to all corners of the globe is featured on our website. You'll find guidebooks to suit every type of traveler, no matter what their budget, lifestyle, or idea of fun.

Adventure Guides – There are now over 40 titles in this series, covering destinations from Costa Rica and the Yucatán to Tampa Bay & Florida's West Coast, Canada's Atlantic Provinces and the Alaska Highway. Complete with information on what to do, as well as where to stay and eat, *Adventure Guides* are tailor-made for the active traveler, with all the practical travel information you need, as well as details of the best places for hiking, biking, canoeing, horseback riding, trekking, skiing, watersports, and all other kinds of fun.

Alive Guides – This ever-popular line of books takes a unique look at the best each destination offers: fine dining, jazz clubs, first-class hotels and resorts. In-margin icons direct the reader at a glance. Top-sellers include *St. Martin & St. Barts*, *The US Virgin Islands* and *Aruba, Bonaire & Curaçao*.

One-of-a-kind travel books available from Hunter include *Best Dives of the Caribbean; London A-Z; A Traveler's Guide to the Galapagos Islands* and many more.

Full descriptions are given for each book at www.hunterpublishing.com, along with reviewers' comments and a cover image. You can also view pages and the table of contents. Books may be purchased on-line via our secure transaction facility.

Photo Credits

We are grateful to the following companies and organizations who allowed use of their photos in this book.

Vallarta Adventures: Pages 23, 71, 91, 130.

Chicos Dive Shop: Pages 119, 120, 122.

Puerto Vallarta Tourism: Pages 10, 19, 29, 54, 101, 105, 115, 116, 118, 122, 123, 126, 134, 135, 175.

The Author, Vivien Lougheed: Pages 4, 15, 39, 51, 53, 111, 119, 157, 203, 221.

All other images credit as shown.

Contents

MAPS

DEDICATION

This book is for Joy, Donna,
Iris and Heather,
Cinco mujeres bonitas.

Introduction

The lure of isolated beaches rimmed with palm trees brought John Huston to Puerto Vallarta in the 1960s to film *Night of the Iguana*. His cast included Elizabeth Taylor and Richard Burton. While working, the two fell in love. Richard bought Elizabeth a house similar to his own that was perched on the

side of a hill overlooking Bandera Bay. The houses were across the road from each other. The couple then built a walkway between the two places so they could visit each other more discreetly. Elizabeth left Eddie Fisher, her husband at the time, and married Burton. Their story became one of the great love stories of that century.

This romance resulted in thousands of people swarming to the shores of Mexico's west coast in search of sun, sand, palm trees and love. Some even came looking for iguanas. The Mexicans soon realized the potential of tourism and, with the help of international companies, built a first-class infrastructure of hotels, shops and restaurants around the bay.

However, not all visitors wanted what had been built, so they moved up and down the coast to little villages where they could ride horses or donkeys, snorkel among the tropical fish, trek in the jungle looking for exotic birds and animals, watch cliff divers perform or just lay where it was quiet and sip on tequila.

In the jungles along the shore, Mexicans built viewing stations connected by cables where tourists could swing like monkeys while looking for exotic birds and strange amphibians. The usual adjustments took place. Some Mexicans and tourists didn't like the environmental effects caused by chasing around in motorboats looking for big fish, building hotels on the beach, and bungee jumping off bridges. Ecologically-sensitive practices were followed so that wildlife was protected. Garbage was picked up and pollution-control devices were put on vehicles. They left some of the jungle in its wild state and planted flowers in their gardens. More people came.

Today, the west coast of Mexico is as popular as ever. This is because it offers every possible recreational activity, suitable for almost any skill level and budget. The area has both economical and lush accommodations. The food is safe to eat and the bottled water, found in every hotel hallway, grocery store and café is safe to drink. The crime rate is low in tourist areas and the locals are friendly, though the usual pressures of tourism often show. But the best draw of all is that the price for a comparable vacation in any other tropical paradise is about twice what it is here.

The best time to visit the Pacific coast of Mexico is between November and May, when humidity and temperatures are down. This is when most North American and European countries are cold. It is also when the whales move south looking for warmer waters and when the migratory birds are passing by on their way to winter nesting grounds.

But Mexico also has lots to offer during the summer. The Sierra Madres butt up against the ocean, offering relief from the heat just a few hours away by car or public bus. At higher elevations, muscle-powered sports like hiking or cycling are possible any time of year. Museums in the state capitals offer endless intellectual stimulation and the live entertainment often found in towns and city plazas is enthralling. There are ruins to visit and architecture to admire, history to relive and exotic foods to taste.

The city of Puerto Vallarta is spread around the **Bahai de Banderas**, a sandy bay with a backdrop of the Sierra Madres. The town is divided by the **Cuale River**, and everything is referred to as being either north or south of the river.

The airport is about four miles/seven km north of the Cuale River. Just south of the airport, large hotels, condominiums and resorts line the beach and main drag, along with restaurants, souvenir shops, dress shops, shoe shops, Internet cafés, night clubs, juice shops, tour agencies, massage parlors, car rentals and time-share hawkers.

East of the beach, residential homes climb the hills, dotting the lush vegetation with white-plastered walls and red-tiled roofs. This is where Elizabeth Taylor and Richard Burton first shared their love for each other. Ever since, millions of tourists have come to PV looking for the same type of romance.

WARNING: Puerto Vallarta has been a travel destination for a long time. The town has grown and changed. At one time, it wasn't safe to walk down the beach at night after you'd had a couple of drinks. However, the government has made the city safe for visitors by posting tourist police around town. As tourism increased, the occasional (and it takes only one in a thousand) visitor has behaved in a way that has been anything but commendable. They have been drunk, abusive, rude or insensitive to a Catholic culture. This has resulted in some locals losing their fondness for tourists. I was called a cheap Canadian because I wouldn't pay US $20 for a child's baseball cap. Bus drivers have taken tourists on goose chases – this happened to me and to others I spoke with. The timeshare salesmen are a big nuisance, though they are just trying to earn a living. If this type of treatment is going to bother you, do not go to PV; try someplace like Manzanillo or Mazatlan that hasn't been so inundated with visitors, or take an all-inclusive package and stay at your hotel.

HISTORY

Anywhere I go I want to know who was there before me. I want to know their stories.

20,000 BC Icepack in North America recedes and land bridge is formed between Asia and North America.

12,000 BC Mesoamerica is populated.

8000 BC Agriculture is practiced in Mexico.

5000 BC Corn is cultivated in Southern Mexico.

3000 BC Pit houses are constructed.

2300 BC Pottery replaces stone dishes.

1700 BC Olmecs and Totonacs become powerful. They develop hieroglyphics.

600 BC Olmecs disappear.

700 AD Teotihuacans gain power in Mexico.

Signs of the Teotihuacans are visible today in original rock and wall paintings.

1100 AD Maya living in Mexico disappear and Aztecs become ruling group.

1517	Diego Velasquez and Francisco Fernandez de Cordoba start exploration of Mexico, and were followed by Hernan Cortez.
1519	Aztec chiefs and thousands of civilians are killed by Cortez.
1524	Francisco Cortez de San Buenaventura came to the bay and started to explore the area.
1528	Antonio de Mendoza became the first viceroy of New Spain.
1535	Luis de Velasco becomes a harsh ruler. This is the beginning of 300 years of Spanish rule in America.
1810	Miguel Hidalgo inspires peasants to start the War of Independence and on September 16th, they succeeded.
1821	Agustine de Iturbide declares Mexico a nation with independent rule and himself emperor.
1824	A Constitution is adopted.
1836	Antonio Lopez Santa Anna is president and leads war against United States, but after his capture, Texas is seceded to the US.
1841	The village of Las Peñas was founded by Don Pedro de Alvarado, although it was habited by locals for over 600 years before that.
1854	Benito Juarez overthrew Santa Anna from office and made himself president.
1864	French succeed to take over Mexico and put Maximilian into power.
1869	Juarez and followers throw Maximilian from power.
1876	Porfirio Diaz comes to power and the economy flourishes.
1910	Francisco I. Madero overthrows Diaz.
1911	Victoriano Huerta succeeds Madero after his death.

1914	Francisco (Pancho) Villa, Alvaro Obregon, Venustiano Carranza and Emiliano Zapata, with the help of the Americans, brings down Huerta's government.
1917	Present Constitution is drawn up.
1918	The name of the area is changed from Las Piñas to Puerto Vallarta.
1928	Obregon assassinated.
1930s	Lazaro Cardenas rules and implements land reform, education for all and nationalized petroleum industry.
1940s	Pan American Highway constructed.
1982	Miguel de la Madrid comes to power but, due to world oil crises, country falls into debt.
1988	Carlos Salinas de Gorari wins election and signs NAFTA.
1994	Zapatistas capture many small villages in Chiapas.
2000	Vincente Fox comes to power under the National Action Pary (PAN), putting PRI's 71-year rule to an end.

POLITICAL PARTIES

The three main parties active today are the **National Action Party** (PAN) headed by Vincente Fox, the **Institutional Revolutionary Party** (PRI) that is headed by Francisco Labastida, and the **Party of the Democratic Revolution** (PRD), headed by Cuauhtemoc Cardenas.

GOVERNMENT

The **United Mexican States** is the official name of the country commonly known as Mexico. The capital of the country is **Mexico City**. Mexico is a federal republic with 31 administrative divisions called states.

States of Mexico

N

1. Baja California Sur
2. Baja Sur
3. Sonora
4. Chihuahua
5. Sinaloa
6. Durango
7. Coahuila
8. Nuevo León
9. Zacatecas
10. Tamaulipas
11. Nayarit
12. Aquascalientes
13. San Luis Potosi
14. Jalisco
15. Guanajuato
16. Querétaro
17. Hidalgo
18. Veracruz
19. Colima
20. Michoacan
21. México
22. Distrito Federal
23. Tlaxcala
24. Puebla
25. Morelos
26. Guerrero
27. Oaxaca
28. Chiapas
29. Tabasco
30. Campeche
31. Yucatan
32. Quintana Roo

© 2007 HUNTER PUBLISHING, INC

The following is a list of all Mexican states.
Aguascalientes, Baja California, Baja California Sur, Campeche, Chiapas, Chihuahua, Coahuila, Colima, Distrito Federal, Durango, Guerrero, Guanajuato, Hidalgo, Jalisco, Mexico, Michoacan, Morelos, Nayarit, Nuevo Leon, Oaxaca, Puebla, Quntana Roo, Sinaloa, San Luis Potosi, Sonora, Tabasco, Tamaulipas, Tlaxcala, Veracruz, Yucatán, Zacatecas.

OFFICIALS

The government is made up of an executive branch headed by a president, who is both the chief of state and the head of government. The elected government includes a National Congress and a Federal Chamber of Deputies.

The **Cabinet** is appointed by the president after an election, but the assigning of an attorney general requires the consent of the Senate. The **National Congress** is made up of 128 seats, with 96 of those being elected by the people in each district. The 32 non-elected seats are given to members of the elected parties and are proportionally split up according to the number of votes won in the election. This provides for fairer representation. Each member serves a six-year term.

The **Federal Chamber of Deputies** consists of 500 seats, 300 of which are elected by popular vote. The other 200 seats are given to members of the elected parties and, as in Congress, are proportionally split according to the number of votes each party has won in the election. The deputies serve a three-year term.

The **Supreme Court of Justice** is appointed by the president, but must have the approval of the Senate. There are 21 judges who function as the full court or tribunal. Circuit judges and district judges are appointed by the Supreme Court and they must all have law degrees awarded from recognized law schools.

MILITARY SERVICE

Men and women can enter the military at the age of 18 and the forces consist of an army, navy and air force. There are presently almost 200,000 active persons in the military working under an annual expenditure of $4 billion. There are also 300,000 on reserve. It is compulsory for men at the age of 18 to enlist and those 16 years of age may volunteer to receive training as technicians. Women may volunteer at the age of 18. Conscientious objectors are not exempt from service. Which sector of the military one serves is a game of chance. Those who draw a white ball from the bag go into the army or air force, while those who get a blue ball must enter the navy. Mexico offers those in the service an opportunity for secondary education or special training in fields such as social work.

THE POLICE FORCE

The Mexican police force is notorious for its corruption. Getting into trouble is usually dealt with by paying a bribe. Because of the low pay, police officers are often people with low education, and many are interested only in expanding their criminal connections. These facts were researched and reported in the *World Policy Journal*, Volume 17, No. 3 in the fall of 2000. The story was also published in *Nexos*, a monthly magazine based in Mexico City, in April and August of 1998. Andrew Reding, a director of the Americas Project at the World Policy Institute, translated the article. For a complete report, go to www.worldpolicy.org/globalrights/mexico/2000-fall-wpj-mexpolice.html.

But there is a good side to the Mexican police force. The **tourist police** found in areas popular with visitors don't seem too corrupt. It appears to me that they have managed to clean up most of the crime in those regions of the country. While walking around I never felt threatened or that I was being watched by potential robbers.

However, I still wouldn't take a chance of walking on the beach alone after dark. I also highly recommend that you don't wander around drunk in a public place, that you stay away from the drug trade (of which there is plenty) and that you avoid things like nude bathing except on beaches designated as such. These things are not tolerated and will get you a jail sentence.

Those driving may be stopped and asked for a small contribution, called a *mordida*. Whether you are guilty or not, I suggest you ask for the ticket, or *boleto*. The best that can happen is that the officer will walk away and let you go.The worst that can happen is you will pay a fine for the infraction you have committed. If you pay a traffic ticket within 24 hours, the cost is half.

ECONOMY

Tourism plays a big part in Mexico's economy.

Mexico is a free market economy with industry, public services and agriculture owned mostly by the private sector. Tourism is a big draw for the Mexican government and it works hard to attract investors to build the infrastructure tourists require. When visiting the resorts, you will find high-quality rooms, service, food, entertainment and security.

The signing of NAFTA, the **North American Free Trade Agreement**, was done in the hope of improving the economy. According to *The New York Times*, November 19, 2003, the agreement has tripled trade with the US and Canada, but the wages of workers in the manufacturing industry, in agriculture and in the service industry have decreased. The inequality of wages between the middle class and the peasant class has increased, and immigration to the US has continued to rise. The World Bank reports that Mexico has benefitted from the agreement. The main problem seems to be that small farmers, who are no longer subsidized for growing staple crops, have left the farms for the factories, but there aren't enough jobs to go around.

At present, Mexico has free trade agreements with the US, Canada, Guatemala, Honduras, El Salvador and Europe. Over 90% of the country's trading power is under these agreements. In 2002 this increased Mexico's purchasing power to $900 billion, which resulted in a growth rate of 1%.

The **GDP** in 2004 was $1.006 trillion, or $9,600 per person. Of this, 4% came from agriculture, 26.6% from industry, 8.9% from manufacturing, and 69.4% from services. This results in 40% of the population living below the poverty line. Although only 3% of the population is unemployed, there is a huge underemployed group. But it's not all bad. The inflation rate dropped from 52% in 1995 to 6.4% in 2002, the lowest rate in 30 years.

THE MAQUILADORAS

An unpredicted result of the free trade agreements and foreign investment was the emergence of the Maquiladora. Maquiladoras are towns along the Mexican/American border where there are no tariffs on exports. Mexico has few ecological restraints in these areas, so cheap construction and operation costs are also a big draw. Additionally, the companies can hire cheap labor. The results are cheap goods going back into the rest of North America with no tariffs attached. The backlash of this is that the people of United States and Canada have lost millions of jobs and, in turn, millions of dollars in tax revenue. The Mexican workers living in these towns are underpaid. The results are that the Maquiladoras are huge slums.

PEOPLE & CULTURE

CULTURAL GROUPS

After the Spanish came, it took just two generations to depopulate Mexico of its indigenous peoples. This happened through disease, war and intermarriage. The population is now predominantly *mestizo*, people with a mixture of Spanish and Indian or Negro blood. Today, this group makes up about 60% of the total population. Pure indigenous people are 30% of the population, and whites are about 9%.

There is an unspoken class system that puts the pure European white person at the top. These are the **Creoles**, those born in the country but originating from unmixed European stock. The first Creoles to populate Mexico were the children of the Spanish settlers. Later, they came as refugees from the Spanish Civil War.

Beneath the Creoles on the class scale are the ***mestizos*** and beneath them are the pure **Amerindians**.

There are also a number of **Asians** in the country, who arrived after they were refused entry into the United States in the late 19th and early 20th centuries. This group shares equal status with the Amerindians.

TRADITIONAL ARTS

As of late, a resurgence of cultural pride among cultural groups has resulted in shows of traditional art, theater and dance.

Mexican art includes everything from painted wild fig tree bark to black Oaxaca pottery. Silver and gold have always been a popular medium and the quality of workmanship now found in Mexico is world class. Weavings and carpets have been finding their way into visitors' homes for half a century and the embroidered pieces that can be used as place mats, pillowcases or framed pictures come in colors and designs to accent any décor. Prices for these art pieces are less than half of what you would pay for comparable art in the States.

EMBROIDERY & WEAVINGS

Cotton *rebozos* (ray-BO-zoz), which are handwoven shawls, originated in the Oaxaca area, but can be purchased throughout the western states. This style of weaving, which is rather loose and usually of cotton, is now also being used to make dresses and skirts in fashionable designs that are especially attractive to visitors.

There are embroidered pillowcases or dresser scarves. Some are unique and of high quality, but you must usually hunt for those. Factory-made pieces are far more common and cost much less.

Wool and cotton are used to make the Zapotec handwoven **carpets**. The better ones are made with natural dyes that come from pomegranate, bark, nuts and flowers. They feature intricate geometric designs similar to those on Navajo rugs. The ubiquitous cotton **blankets** woven in simple stripes come in every color and quality.

The weaving of reeds, straw, needles and leaves has been tradition for about 5,000 years. Weavers make things like small mats that are far better for lying upon in the sand than towels.

Pine needle **baskets** have been used as containers for everything from food to babies and can be plain, or with geometric, floral or other intricate designs. Though these pieces are not colorful, their beauty lies in the design. Reeds, on the other hand, are often colored and woven into geometric designs, usually for baskets.

HUICHOL ART

Huichol art, made with beads, is seen in the shops throughout western Mexico. Some pieces are life-size replicas of animals; others are small. The work is colorful and intricate and depicts images representing stories and deities from Indian myths. Each piece is made by carving the desired shape out of wood or by using a gourd

A Huichol artist.

and covering it with a bees-wax and pine resin mixture. The colored beads are then placed, one at a time, onto the wood or gourd to create the design.

There are many imitations of this art form made in factories with the profits going to the industrialists, rather than artists. To avoid buying factory-made ones, ask if you can purchase another piece exactly the same. If you can, it's a sign that the piece is produced en masse.

> **AUTHOR TIP:** *If you purchase a piece of Huichol art, don't leave it in the sun, as the wax can melt.*

LEATHER GOODS

There is a **shoe store** on every street in Mexico. Although you can see the cheap offshore imitations of good quality shoes taking their place on the shelves, there are still many shops that sell the best. Prices are usually a third of what you'll find at home.

And the market isn't restricted to shoes. For reasonable prices, you can purchase purses, belts, jackets, pants, boots, hats and almost anything else that can be made out of leather. The best thing to do if shopping for leather is head to the closest highland town on market day. For example, if staying in Puerto Vallarta, take a trip to Guadalajara.

MASKS

Masks have been worn by traditional dancers for centuries. They can be made out of ceramic, wood, leather or papier mâché and decorated with paint, stones and metals.

As long as 3,000 years ago, masks were used to imitate gods that had re-incarnated into exotic animals. During the conquest, masks were used to depict oppressors and to emphasize a specific aspect of a story. Now they are used in religious ceremonies and for artistic expression. No matter which mask you purchase, it will be an original.

Masks are often made of wood and painted in bright colors.

For an interesting display and brief description of collectors' masks, visit www.mexicanmasks.us.

POTTERY, GLASS & CERAMICS

Pottery and ceramics have been a part of Mexican culture since ancient times, even though many of the religious beliefs that inspired specific works of art have not. Indigenous styles are popular, but the most popular style is **Talavera**, from Arabia via Spain. Talavera pottery is produced only in Puebla. The more Persian-styled works come from Jalisco state. These pieces are usually decorated with gold and silver. If you're in search of something more Mexican-looking, you will be able to find finely decorated ceramic pieces called the "tree of life." They are

Tree of Life.

very ornate and come from post Catholic times.

Stoneware is also common. The most popular piece is a **chess set** made with Aztecs facing conquistadors as opponents. The pieces are usually made of obsidian or onyx.

DRESS

Most mestizo dress like you, in comfortable pants or skirts of the latest fashions (although the women tend to dress on the conservative side). Shorts are worn in the country's western states. Down jackets help keep people warm in the highlands.

On market day or during a fiesta, it is common to see hand-embroidered clothes in myriad colors adorning the Amerindian people.

MUSIC

Mexican music has been popular in European countries as well as the US and Canada since the beginning of the last century. This is probably because of the huge Mexican population in the southern US, especially Texas and California areas, which were once part of Mexico. In recent times, artists like Joan Baez and Linda Ronstadt sang for a large Hispanic audience and popularized Mexican songs like *Gracias a la Vida.*

MARIACHI

Although I often listen to the music of Ronstadt and Baez, for me, Mexican music is the traditional mariachi band. Before the Spanish came, locals used five different instruments to play mariachi. These consisted of various styles of wooden drums and rattles.

After the Spanish arrived, they used music to draw the locals into the Catholic religion. They opened a music school as early as the mid-1500s and introduced such string instruments as the violin, harp and guitar. It didn't take long for the Mexican musician to combine these sounds and make new music not only for the church, but also for fiestas.

By the revolutionary period in the early 1800s, the music had blended traditional Indian tunes with Spanish and Negro tunes. The instruments commonly used were a harp, a violin, a guitar, a drum and a flute. During the battle for independence, music became a unifying symbol. At that time, musicians wore peasant clothing; it wasn't until after independence that they started dressing in what we associate with the Mexican musicians today – tight pants, a black jacket fitted snuggly at the waist, an embroidered belt and a wide bow tie. (See Antonio Banderas in the movie *Desperado*.) On their heads are huge sombreros that were not so much a symbol of music, but a symbol of wealth (sombreros were once worn only by wealthy hacienda owners).

A modern mariachi band at the Guadalajara festival.

THE CLAIM ON MARIACHI

The word "mariachi" comes from the no-longer-used Coca language of central Jalisco state. However, the French like to think that it comes from the French word *mariage*, and that they gave the word to Mexico. Historical documents indicate that the Coca, not the French, are responsible for the word.

DANCE

Mexican dance is a sensual expression often performed with masks. Before the Spanish arrived, dances depicted the relationship between the gods and mankind. Later, once Christian priests saw the advantage of the enactment, they used dance to stress good and evil in the world according to Christ. However, the Mexicans occasionally used dance as a mockery and to poke fun at the all-powerful forces. The Christians were much too serious to do this.

Each area has its own style of dance. For example, residents of Jalisco dance the jarabe, a romantic display about love and courtship. "Jarabe" means syrup. The dances of Nayarit show the joy of a party and the excitement of becoming an adult. Those in the state of Colima dance after the harvest and their exuberance often includes the throwing of knives. Not, I hope, at one another.

There are numerous **folklorica** shows in all major tourist centers. The acts are usually colorful and fun, and also give an interesting history of the culture and its relationship to the dances you see.

THE LAND

Mexico has almost 772,200 square miles/two million square km of land and is bordered by Belize, Guatemala and the US. It has 5,831 miles/9,330 km of coastline.

GEOLOGY

The land forms a bridge between North and South America and consists of high rugged mountains, plateaus, deserts and low coastal plains. Of these lands, 12% is farmland, 40% is pasture and 25% is forest and woodland.

Within the vegetated hills are plateaus and basins that form rich valleys like the Atemajac Valley near Guadalajara. A number of rivers drain these valleys into the Pacific Ocean.

The American Pacific coast from Alaska down to Tierra del Fuego is rock interspersed with sandy beaches. Just offshore most bays are dotted with tiny islands rich with wildlife. There is a limited amount of coral off the coast.

ENVIRONMENTAL CONCERNS

Environmental issues have been a big problem in Mexico. Hotels and cities along the oceans often dump their raw sewage into the ocean. Water purification plants are inefficient and below standard. Wildlife has been hunted almost to extinction. Air pollution is extreme and deforestation has resulted in erosion. However, there is a good side. Tourism is creating a market that demands clean air, clean water and lots of wildlife. The Mexicans are realizing this and their

Despite deforestation and air pollution, hikers still enjoy nature.

environmental practices, although still not up to the standards of places like Switzerland, are improving. People in the tourist industry are starting to insist on catch-and-release fishing and no-touch viewing of animals. More people are hiking rather than taking all-terrain vehicles into the jungle and Mexicans are putting emissions controls on their vehicles.

The best you can do, as a visitor, is insist on traveling only with tour companies who are environmentally sensitive. Below are a few examples of environmental groups working in Mexico. All are open to enlarging their membership and their bank accounts.

- La Systema Nacional de Areas Naturales Protegidas (Sinap) – type in "sinap Mexico" on the Internet and you'll see many references to their programs. Click on one that appeals to you.

- Audubon Society, www.audubon.org.
- Greenpeace, www.greenpeace.org.
- Cetacea Defence, www.cetaceadefence.org.
- Sea Turtle Survival League, www.cccturtle. org/ccctmp.htm.
- Earthjustice, www.earthjustice.org.
- Sierra Club, www.sierraclub.org.
- World Wildlife Fund, www.panda.org.

PARKS

There are numerous categories for protected public land, but the ones of most interest to us are the national parks and reserves. National parks are used for recreation or have historical value. These can be large, wild areas with few trails or small parks that are used mainly for strolls. Reserves are wildlife sanctuaries or areas set aside for scientific study.

NATIONAL PARKS & RESERVES

Cumbres de Cuixmala Reserve, Jalisco state, runs from the ocean into the mountains. It covers 32,500 acres and encompasses eight vegetation zones, each with its special communities of animals and birds. See page 242.

Sierra de Manantlan Biosphere Reserve, also in Jalisco, is a cultural reserve, rather than a natural one. It features gargantuan stone carvings. In the reserve, the most traditional town is **Ayotitlan**.

Nevado de Colima National Park, Colima state, has two volcanoes. **Volcán de Colima**, the taller of the two, is almost 14,000 feet/ 4,300 meters high. The other one, **Volcán de Fuego**, is still spewing fumes. There is hiking, climbing and camping in this park.

CLIMATE

The climate varies from tropical to desert and is dictated the most by elevation. Between November and March, it is warm and dry along the coast. Temperatures run around 26-28°C/80-85°F during the day and drop about 16°C/60°F at night. If you go up to Guadalajara (5,000 feet/1,500 meters), the temperatures average 16-21°C/60-70°F, with 60% humidity during the day. Nighttime temperatures drop as they do along the coast.

In the wet season, from April to the end of October, the coast experiences around 90% humidity that, coupled with temperatures of over 30°C/90°F, makes walking more than three minutes a huge effort. Guadalajara temperatures average 21°C/75°F during the day, with 80% humidity. This is what locals call the eternal spring climate.

HURRICANES

Because of high temperatures during the wet months (May to November), the water in the ocean heats up, causing a draft sometimes strong enough to create a hurricane. A hurricane forms when there's an area of low pressure in the upper atmosphere and the tropical waters warm to over 26°C/80°F to a depth of 200 feet/60 meters. The heat of the water causes circulation of the winds to accelerate.

The good news is that the west coast does not have as many hurricanes as the Caribbean because most hurricanes move northward in an east-to-west direction. This means that those over the Pacific often miss the mainland because they move toward the ocean. As they move north, the colder temperatures decrease the velocity of the winds. However, the winds and water currents on the swimming and surfing beaches during hurricane season are dangerous.

TSUNAMIS

Since Mexico sits on a tectonic plate, the country is subject to frequent tsunamis. The last one to hit the west coast of Mexico was in 1995, when Manzanillo was struck. Tsunamis can be expected after an earthquake or any other underwater volcanic activity. Occasionally, an underwater mountain will collapse or a landslide will occur and start a wave.

Tsunamis consist of huge waves that are formed far out at sea and can measure up to 90 feet/30 meters in height when they finally hit land. Moving toward land, they can travel as fast as a jet liner, up to 500 mph/800 kmph. They can move back and forth across the ocean for hours, over distances of up to 12,000 miles/19,000 km, before they finally peter out.

DEADLIEST RECORDED TSUNAMIS IN THE AMERICAS		
LOCATION	**DATE**	**LIVES LOST**
Chile	May 22, 1960	1,260
Colombia/Ecuador	Dec 12, 1979	500
Venezuela	Jan 31, 1906	500
Guatemala	Feb 26, 1902	185
Nicaragua	Sept 2, 1992	170
Aleutian Islands	April 1, 1946	165
US (Alaska)	Mar 28, 1964	123
Chile	Nov 11, 1922	100
Mexico	June 22, 1932	75
Canada (Newfoundland)	Nov 18, 1929	51
Solomon Islands	Oct 3, 1931	50

FACT FILE: *A 1960 tsunami that started near Chile killed 150 people in Japan 22 hours later.*

Tsunamis, when they reach land, throw the sediment from the ocean floor over a half-mile/one km inland; once the water subsides, this sedimentation can be over three feet/one meter deep. Tsunamis cause terrible destruction to the vegetation along the coast and often destroy entire villages.

When a tsunami approaches shore, it appears as a wall of water. A tsunami wave does not crest.

EARTHQUAKES

Earthquakes in the central and south region of the country are common. The one that hit Mexico City on September 19, 1985 had a magnitude of 8.1 on the Richter Scale and was the worst to hit since the Great Jalisco quake of 1932. Quakes occur when tectonic plates under the earth's surface move. When the quake hit Mexico City, the tectonic plate moved seven feet/2.5 meters across and 32 in/80 cm in a vertical direction. When an earthquake occurs under manmade structures, the damage is immense. The 1985 quake covered an area of almost 5,405 square miles/14,000 square km. It caused a tsunami that hit the coast from Manzanillo to Acapulco, causing most damage in the town of Zihuatanejo, where the wave was 10 feet/three meters high.

The aftershock of the Mexico City earthquake hit two days later and measured 7.5 on the Richter Scale, but that occurred 60 miles/100 km from the main site. It too, caused some tsunami activity.

PLANT LIFE

When we think of the Pacific coast of Mexico, we see swaying palms along sandy beaches and bougainvillea hanging over stone fences. Panning the landscape a bit farther inland we see giant cactus and spiked shrubs; lizards and snakes skittering around the dry ground. In the higher elevations, we see lush rainforest with canopies so solid they hide the sun and the parrots, monkeys, scorpions and snakes that live there.

ECOLOGICAL ZONES

The flora can be described in terms of seven distinct ecological zones between the Pacific coast and the highlands of Guadalajara or Mexico City. Each zone supports a huge variety of plants, animals, birds, amphibians and reptiles. The ocean has a vast array of vegetation, corals, mammals and fish. It is beyond the scope of this book to describe the entire natural habitat of western Mexico but, for the beginner, below are a few of the common characteristics of this unique environment.

TROPICAL DECIDUOUS FOREST

A tropical deciduous forest follows the west coast from the north to the south. It contains such plants as the palm tree (of which there are about 3,000 species worldwide), strangler fig or *mato palo* (in Spanish), pink trumpet tree (highly poisonous), cardinal sage, spider lily and the *mala raton* (bad rat). These plants usually lose their leaves during the dry season and flower between May and September, during the rainy season.

The **palm tree**, so common in the tropical deciduous forest, has been used for everything from baking ingredients to home construction to basket weavings to the promotion of paradise. The ones seen on the coast are usually the coconut or fan palm. The coconut palm is tall, with green-husked fruit clustered near the base of the fronds. You can recognize the palm that produces palm oil by the thousands of crab apple-sized nuts hanging below the fronds. On the fan palm, each leaf looks like a huge fan. The **strangler fig** is often associated with Tarzan and the deep jungle. This plant is a parasite that winds itself around a host tree and eventually sucks all the nutrients out of its captive. The strangler has numerous aerial roots that hang down from the host. Some of these roots can be quite thick and are strong enough to swing upon.

The **pink trumpet**, with its huge bell-shaped flowers that hang from every limb, is beautiful to look at but deadly to eat. **Cardinal sage**, also known as *Salvia fulgens*, should not be confused with *Salvia divinorum*, a hallucinogenic plant that was once used by shaman of the Oaxaca region for religious purposes. The cardinal version grows about three feet (one meter) in height, has red flowers and seems to be especially attractive to hummingbirds. When the Spanish arrived, the **spider lily** could be found growing near the swamps of Mexico City and has since spread to the swamps of the Pacific coast. The flower clusters grow in all shades of red, from light pink to deep maroon, and are found on leafless stems. The bulbs are poisonous. A sister plant to the Mexican variety grows in Japan and is planted at the entrances to temples.

Red Spider Lily.

PACIFIC THORN FOREST

The Pacific thorn forest is located around Mazatlan, south of Puerto Vallarta and between Manzanillo and Ixtapa. This vegetation zone, located in a fairly dry environment, includes such plants as the morning glory tree, the acacia, the mimosa, the fishfuddle tree and the candelabra cactus. Because of the climactic dryness, these plants are generally scrub or cactus-like in appearance.

The **morning glory tree** grows to about 30 feet/10 meters in height. Its cream-colored flowers are about two inches wide with bright red centers.

THE ROOT OF THE PROBLEM

The morning glory tree is also called *Palo del Muerte* (Tree of Death) or *Palo Bobo* (Fool Tree) because it was believed long ago that if one drank the water that flowed near the roots of the tree, he would either die or go crazy.

The **mimosa**, of which there are about 2,500 varieties, is often associated with the dry lands of Africa. However, some types can be found along the Pacific coast of Mexico. They can grow as high as 35 feet/10 meters, with a foliage spread of about the same. In some places the mimosa is known as the shaving brush tree because of its delicate thread-like flowers that resemble the edge of a shaving brush.

The **acacia** is similar to the mimosa in that its leaves are six to 12 inches long with anywhere from 11 to 23 leaflets attached symmetrically to a single stem. The thorn acacia has a double thorn at the base of the leaf stem and houses ants that bite any possible intruders. In return for this protection, the plant provides nourishment to the ant. The thorns were once used as sewing needles by those living in the area. The yellow clusters of flowers that appear in May are highly scented and leave a seedpod that is often eaten by birds.

The **candelabra cactus** looks like its name suggests, except it always has more than the seven branches (the candleholders). The plant grows three-12 feet/one-four meters high. Its branches have six to eight ribs and a long central spine. When the skin is ruptured, the plant oozes a milky sap that is poisonous to humans.

SAVANNAH

The savannah or plains grasslands are common in the state of Sorora and farther east. These semi-desert areas are often called *pastizales* (pastures) and are characterized by the abundant grasses (usually bunchgrass) that grow there. However, shrubs and small trees also flourish. The hot, dry climate receives less than 12 in/30 cm of rain a year and often has daytime temperatures of over 100°F/38°C. Over 700 invertebrate species make this environment their chosen home.

MESQUITE GRASSLAND

Generally, this land has been overgrazed, causing damage to the grassland. Mesquite grassland is where the **mescal cactus** is grown. There are numerous species of mescal grown and used in Mexico, but the most famous is the one from which tequila is made. It comes in two varieties, the agave tequelana and the aguey azul. In and around Guadalajara, Tequila and Tepatitlan huge plantations (a total of 62,000 acres is presently under cultivation) produce the aguey azul. These plants ripen in about six years, at which time the leaves are hacked away and the heart of the plant is chopped and roasted. It is then shredded and pressed, sugars and yeast are added and it is left to ferment. After fermentation, the liquid is distilled and we get to enjoy a delicious margarita.

PINE-OAK FORESTS

The pine-oak forests of the Sierra Madres hold many endangered species. This ecosystem lies between 4,500 and 7,500 feet/1,400 and 2,300 meters in elevation and trees here grow to a height of 75-125 feet/25-40 meters. Pine-oak regions usually have a thick undergrowth that includes many endangered ferns and water lilies.

> **FACT FILE:** *Forty percent of vertebrates known to live in Mesoamerica make the pine-oak forests their home, including the canyon tree frog. This is one of the most endangered ecosystems in Mexico.*

CLOUD FORESTS

Cloud forests or rainforests are defined as areas that receive 160-400 in/400-1,000 cm of rain annually and have little temperature change throughout the year.

> **FACT FILE:** *All of the world's rainforests lie between the Tropic of Cancer and the Tropic of Capricorn and are on land that has never been glaciated. This long period of consistency may be the reason that rainforests play host to such a huge number of different species.*

Typically, trees in the rainforest grow over 150 feet/45 meters and their branches spread out, forming a lush canopy over the creatures living below. This canopy prevents most of the sunlight from reaching the forest floor, leaving the ground with few nutrients. Since the root systems of these trees must compete for the small amount of available nutrients, roots spread out sideways rather than heading deep down into the ground. This type of growth leaves trees somewhat unstable. To counter this instability, many trees, such as the ceiba, have developed buttresses at the base of their trunks that act like stabilizing arms. Long woody vines called **lianas** are common in the cloud forest, as are orchids and bromeliads, or air plants. **Orchids** are members of the most highly evolved plants on the planet. There are about 25,000 species worldwide. Their evolution has developed thick leaves that hold moisture for the plant. Some of the flowers are highly perfumed to attract creatures for pollination. The vanilla is the most aromatic of the orchids.

Similar in appearance to the orchids are **bromeliads**, plants of the pineapple family. Unique to the Americas, bromeliads will grow in any elevation up to 8,000 feet/ 2,500 meters and anywhere from rainforest environment to desert. Also like orchids, these plants gather nutrients and moisture in their leaves; their roots serve only as anchors and are not used to gather food. Some bromeliads are as small as one inch across, while others grow to three feet. The pineapple is the most commonly known bromeliad.

TROPICAL REGIONS

This moist environment below 1,500 feet/500 meters has many **heliconias**, plants like the ginger, bird of paradise, prayer plant and banana. These plants all have large leaves and brilliant flowers. Banana trees (not actual trees, but heliconias) are abundant in Mexico. The fruits of different species vary; some are tiny, some large, some sweet and some bitter. You'll often see banana stalks hanging from trees wrapped in blue plastic bags designed to protect the fruit from insects. After the fruit stalk is removed from a tree, the treetop is chopped off and left at the base as fertilizer. New shoots grow and, eight months later, a new stalk of bananas is growing on the new tree.

NOPAL CURES

Nopal is a plant that has been eaten for thousands of years. Its fruit comes in different colors and tastes like watermelon or raspberries or pears, depending on the color. The green leaf is used in herbal medicines to cure diabetes, kidney infections and burns. The fruit is also used in salads and soups.

ANIMAL LIFE

The wildlife in Mexico is making a comeback after years of abuse – over-hunting of animals, over-grazing of grasslands, over-logging of forests and over-fishing of waters. Because tourists are more interested in whales and dolphins than in marinas, Mexicans are cashing in and again trying to give the tourists what they want. Parks and reserves are numerous and locals are relentless in their attempts to educate people about the environment.

Mammals common to the country are armadillos, coatis, spider monkeys and jaguars. Coyotes are numerous, as are rabbits, squirrels and deer. Reptiles include crocodiles, turtles, snakes and lizards. There is no greater thrill than to walk alone in the jungle and see a huge reptile slither away to the safety of the bush as you pass by. On the other hand, there is nothing more frightening than to come across the aggressive fer-de-lance snake while walking in the jungle.

Marine life is also rich, with gray and humpback whales, dolphins, swordfish, sailfish, marlin and roosterfish. There are many sportfishing operators who practice catch and release. The photos so common a few years ago of a dozen sailfish next to the proud white hunter are no longer popular.

ON LAND

RODENTS

There is the usual array of rodents, including the **squirrel, gopher, rat, rabbit** and **porcupine**. Distinct for their gnawing abilities, these animals have teeth that never stop growing and must be worn down in order for the animal to survive. Rodents are generally small and eat mostly vegetation, although their diets are often supplemented with eggs, birds and insects. Rodents are also a highly reproductive group, having at least one and sometimes numerous litters every year. **Audubon's ground squirrel** is seen near the beaches. Yellowish-brown in color, these two-foot-long, short-necked rodents live underground and are both gregarious and social. They live in underground communities, eat insects, fruits and grasses and usually have five kids per litter. They store food in ground holes and their keen sense of smell allows them to find the food again. The **Colima squirrel** is gray, with large eyes and small flexible ears. It grows up to three feet/one meter long, including the tail. Colima squirrels like to live in mango plantations and palm groves, where they feast on the fresh fruits. These sociable animals live in groups of 10 to 12 adults. Each female will give birth to about five kids, which she keeps close for eight to 10 weeks.

BATS

Bats are the only mammals that fly. In the Americas, bat wingspans range in size from a tiny three in/seven cm to six feet/two meters. There are over 1,000 types of bats in the world and Mexico has its fair share.

The wing of the bat is like a webbed hand, with a thumb and four fingers. It is used to scoop up food, cradle young or hug itself for warmth. Bats like their own homes and live an average lifespan of 30 years in the same cave, near the same hanging spot. All bats in a cave are related, except for one reproducing male who

always comes from another family and area. The females give birth to one baby a year, but the infant mortality rate is high, up to 60%. During the first year of life, the mothers leave their babies only when hunting for food. When they return to the cave, they call to their young, who recognize their parent's sounds and answer. Following the sound, the mother joins her youngster.

> **FACT FILE:** *Bats can eat up to 3,000 insects in one sitting and up to 1,000 mosquitoes in an hour. I don't know who does the counting but, if the figures are correct, I really like bats.*

CATS

JAGUAR: Jaguars are the largest and most powerful cats in the Americas. Often referred to as *el tigre*, the jaguar stands 20-30 in/50-75 cm at the shoulder and has an overall length of six-eight feet/two-three meters. Its slender but strong body can weigh 250 lb/115 kg. The jaguar is built to hunt, with strong shoulders, sharp teeth, good eyesight and hearing, and claws that can rip the hamstring of a deer with one swipe. The jaguar's short fur is usually yellow with black spots, or black circles with a yellow dot in the center. Some jaguars appear all black, but it is just that the black circles are so big they override any trace of yellow. There is no specific breeding season for the jaguar. Both parents care for the kitten for about one year after birth, at which time everyone splits and fends for themselves. With good luck and lots of food, the jaguar lives about 20 years.

PUMA: The red tiger, or puma, is also called the mountain lion, cougar or panther. Just a bit smaller than the jaguar, this animal lives throughout North and South America wherever deer, its main source of food, is found. Comparable in strength to the jaguar, the puma can haul an animal five times its size for a considerable distance. When hunting, it strikes with lightening speed and can spring forward 25 feet/7.5 meters in one leap and jump down 60 feet/18 meters to land safely. Like the jaguar, the puma can mate at any time of year and both parents help look after the young. The puma's life expectancy is 15 years.

COATI: The coati is a tree-climbing mammal related to the raccoon. It has a long snout (tipped white) and an even longer tail that is usually the same length as its body. It keeps its striped tail high and, as it walks, the tail swings from side to side. Coatis are sociable animals and the females often travel with their young in groups of up to 20. When a group of these animals attacks a fruit tree, they often devour the entire crop in a few minutes. A full-grown male stands 10 in/25 cm at the shoulder and will grow to two feet/50 cm long. As this omnivore hunts both in the day and at night and eats just about anything, you have a good chance of seeing one moving along in tall grass or along rocky hillsides.

© Photographer: Ramon Berk/Dreamstime

MONKEYS

Spider monkeys have grasping hands that have no functional thumbs and a grasping tail that is hairless at the end. These five "hands" make the spider monkey efficient in maneuverability. They travel in bands of 20 to 30 and will attack threatening invaders. They use fruits and branches as weapons and have been known to urinate on enemies walking below. There are signs in Manuel Antonio Park, Costa Rica, warning tourists of this possibility.

AMPHIBIANS

Amphibians include **frogs**, **toads**, **newts**, **salamanders**, **sirenians** (sea cows) and **caecilians** (creatures that look like earthworms). Although amphibians have lungs, they also do some air exchange through their skin. They are found worldwide, except on the poles and in extreme deserts. Amphibians are hatched from eggs and usually go through a tadpole or larvae stage, where breathing is done through gills. They metamorphose and then use lungs. Their skins are moist, glandular and pigmented, although if living away from light, pigmentation is minimal. Some, like the salamander, are able to rejuvenate lost body parts (for some reason, the back end of the creature is quicker to respond to regrowth than are the front limbs). The most endearing feature of the amphibian is its ability to consume large amounts of insects, especially mosquitoes.

The red-eyed tree frog is just one of many frogs found in Southern Mexico.

REPTILES

Reptiles are prominent in Mexico and it would be a rare visit if you didn't see at least one iguana, snake, turtle, or gecko while there. Reptiles control their temperature by moving in their environment. If it is too hot in the sun, they move to the shade. They all have a tough dry skin that is used primarily to preserve body moisture.

SNAKES: The **fer-de-lance** is the most dangerous of Mexico's snakes and its bite is usually fatal. It is an aggressive, nocturnal viper that can be found almost anywhere – in a tree, on the jungle floor, in the grass or out in the open. Its markings are not distinct, so it is hard to identify. It has an arrow-shaped head and a mouth with two retractable fangs appearing too big for the snake's head. The fer-de-lance comes in many colors, from dark brown to gray to red, and has a row of dark-edged diamonds along its sides.

> **WARNING:** If you are attacked by one of these snakes, you must get to a doctor immediately. Twenty-four hours is too long to wait; some people say that you have only 20 minutes to receive treatment before you die.

The **rattlesnake**, found only in North America, is in danger of becoming extinct. Identified by the rattle sound made by the animal shaking its tail, rattlers are not as dangerous as the fer-de-lance, although their bite can be fatal. If bitten, you should see a doctor who will administer some antivenin, a drug obtained from horses that neutralizes the snake's venom.

FACT FILE: *More people die every year in the US from bee and wasp stings than those from snake bites.*

Coral snakes are nocturnal, but are far less aggressive than the fer-de-lance and are hard to find as they like to hide in ground vegetation. They also prefer eating other snakes, rather than sharpening their teeth on you. However, if you step on one and are bitten, get to a doctor immediately as they are one of the most poisonous snake in the tropics.

The yellow-bellied **sea snake** is a carnivorous snake that seldom grows over 45 in/113 cm. It hunts fish during the day. The snake sleeps on the ocean floor, rising to the surface once every one to three hours to breathe. It is mild-mannered and often swims in groups of up to a hundred. If washed ashore by wave action, it has a hard time getting back to the water and it often dies. Sea snakes expel only a small amount of poison when they bite. If bitten, your life is not in danger, but you should still see a doctor.

TURTLES: The **green turtle** is so named because of the color of its fat. The **black turtle** is a subspecies of the green. These slow-growers do not reach sexual maturity until 20 years of age, and some take up to 50 years. The green turtle will grow to 39 in/one meter and weigh about 330 lb/150 kg. In the recent past, these creatures would grow to twice that size. Today, we harvest them so rapidly that they no longer have time to grow.

The green turtle is vegetarian and likes to graze on meadows of sea grass that grow in warm ocean waters. However, immature greens are known to eat a bit of meat. The females nest once every two to four years. Each nesting season results in two

Green turtle.

or three breeding sessions that are about 14 days apart. The female lays about 100 eggs each time and the young hatch 60 days later. The largest known nesting beach is at Colola in the state of Michoacan.

Leatherback turtles are in great danger of extinction worldwide. This is the largest living turtle, growing up to 110 in/270 cm long and weighing up to 2,000 lb/900 kg. The leatherback is so named because it has a flexible shell that resembles leather. There is no separation from the sides of the shell and the underbelly, so it appears a bit barrel-shaped. An old study from the early 1980s found that of all the leatherbacks known to exist world-wide, almost half of them nested on the western shores of Mexico. However, more recent studies have indicated that the turtles travel to Japan to nest and, when the young hatch, sea currents return the babies to the western shores of America. One of the greatest threats to the leatherback is that it mistakes plastic bags and Styrofoam pollutants for food. Once the garbage is ingested, the turtle's gut becomes blocked, nutrition is limited and death is close.

The **Olive Ridley turtle** is the most abundant turtle in the Pacific Ocean. It is small, merely 22-30 in/56-76 cm long. Some of the females nest in arribados, or groups. The grouping of turtles is believed to have evolved so they can help each other protect their eggs.

THE WAITING GAME

Some turtles have been known to stay in the water waiting for a safe moment to lay their eggs and, while waiting, the eggs develop hard shells. When the turtle eventually tries to lay her eggs, they are very difficult to pass and, because of the rigidity, they break.

The Ridley Turtle nests every year, three to four times during each season, as opposed to the green turtle who has a nesting season only every two to four years but nests three times each season. It takes 14 days for eggs to hatch from the females who nest alone, and up to 28 days for the arribado nesters. Only 5% of eggs actually produce offspring. One scientific theory for this is that 90-95% of the eggs produced are unfertilized (without a yolk) and left at the top of the nest so predators will eat them and not bother with the fertilized eggs lying below. Olive Ridley turtles are omnivorous and include crab, shrimp, lobsters, jellyfish, algae and sea grasses in their diets.

INSECTS

Insects and arachnids include mosquitoes and cock-roaches, botflies and butterflies, houseflies and fireflies, fire ants and leaf-cutter ants, termites and scorpions. Some bite and others don't. Some are good to eat (like ants, which you can cover in chocolate) and some are not even wanted by birds, toads or frogs (like fireflies). Below I have mentioned just a few of the more interesting ones.

Scorpions should be avoided because they do bite; shake out shoes and clothes before putting them on when in the jungle. Apparently, the smaller the scorpion the more lethal its bite.

For the most part, **ants** work in the service industry, cleaning up garbage left around the jungle floors (and your room, if you are careless). Highly organized, their hills can measure many feet across and be equally as high. A colony of leaf-cutter ants (also called wee-wee ants) can strip a full-grown deciduous tree within a day. These ants chew and swallow the leaves, which they re-gurgitate shortly after. The vomit grows a fungus, which the ants then eat for nutrition. The excretion left by the ants helps to fertilize the jungle floors. The ants' colonies consist of females only and the queen is the size of a small mouse. Her job is to lay eggs; she has workers to clean and feed her.

There are hundreds of species of **butterflies** and **moths** in Mexico and their colors and designs are fascinating. Some have eye markings at their tail end (to fool predators as to the direction they will be going), while others are so bright they attract the attention of all. Butterflies and moths have no jaws, so they don't bite. Instead, they suck up nutrients in liquid form. For protection from rain, high winds and extreme heat, they sit on the undersides of leaves.

OTHER BEASTS

Skunks are often incorrectly referred to as polecats. A polecat is native only to Europe and Asia; skunks are found in America anywhere from northern Canada all the way down to Patagonia. Related to the weasel, the skunk is able to spray a foul-smelling substance a distance of 12 feet/3.5 meters. The skunk actually aims for the eyes of its enemy. The liquid produces temporary blindness in the recipient. A night hunter, the skunk comes out of its den when the temperatures cool and it forages for insects, larvae, mice and fallen fruits. Skunks mate in spring and have litters of five or six young that are ready to look after themselves after about two months. Their life span is around 10 years.

The **peccary** is a pig-like creature that has been around for about 40 million years (according to fossil finds). Not very big, it weighs about 65 lbs/30 kg and travels in herds of a few individuals to as many as 300. The peccary has two distinct features. One is the smell it exudes from a musk gland on its back whenever it is irritated. The second is its amazing nose, the tip of which is flat and reinforced with a cartilaginous disk that can lift logs and dig underground for roots and insects. A true omnivore, the peccary will eat anything from poisonous snakes to cactus. There is no fixed mating season and the female usually gives birth to one or two young about the size of a full-grown rabbit. By the time the young are two days old, they are ready to take their place in the herd.

Peccaries cannot be tamed.

The **armadillo** is an insect-eating mammal that has a bony-plated shell encasing its back. This shell is the animal's protection. The armadillo has teeth that are simple rootless pegs in the back of its mouth. Because of these teeth, the armadillo is able to eat snakes, chickens, fruit and eggs. It also likes to munch on the odd scorpion. The female gives birth to a litter of young that are all the same sex; the theory is that they develop from the same egg. The young are born with shells, but the shells don't harden until the animal is almost a year old. This is when it leaves its mother.

AIRBORNE

BIRDS

Because Mexico lies on the migratory path, seeing both common and rare bird species is possible, often in larger numbers than elsewhere. Numerous bird tours come to this area from the United States. Many environmental groups are involved in preserving areas that the birds use so their numbers are again increasing. If you have more than a passing interest in birds, bring your favorite identifying book and binoculars with you.

Parrots are brightly plumaged, gregarious creatures that have no problem imitating human speech. They will be the most ubiquitous bird (next to the frigate and pelican) you will see. In total, there are 358 parrot species worldwide. Along with bright colors, all parrots have strong hooked beaks with moveable upper jaws and thick tongues. They eat fruit and seeds. Captive parrots make strong bonds with their

Colorful macaws are always a pleasure to see.

owners and are known to become physically ill if abandoned. The species most commonly seen on Mexico's west coast are the tiny (four-six inch/10-15 cm) Mexican parakeet, the orange-fronted parakeet, the lilac-crowned parrot and the military macaw.

The **frigate** is the big, black bird you see soaring over the water with a "W" shaped wing. It can soar for hours over the sea, although it seldom goes more than 50 miles/80 km from its home island. Because it does not lift off from water very well, it doesn't fish much. Instead, it steals from other birds or swoops down and catches fish swimming near the surface.

The brown pelican is the smallest of the pelican family.

Pelicans come in eight varieties, the most common of which is the brown pelican. Their pouch bills could easily hold a newborn human. Their bodies are about 40 in/100 cm long and their wingspan is a mighty 90 in/228 cm. These birds, when fishing, torpedo into the water from great heights. Their ancestors can be traced back about 40 million years, but in the 1950s and 1960s pelicans almost disappeared from earth due to DDT poisoning. They are now making a comeback. Each female lays about three eggs per year and the hatchlings are born four weeks later.

An indiscriminate scavenger, the **cara cara** is a raptor with black and white plumage and a featherless face. It is Mexico's national bird. Its legs are bare and its tearing beak is hooked like an eagle's and long like a vulture's. It will eat garbage, dine with both eagles and vultures, or kill its own mammal for dinner. Cara caras love to eat anacondas, boa constrictors and caimans. When they leave the nest, young cara caras are 21 in/55 cm long, with a four-foot/1.3-m wingspan. Due to loss of savannah and wetlands, the cara cara is endangered. But loss of habitat is just part of the problem. Throughout Central and South America, their claws were used for jewelry and their feathers used to make ceremonial robes for priests and kings. More recently, the claws and beaks have been ground and sold as aphrodisiacs. The use of DDT in the last 25 years has also taken its toll on the development of eggs. Cara caras are slow reproducers.

RECOMMENDED BIRDING BOOKS

The most comprehensive tome available is the *Field Guide to the Birds of Mexico and North Central America*, by Steve Howell and Sophie Wedd, published by Oxford Illustrated Press. It has color plates and black-and-white drawings that illustrate 750 species. It has 1,010 pages and is heavy to carry.

Mexico: A Hiker's Guide to Mexico's Natural History, by Jim Conrad, was published by Mountaineer Books in 1995. This 220-page book combines wildlife information with 20 trail descriptions.

Bird-Finding Guide to Mexico, by Steve NG Howell, Cornell University Press, 1999. The book's 512 pages describe 100 sites where birders may see more than 950 species.

Birds of Mexico and Adjacent Areas, by Ernest Preston Edwards, University of Texas Press, 3rd edition, 1998. Lists 870 species, with 300 that are not included in other guides. The names include English, Spanish and the scientific names.

IN THE OCEAN

Dolphins are playful and intelligent. They mature between five and 12 years and a female gives birth to one calf every two or three years. The life span of a dolphin is up to 48 years. Dolphins travel in pods and it is sus-

Playful dolphins.

pected that each member of a pod is related. They like to stay near their home waters for their entire life. They hunt for fish using the echolocation method similar to bats. A dolphin will eat up to 150 lb/68 kg of fish a day.

Hammerhead sharks are one of nine species of sharks. They grow anywhere from three feet/one meter to 20 feet/six meters, but most average 11.5 feet/four meters long. They weigh around 500 lb/230 kg, but can weigh up to 1,000 lb/450 kg. They kill their prey by smashing them with their heads and they especially like to eat squid, rays, crustaceans and each other. They generally swim at a depth of 250 feet/75 meters, migrating north in summer and south in winter. Females give birth to 20 to 40 live pups that are about 27 in/70 cm long.

WHALES: **Great gray whales** migrate down the Pacific coast from the Arctic waters each year around October and return the following spring around May. The gray whale belongs to the baleen whale classification because it has baleen, a substance made of keratin similar to fingernails, instead of teeth. The baleen grows in strips down from the upper jaw.

> **FACT FILE:** *There can be up to 180 plates of baleen on each side of a whale's or shark's jaw. The strips grow two-10 in/five-25 cm and, since the ends wear down from eating, they must continue to grow during the animal's entire life.*

Baleen is used to filter amphipods from the ocean bottom. Land deposits due to erosion of the earth along the oceans cause death to these tiny bottom growers and results in the grays having to go farther afield in search of food. An average-size gray measures 40-50 feet/12-15 meters long and weights up to 40 tons. Grays are known to live about 50 years, are gray in color and have scars caused from barnacles. It is also common to see orange whale lice growing on their skin. Gray whales have 10-12 dorsal nodules rather than fins and their tails are 10 feet/three meters across. Grays have hair, are warm-blooded and suckle their young for six months. During the suckling period, babies drink around 50 gal/200 liters of milk a day, gaining 50 lb/23 kg of body weight per day.

A female must be 36-39 feet/nine-10 meters in length before she is mature enough to mate. A 15-foot/five-meter), one ton/1,000 kg calf is born a year later. During delivery, a second female may help with the birthing by holding the mother up near the surface so she can breath. After birth, the youngster does some practice swims back and forth against the current in preparation for the 10,000-km/6,000-mile migration north.

Humpback whales also belong to the baleen classification of mammals. They, too, have patterns on their dorsal fins and tails that are as unique as fingerprints on humans. Humpbacks are black on top and white on their bellies, have irregular-shaped dorsal fins and tails that can be up to 18 feet/5.5 m wide. They are usually 40-50 feet/12-15 meters in length and weigh 25-40 tons. They feed on small crustaceans and fish. Humpbacks consume around a ton of food every day.

A pair of humpbacks "lunge-feeding."

Humpbacks reach maturity when they are 36-39 feet/11-12 meters long, which is usually reached by six to eight years of age. Females have a calf once every two to three years and the gestation period is one year. The calf weighs around a ton at birth and suckles for a year. Humpbacks, like gray whales, migrate north in summer and return south to mate and give birth in winter.

SPORTFISH: **Swordfish** are part of the billfish family and are identified mainly by their long sword-like upper jaws. They have large eyes, brown bodies with white bellies and have no scales or teeth. They have been known to grow up to 200 .lb/90 kg but, due to over-harvest, are now much smaller. They like to eat other fish, squid and octopus.

Sailfish are also part of the billfish family and have a large upper jaw that looks like a spear. But it is the enlarged dorsal fin that gives the fish its name. Sailfish grow to four-five feet/one-two meters in their first year of life and usually reach seven feet/two meters and 120 lb/ 60 kg at maturity. The sailfish is a fast swimmer, often traveling up to 50 knots.

Blue and **black marlin** are more often found in the Atlantic than the Pacific. However, those in the Pacific grow to 14 feet/four meters and can weigh one ton/900 kg. The largest marlin found in the Pacific was 1,376 lb/624 kg. Marlin eat dolphin, tuna and mackerel. Spawning season is May to November, and the eggs hatch about one week after being deposited. The marlin's biggest predator is the white shark, but man, too, has over-fished this species. The catch-and-release practice of fishing has not been so good for this group because the damage occurred during the catch usually kills the fish.

The **rooster fish** has a spiked dorsal fin with eight thorns. It is gray-blue in color, with a silver underbelly and two dark spots, one on the nose and another on the nape of the neck. It likes to swim near shore where there is a sandy bottom and is also found around reefs. Rooster fish usually grow to 10 in/25 cm long and weigh about 115 lb/55 kg. Because of their great fighting ability, they are a desired sportfish.

Tuna are found around the world between the cold northern or southern waters to the equator. The bluefin tuna, the largest of this group, can reach 180 in/455 cm and can weigh 1,500 lb/680 kg. However, the most common size is about 75 in/200 cm.

Because of the quality of the meat, these fish can sell for up to $45,000 each in Japan. Tuna become sexually mature at about four or five years and live to 15 years on average. They travel in schools when young. The schools are often a mixed bunch of students determined by size rather than species.

Tuna like to swim as deep as 3,000 feet/ 1,000 meters and can cross the Atlantic Ocean in 60 days, swimming an average speed of 45 mph/75 kph.

A trio of yellowfin tuna.

Dorado is also called mahi mahi or dolphin. It has a flat face, large dorsal fin and is a metallic blue-green in color with orange-gold specks. It is grows from 15-30 lb/five-12 kg and eats mainly smaller fish. The dorado is known to travel in pairs.

The **king mackerel** is a long, narrow fish with a dark thin stripe along its side and spots below the stripe. The largest of the mackerels, it grows to 35 in/90 cm; the largest ever found measured 72 in/180 cm and weighed 100 lb/45 kg. King mackerel usually live to be 14 years old, although some studies show them to live almost twice that long. Size determines sexual maturity and they spawn from May to September.

NATIONAL EMBLEMS

NATIONAL FLAG

The national flag has three vertical stripes of equal size. The colors are green, white and red, with the white center stripe holding the coat of arms. The present flag was adopted in 1968 to update it for the Olympics being held in Mexico that year.

NATIONAL ANTHEM

The lyrics of the national anthem were written by **Francisco Gonzalez Bocanegra** and the music was composed by **Jaime Nuò**. It was declared the national anthem in 1854.

Mexicans, at the cry of battle,
prepare your swords and bridle;
and let the earth tremble at its center
at the roar of the cannon.

O Fatherland! Your forehead shall be girded
with olive garlands, by the divine archangel of peace.
For in heaven your eternal destiny
has been written by the hand of God.

But should a foreign enemy dare to profane
your land with his sole.
Think, beloved fatherland, that heaven gave you
a soldier in each son.
War, war without truce against who would attempt to blemish
the honor of the fatherland!

War, war! The patriotic banners drench in waves of blood.
War, war! On the mount, in the valley,
the terrifying thunder of the cannon and the echoes nobly
resound to the cries of the Union! Liberty!

Fatherland, before your children become unarmed
beneath the yoke their necks in sway,
and your countryside be watered with blood,
on blood their feet trample.
And may your temples, palaces
and towers crumble in horrid crash
and ruins remain saying: the fatherland
was made of one thousand heroes.

Fatherland, fatherland, your children swear to exhale their
breath in your cause if the bugle in its belligerent tone should
call upon them to struggle with bravery.

For you the olive garlands!
For them a memory of glory!
For you a laurel of victory!
For them a tomb of honor!

COAT OF ARMS

The coat of arms is designed after the legend of the Mexican people. The gods told them to find a place where an eagle, eating a snake, landed on a prickly-pear cactus. After years of wondering, the people found the site and in 1325 started building a city on the island in the swamp where the eagle was found. The place became the center of religion, politics and commerce until it fell under the cannons of Hernando Cortez. To the Mexican people, the eagle was a symbol of war and in other pieces of art it can be found attacking a snake or a jaguar.

NATIONAL PRAYER

National prayer, or the Initial Prayers for Mexico, are the traditional devotions of the Roman Catholic Church. During an Act of Contrition (during confession) a Mexican will recite:

O my God I am heartily sorry for having offended you, and I detest all my sins because I fear the loss of heaven and the pains of hell, but most of all because they offend you my God, who are all good and deserving of all my love. I firmly resolve, with the help of your grace, to sin no more and to avoid the near occasions of sin. Amen.

NATIONAL BIRD

The national bird is a raptor, a scavenger and, sadly, now on the endangered list. To learn more about the **cara cara**, see page 40.

Travel Information

FACTS AT YOUR FINGERTIPS

AREA: 742,474 sq miles/ 1,923,000 sq km of land, with 19,112 sq miles/ 49,500 sq km covered by water.

BORDERS: USA, 2,414 km/ 1,500 mi, Guatemala, 800 km/500 mi and Belize, 200 km/125 mi.

CAPITAL: Federal District of Mexico (Mexico City).

COAST: 450 miles/725 km of coastline, more than half of which is on the western shore.

CURRENCY: The peso, the value of which fluctuates. At time of writing, it was 10.4 pesos for US $1.

ETHNIC GROUPS: 60% mestizo (American Indian and Spanish mix), 30% American Indian, 9% white and 1% other.

GDP: US $9,600 per person, but 40% of the population is under the poverty line. There is a labor force of 40 million people.

HEAD OF STATE: The new head of state is Felipe Calderòn who is the Head of State, Head of Government, and Commander-in-Chief of the military. He became president in September, 2006 and is a member of the National Action Party (PAN). Opposed to abortion, gay marriage and contraception, he will be in office until December, 2012.

Pico de Orizaba.

HIGHEST/LOWEST POINT: Pico de Orizaba, 17,500 feet/5,350 meters; Laguna Salada, at 30 feet/10 meters.

LANGUAGES: Spanish, Mayan, Nahuatl.

LIFE EXPECTANCY: Average is 69 for males and 75 for females.

POPULATION: 105 million (estimated), with a growth rate of 1.43% and 2.53 children per family.

RELIGION: 89% Roman Catholic, 6% protestant and 5% other religions, including Buddhism, Hinduism, Sikhism and Taoism.

RESOURCES: Petroleum, silver, copper, gold, lead, zinc, natural gas and timber.

TRANSPORTATION: 10,000 miles/16,000 km of railway; 175,000 miles/282,000 km of highway; and 1,500 miles/2,400 km of navigable rivers and coastal canals. There are 231 airports with paved runways and 1,592 without.

WHEN TO GO

Mexicans travel within their own country a lot, so be certain to have your room booked during the peak seasons like Christmas, Easter and summer vacation, from June to mid-August.

At Easter and Christmas, most Mexicans close shop and spend time with their families. During these holidays, the large hotels will serve meals, but almost everything else will be closed. During any other festival, everything remains open. This is especially true in tourist areas. Only in the smaller villages may you find things closed; if you need anything, seek out the local proprietor.

NATIONAL & RELIGIOUS HOLIDAYS

■ January
1st – **New Year's Day**

6th – **Dia de los Santos Reyes** is when Mexicans exchange Christmas presents. The day corresponds to the day the Three Wise Men brought Jesus gifts.

17th – **Feast Day of San Antonio de Abad** is when animals are blessed in the church.

■ February
5th – **Dia de la Constitución** is when the constitution was inaugurated.

24th – **Flag Day** honors the national flag.

March

Carnival is the weekend before lent, 40 days before Easter. The date changes every year. Carnival is celebrated with parades, street dancing, partying and feasting. Mazatlan is the best town on the west coast in which to enjoy this celebration.

21st – Birthday of **Benito Juarez**, a national hero and one of the early presidents.

April

Semana Santa is the week of Easter and includes Good Friday and Easter Sunday. To celebrate, Mexicans like to break eggs filled with confetti over the heads of friends and family.

May

1st – **Primero de Mayo** is equivalent to Labor Day in the US.

5th – **Cinco de Mayo** honors the battle and victory over the French at Puebla de los Angeles in 1862.

10th – **Mother's Day** is especially important in Mexico.

June

1st – **Navy Day** is when coastal cities celebrate the importance of the Navy for defending the country. They have regattas and parades with decorated ships.

September

The annual **State of the Union**, when the president addresses the nation, is held at the start of September; the date changes.

16th – **Independence Day** is the day Miguel Hidalgo announced the revolution against the Spanish.

October

12th – **Dia de la Raza** commemorates the arrival of Columbus in America.

November

1st & 2nd – **Dia de los Muertos**, Day of the Dead, is when Mexicans honor the spirits of their ancestors by visiting their graves, decorating them and feasting.

© Velusariot/Dreamstime

Festive skulls and an angel on top of an altar to celebrate Dia de los Muertos.

20th – **Revolution Day** commemorates the Mexican Revolution of 1910.

December

12th – **Dia de Nuestra Señora de Guadalupe** honors the patron saint of Mexico.

16th – **Las Posadas** starts the Christmas celebrations with a candlelight procession and commemorates the search for shelter by Joseph and Mary.

25th – **Christmas Day**

Travel Information

■ SEASONAL CONSIDERATIONS

Head to the Pacific coast between November and February if you want ideal weather. If you don't mind high heat and humidity, you can go at other times. The farther north you are, the longer the "winter season" of warm days and cool nights. During this season, daytime temperatures at northern beaches hover around 70°F/21°C, while evenings are cool, sometimes as low as 50°F/10°C. The humidity is between 30 and 50% and the rains have generally stopped. However, during the summer months, humidity is often around 80%, and temperatures are quite a bit higher than in winter.

From December to March, the central coast has warm weather, with daytime temperatures in the low to mid-80s and evenings in the mid-60s to 70s F (15-21°C). Summers are oppressively hot and hurricanes threaten between June and September. This is also rainy season.

The southern coast has much less rain than the north, and the humidity is generally never below 50%. Coupled with temperatures between the mid-70s and low 90s F (21-32°C), this makes for a hot visit. The best months to visit are between December and February. The rest of the time, the high temperatures and humidity can be too much to bear.

WHAT TO TAKE

REQUIRED DOCUMENTS

Under new government regulations, by January 8, 2007, travelers going to and from the Caribbean, Mexico and Canada – plus Bermuda and Panama – will be required to have a passport to enter or re-enter the United States. On December 31, 2007, the requirement will be extended to all land-based border crossings as well.

> **AUTHOR NOTE:** *I recommend that every member of the family carry a valid passport for international travel.*

Children under 18 who are citizens of Canada or the United States may travel with a birth certificate but without a photo identification card. However, it is advisable to have a photo ID also. Children not traveling with both their legal guardians must have a notarized letter of consent from the non-traveling parent with permission for the child to cross international borders. A child too young to have received his birth certificate must have a notarized letter from the pediatrician or hospital identifying the child as belonging to the adult.

> **AUTHOR TIP:** *In our technological age you can scan your passport and e-mail the scan to your traveling e-mail address (i.e., Yahoo, Hotmail). This way, you always have a copy. You can do this with your postcard or e-mail address list also.*

Mexicans residing in the US may travel one way with a Mexican passport (even if it is expired) or they may present a Matricula Consular that is a Certificate of Nationality issued by the Mexican Consulate. Those using the Matricula Consular must have a photo identification card and birth certificate. If this is not possible, the Matricula Consular may be presented with a Mexican voter registration paper and a photo identification card. An American green card will not allow Mexican citizens permission to enter into Mexico, but the green card will get them back into the US.

Travel Information

Once in Mexico, and if staying more than 72 hours past the border zones like Tijuana, you will receive a **tourist card**. Do not lose this card as it will take a lot of complicated bureaucracy and a bit of money to get another. There is no charge for a tourist card when it is issued.

Depending upon your reasons for traveling to Mexico, as well as your country of citizenship, you may be required to obtain a **visa**. Residents of some countries must apply for a visa to the Mexican consulate or embassy in their own countries before they arrive at the Mexican border. If there is no embassy or consulate, you must apply by mail to the immigration authorities in Mexico City (Mexican Ministry of the Interior, National Institute of Migration, Ejercito Nactional #862, Col. Los Morales/Sección Palmas, Mexico, DF, 11540). For more specific information, visit www.embamexican.com. It takes six to eight weeks to process this type of visa and only those applying for a visa may enter the Mexican consulate or embassy in their country. The cost is US $37 and must be paid in cash or money order.

People who want to retire or reside in Mexico must have a special visa. For this one-year, multiple-entry visa you must present a valid passport, application form, photos, health certificate, letter from your local police department stating that you are free of a police record, letter from the bank stating that your monthly income exceeds $2,000 plus $1,000 for each dependent. And finally, you must pay a consular fee of $136 in cash or money order. This type of visa takes three days to process and can be extended on a yearly basis for a period of five years, after which permanent residence status must be obtained.

> **FACT FILE:** *If you make money in Mexico, you are subject to Mexican taxes and are eligible for Mexican social security.*

For more information about immigration laws for retirees, contact the **Mexican Ministry of the Interior**, National Institute of Migration, Ejercito Nactional #862, Col. Los Morales/Sección Palmas, Mexico, DF, 11540. Specifics about becoming a Mexican resident is offered at www.embamexican.com/consular/resident.html.

Canadian and American journalists traveling in Mexico for a special event (or to write a book like this) must get an FM-3 migratory form from the nearest consular office in their country. This document allows the journalist to remain in Mexico for 90 days and to make multiple entries.

VISAS, PLEASE

Citizens of the following countries are not required to show a visa to enter Mexico for tourist purposes, but they must have a valid passport: Andorra, Argentina, Australia, Austria, Belgium, Bermuda, Brazil, Costa Rica, Chile, Czech Republic, Denmark, France, Finland, Germany, Great Britain, Greece, Hungary, Ireland, Iceland, Israel, Italy, Japan, Liechtenstein, Luxembourg, Monaco, Norway, New Zealand, Netherlands, Poland, Portugal, San Marino, Singapore, Slovenia, South Korea, Spain, South Africa, Switzerland, Uruguay, Venezuela and Sweden.

Citizens of the following countries are required to obtain a visa, as outlined above: Afghanistan, Albania, Angola, Armenia, Azerbaijan, Bahrain, Bangladesh, Belarus, Bosnia-Herze-govina, Cambodia, Congo, Croatia, Estonia, Georgia, Haiti, India, Iraq, Iran, Jordan, Kazakhstan, Latvia, Lebanon, Libya, Lithuania, Macedonia, Mauritania, Moldavia, Mongolia, Morocco, Niger, North Korea, Oman, Pakistan, Palestine, Qatar, Russia, Sahara Democratic Republic, Saudi Arabia, Somalia, Sri Lanka, Sudan, Syria, Tunisia, Turkmenistan, Turkey, Ukraine, United Arab Emirates, Uzbekistan, Vietnam, Yemen and Yugoslavia.

Citizens of the following countries must also apply for a visa to visit Mexico, but they need not pay the US $37 consular fee: Bolivia, Colombia, Dominican Republic, Jamaica, Nicaragua, Peru, Ecuador, Rumania, Belize, Panama, Guatemala and Malaysia.

Travel Information

Working in Mexico requires a special visa. Workers may fill positions in the country that cannot be filled first by Mexicans. Companies big enough to require a foreign president, treasurer, general manager, and so on, must comply with the 90% Mexican employee to 10% foreign employee ratio. Professionals such as doctors, lawyers and engineers may receive immigrant status if they have their degrees and a special license to practice in Mexico. Investors must have 26,000 times the current daily minimum wage (between 46 and 49 pesos) to invest in Mexico before opening a company. At today's exchange rate, that's US $120,000 to US $128,000, but the peso value fluctuates regularly. This money must be in the Mexican Development Bank guaranteeing that investment will be made within a specific time period. This time period is determined by the National Institute of Migration.

TRAVELING WITH PETS

You can bring pets into Mexico as long as you have a certificate from a veterinarian, issued within the last seven days, stating the animal is free of communicable diseases. You also need a rabies vaccination certificate showing that the pet was vaccinated at least one month and less than one year before crossing the border. It is advisable to have pet travel insurance. Taking any exotic or endangered pet like a macaw into Mexico is not permitted and the animal could be confiscated at the border.

Returning to the US with a traveling pet, you must have a vet's certificate saying the pet had a rabies shot within the preceding three years.

PACKING LIST

Binoculars are a must if you are a birder. There is an abundance of exotic and migratory birds that are well worth scouting out. Binoculars are also fun to use on the beach to watch boats (and those on the boats) as they pass by. I even use mine on bus trips to look at distant hills and volcanoes.

Shorts and **t-shirts** are great. Everyone wears shorts, but a skirt or pants are acceptable too. Keep your clothing loose and comfortable – let the heat determine your attire, but keep in mind that revealing outfits are not acceptable. If you are a touch stodgy (like me) be prepared to be shocked by some of your fellow tourists as you wander the beach.

If going during the rainy season, May to September, pack some type of **rain protection**. **Sandals** are good at the beach, but **running shoes** or light **hiking boots** are needed for jungle walks, playing golf or touring the museums.

You will need at least one **bathing suit** and two would be better. A beach towel or grass mat is good for lying on the sand. Mats can be purchased along the beaches for less than $5.

Cameras are a great way to record memories. Bring one that you are familiar with so that you don't make mistakes on critical images. Humidity is high, so keeping your camera dry is an issue. I use a foam-padded carrying bag. Putting cameras in plastic bags is not advisable as the moisture condenses inside the bag. Non-expired film, camera batteries and flashes are readily available. Because there is so much intense sunlight, a slow-speed film is recommended (ASA 50 to 100). A flash should be used when photographing people during the day so that the harsh shadows are eliminated.

Money belts are necessary if you want to carry money with you rather than using an ATM each time you need cash. They are also good to hold credit, bank cards, and your passport. The belts should be of natural fiber and worn at the midriff. Always have a stash of emergency money somewhere in the event that you are robbed and lose your bank card and credit card in the process.

Daypacks are far more convenient to carry than handbags or beach bags. They are also harder to pickpocket or snatch. In cities, on buses or crowded places like markets, wear your daypack at the front, with the waist strap done up. That way, your hands can rest on the bag while you walk. In this position, it is almost impossible for pickpockets to access the pack. Keep only the amount of money you need for the day in your daypack and put the rest somewhere secure, like in your hotel safe or your hidden money belt.

Maps are essential. The best I have found is published by International Travel Maps and Books, 530 West Broadway, Vancouver, BC, ☎ 604-879-3621, www.itmb.com, and sells for less than $20. Their maps, Mexican Pacific Coast and Mexico Northwest, are easy to read, but do not have every village and pueblo included.

It seems to me that a map is really hard to follow if you don't have a **compass**. They are not heavy and you need not buy one that can do triangulation measurements. A simple one will do.

Tennis players should bring their own rackets because they, like other sports gear, are quite personal.

Golf clubs are also personal and should be brought with you. However, for those able to adapt to any clubs, rentals are most convenient.

Diving gear like wet suits and face masks can be brought from home or rented from dive shops. You will

need your PADI diving certification ticket. The tour operators check this certificate every time you go out. You should also check their qualifications before heading into the depths.

The marine life attracts many visitors.

Snorkeling mask and **flippers** can be carried with you from home or rented in Mexico. If going to only one resort, bringing your gear is not a problem but if traveling around, you may find it easier to rent.

Surf boards can be taken as a piece of luggage on the plane. Hardcore surfers should definitely bring their own board, but if you are a beginner, you can get away with renting.

Camping equipment should be brought with you if you are traveling around from beach to beach, sleeping in the campgrounds. Sleeping on secluded beaches is not recommended, although I know people do it. You will need a tent with mosquito netting, sleeping pad and a light cover. Cooking stoves should be able to use gasoline rather than white gas because of the availability of these fuels. The extent of your camping will determine what you will bring with you.

An **umbrella** is good if you plan on doing any walking. It keeps off the sun or rain. These can be purchased in Mexico for about the same price or a little less than those at home.

Your **first aid kit** should include things like mole-skin, Advil, tenser bandage, antihistamines, topical antibiotic cream and Band-Aids. All prescription medications and things like batteries for hearing aides or extra eyeglasses should be carried with you. A band that attaches to your glasses and goes around your head to keep glasses from falling off is a good idea if you are even a little bit active.

Reading material is available in English at the magazine stands or bookstores. In addition, many hotels have book-trading services. But for the most part, you need to bring the really good books with you. Leaving them behind when you return home is a good idea.

Sunglasses and **sun hat** should be brought and worn all the time you are in the sun because the intense ultraviolet rays can damage your eyes. If you forget to bring these, they are readily available in all the markets.

FACT FILE: *Paul Theroux, author of Patagonia Express and other travel books, has problems with his eyes due to the damage caused by the ultraviolet rays. He often kayaked without sunglasses.*

Sunscreen is necessary. Do not let yourself become cancer red because you don't like chemicals. If spending time in the jungle, you should bring **insect repellent**.

HEALTH CONCERNS

General health should be kept at optimum level when traveling. Make certain you have rest, lots of clean water and a well-balanced diet that is supplemented with vitamins. This is not difficult to do. Salt intake is important in the heat to help prevent dehydration. Carry some powdered electrolytes in case you do become dehydrated, especially if you are planning some off-the-beach trips.

Bring with you anything you may need in the way of prescriptions, glasses, orthopedics, dental care and batteries for hearing aids. Things like vitamins, bandages, antihistamines and topical creams are readily available.

▨ MEDICAL INSURANCE

Mexico now has almost the same quality medical services as the rest of North America and Europe, but it is still advisable to travel with medical insurance. The cost is far less than any medical bill would be and many policies include ticket cancellation insurance and coverage against theft.

In the event of a serious illness or accident, you will want to get to your own country fast. Without insurance, the cost could be prohibitive.

Good insurance includes emergency evacuation, repatriation, emergency reunion, trip interruption, lost baggage, accidental death and trip cancellation.

INSURANCE COST GUIDELINES		
INDIVIDUAL	**15 DAYS**	**30 DAYS**
Age 18-29	$24	$48
Age 30-39	$31	$62
Age 40-49	$47	$94
Age 50-59	$67	$134
Age 60-64	$79	$158
Age 65-69	$90	$180
Age 70-79	$122	$244
Age 80+	$212	$424

For US citizens, the table above gives you an idea of what it will cost for $50,000 coverage with a $100 deductible. For each additional month but under a year, multiply the monthly premium cost by the number of months you will be staying. Those staying longer than three months are usually eligible for a 10% discount. Groups traveling together are often offered a lower rate.

It is recommended that anyone traveling for longer than a month take out insurance of up to a million dollars.

I worked with Patricia Romero Hamrick from **International Insurance-Seguros**, 1047 W. Madero Mesa, AZ 85210-7635, ☎ 480-345-0191, www.seguros-insurance. net. I found her helpful and quick to answer any questions. She also works through **Global Travel Insurance**, ☎ 800-232-9415, www.globalmedicalplans.com. The best thing about this company's insurance is that it covers emergency evacuation and reunion, which means a loved-one can be brought to your bedside in the event that you are in hospital away from home for a long time. Moderate expenses for this loved-one are included. Global Travel also carries a Hazardous Sports Rider for those partaking in sports such as mountain biking or rock climbing. This is especially important for the serious sportster.

■ WATER

Tap water, called purified water, is considered safe to drink in luxury hotels. If you feel uncomfortable with this, bottled water is available throughout the country. It comes in sizes from half a liter (pint) to four liters (one gallon). When there is no sign, water is considered drinkable. If there is a W1 or W2 sign, it means the water is untreated and not drinkable.

Use your common sense to avoid illness. Eat at places where locals are eating. If they remain healthy, you should too. An empty restaurant usually means a bad stomach. If the sanitation looks dubious, don't eat the salad; have some hot boiled soup instead.

If traveling where creek/lake water must be consumed, I suggest using a chemical such as iodine for purification.

There is also a tablet available that has a silver (as opposed to an iodine) base that is far more palatable than the iodine. Chlorine bleach can also be used as a purifier, but it is the least effective of chemicals.

Mechanical filters take a long time to process the water and they do not filter out all organisms that could cause problems. They are also much heavier to carry than chemicals.

■ COMMON AILMENTS

Should you get a mild case of **diarrhea**, take a day of rest, drink plenty of mineral water and consume no alcohol. This common condition, often caused by the change in diet, usually clears up quickly. Mineral water can be supplemented with yogurt tablets. Imodium can be taken if you must travel and have a bad case of the trots. However, it is not recommended except in very dire emergencies because holding in the cause of your problems will allow them to multiply and make you even sicker, sometimes even causing scaring of the intestinal tissue.

FEVERS & WORSE

According to the World Health Organization, contacting **malaria** is a possibility all year at elevations below 3,000 ft/950 meters anywhere from Guaymas in the north all the way south to the Guatemala border in the south. The states of Sonora and Sinaloa are free of malaria except for the months between May and October, during rainy season.

People staying at major resorts need not use a prophylactic against malaria, but should use mosquito repellent after sunset or if going into the jungle. Anyone traveling around the country – especially those staying in lower-priced hotels – will need to use a prophylactic. Chloroquine is the prophylactic of choice. It should be taken for one week before entering the country, once a week while there, and for four weeks after returning home.

In the event that you develop a fever for no explicable reason like a cold or flu, especially if you are in mosquito country or have been bitten, you should see a doctor as soon as possible. The possibility of malaria should be considered for up to three months after leaving an infected area.

PROTECTION IS BEST

Keep exposed skin covered early in the morning or at dusk when the mosquitoes are most active. Using repellent laced with deet is also recommended. Although traces of deet have been found in the livers of users, this problem is still better than malaria. Use a sleeping net in infected areas.

Dengue fever and **dengue hemorrhagic fever** are caused by four related, but distinctly different, viruses that are spread by daytime-biting mosquitoes. Infection from one of the viruses does not produce immunity to the other three. Dengue cannot be transmitted from person to person.

Symptoms of dengue are high fever, headache, backache, joint pain, nausea, vomiting, eye pain and rash. There is no treatment except to take painkillers with acetaminophen in them rather than ASA (acetylsalicylic acid decreases your blood's clotting abilities, thus increasing the possibility of hemorrhage). Drink plenty of fluids and rest. If dengue hemorrhagic fever is contacted, fluid replacement therapy administered by a medical practitioner may be necessary. The illness lasts about 10 days and total recovery takes between two and four weeks.

Dengue is now on the rise worldwide. In 1960s, the WHO stated that there were about 30,000 cases worldwide. By 1995, this number increased to 592,000, with 240,000 cases in Mexico. Today, with the increase in urbanization and decrease in eradication programs, the WHO believes there are 20 million cases worldwide. This means that mosquito bites are potentially dangerous when traveling in the tropics. For more information, visit the website of the World Resource Institute at www.wri.org/wr-98-99/dengue.htm.

Travel Information

Yellow fever is present in all the jungles of Central America. Though inoculation is not required for entrance to Mexico, it may be required for re-entry to your own country. Inoculation, good for 10 years, is recommended if you want to avoid a lengthy stay in quarantine. Children must also have a certificate of inoculation, but it is not recommended to inoculate children who are less than one year of age.

Routine inoculations common in your home country should be up to date. Besides these, **immune globulin** is recommended against viral hepatitis; the shots are good for about six months. If you have had viral hepatitis, you are already immune. Inoculation against **typhoid fever** is highly recommended. This inoculation is good for 10 years.

BUGS

Worms and **parasites** can be a problem anywhere in the tropics. To name and describe them all would be impossible. Keep your feet free of cuts or open sores so that worm eggs or parasites cannot enter. Use sandals in showers where cleanliness is a question. Wear closed shoes such as runners or hiking boots when in the jungle.

The **bot fly** and the **New World screw worm** are insects that cause a boil-like sore after the larvae (maggot) has started to grow in its host (you). Botflies transport their eggs by way of the mosquito and the screw worm in the fly stage drops its eggs near an open sore or on mucus membranes. Once the egg is in its host, it hatches and lives under the skin. However, the fly must have air. If you have a red, puss-filled swelling that is larger than a mosquito bite, look closely. If you see a small hole in the swollen area cover it with petroleum jelly to prevent the fly from breathing. Without air, it dies. It takes four to eight days for the botfly larvae to hatch and five to 12 weeks for the screw worm.

Chagas, also known as the kissing bug, exists in Latin America and infection can become either chronic or acute. The parasite enters the blood stream when the oval-shaped insect inserts its proboscis into your skin.

As it sucks your blood, its excretion is forced out and into the opening it has formed in your body. It is the excretion that carries the larvae of the parasite.

Once planted, the larvae migrates to the heart, brain, liver and spleen, where it nests and forms cysts. If you wake up one morning after sleeping under a thatched roof and you have a purplish lump somewhere on exposed skin, you may have been bitten. If fever, shortness of breath, vomiting or convulsions occur, see a doctor immediately. Mention your suspicions.

JELLYFISH STINGS

These are a possibility for anyone who enters the water. There are often flags along the beach indicating that jellyfish are present and what their parameters are. Some stings can leave a welt for weeks, but most last only a few hours. When a jellyfish stings you, it is actually the nematocysts attached to the tentacles that touch your skin and release a toxin. This is what burns. If you do get stung, douse the area with vinegar and cover with ice to relieve the pain. A product available in the United States called After Sting Gel, which sells for about $4, can be used for jellyfish and bee stings. For more information on jellyfish, see www.diversalertnetwork.com.

TREATMENT OPTIONS

If you become sick, contact your own consulate for the names of doctors or medical clinics. The consulates can usually recommend doctors who have been trained in your country of origin.

An alternative is to contact the **IAMAT** (International Association for Medical Assistance to Travelers) clinics. The doctors speak English or French and Spanish (in Mexico) and charge between $55 for an office visit to $95 for an emergency call-out at night or on Sundays.

The information reported in this section is taken from either the IAMAT's or the World Health Organization's publications. You can become a member of IAMAT and/or send a donation to them at 417 Center Street, Lewiston, NY 14092, ☎ 716-754-4883, or 40 Regal Road,

Guelph, Ontario, Canada, N1H 7L5, ☎ 519-836-0102, www.sentex.net/~iamat.com. Their services are invaluable. Some of the money they raise goes toward a scholarship program that assists doctors in developing countries obtain medical training in more advanced parts of the world. They also sell, at cost, a portable mosquito net that weighs about five lbs/two kilos.

SAFE INDEED

IAMAT was started when Vincenzo Marcolongo, a graduate of medicine from McGill University, was working in Rome in 1960 and saw an ill Canadian who had previously seen a local doctor. He had been given a drug that was banned in North America because it destroyed white blood cells. Blood transfusions and antibiotics saved the patient's life. Realizing the problems of language and culture for foreign visitors, Dr. Marcolongo started a worldwide list of North American- and European-trained doctors that could be available for travelers. Over 200,000 contributing members now receive the directory containing 850 doctors working in 125 countries.

IAMAT CLINICS

Remember, no area code is needed when making a local call.

■ **Hermosillo, Sonora**
Clinica de Praga #1 Altos, Juarez y Jalisco, ☎ 662-213-2280

■ **Mazatlan**
Clinica Mazatlan, Zaragoza #609, ☎ 669-981-2917 or 669-985-1923

Alternative medicines are popular and as North Americans get more and more into natural health, herbal treatment for minor ailments may be a priority. There are some locals who learned from their ancestors the art of medicine using jungle plants and they are willing to treat or share information with visitors. However, for more serious ailments like a burst appendix or a broken leg, I recommend the use of traditional scientific medicine that uses strong drugs or surgery.

For official government updates on outbreaks and advisories, visit the **Centers for Disease Control & Prevention** run by the US Health Department at www.cdc.gov.

Medic Alert is an emergency response service that has been in business since 1956. Members get a bracelet that has their membership number on the back. If you have a medical condition that could result in your hospitalization while you are in an unconscious state, the medical staff contacts the 24-hour service at Medic Alert, providing your membership number. Medic Alert relays your medical conditions and any necessary precautions that must be taken. They also call your family. Medic Alert can be contacted at ☎ 888-633-4298 in the US or 209-668-3333, from elsewhere, www.medicalert.org.

Critical Air Ambulance, ☎ 800-247-8326 in the US or 800-010-0268 in Mexico. This is a team of medical experts who transport patients with multiple injuries, cardiac failure, severe head injuries, cerebral bleeds, and so forth, to the nearest fully equipped hospital in the United States. If your medical insurance handles air evacuation then they may well use this company. If not, keep the number handy in case you or a member of your group needs to get home quickly. The cost would be around US $10,000.

Sky Med, ☎ 800-475-9633 in US and Canada, 866-805-9624 in Mexico, www.skymed.com, is another company that will take you home in the event of an emergency. They go one step farther by insuring that your vehicle and all belongings also get home. They will allow a companion to travel at your bedside during the trip. Sky Med will take Canadians to a Canadian hospital if time permits, rather than an American one. This is not an expensive insurance, especially for anyone doing extreme sports where chance of accident is high. An evacuation could cost up to $30,000 from Mazatlan to Chicago (for example), so some type of insurance is advisable.

Travel Information

MONEY MATTERS

Mexico is a good deal even though prices have risen with the signing of the North American Free Trade Agreement. You can expect to pay about half of what you would in the United States for a comparable vacation. All-inclusive packages are often almost as cheap as airfare alone and those on a strict budget can almost always find a clean hotel for about $20 a night. The cost of an average vacation in a three-star hotel with restaurant food and at least one activity a day will run about $100 per person, per day. If sharing a room, the cost drops to half for every additional person.

■ BANKING/EXCHANGE

The local currency is the **peso** and it is indicated by the $ sign. Each peso is divided into 100 **centavos**. Coins come in denominations of 10, 20 and 50 centavos and one, two, five, 10 and 20 pesos. Notes come in the two, five, 10, 20, 50, 100 and 200 peso denominations. At time of writing, the exchange rate was about 10 pesos to US $1 and 13 pesos to one Euro.

Foreign money can be exchanged at the banks or Casas des Cambios. Banks are open 9 am-1:30 pm, Monday to Friday, and a few banks are open on Saturday afternoons. Casas are open later in the day, but seldom on Sundays. The exchange rate for cash is always higher than that for traveler's checks.

Traveler's checks issued by Visa, American Express or Thomas Cook are accepted throughout the country. The preferred currency is the American dollar.

There are over 9,000 ATMs in Mexico and, although there are plenty, finding one can sometimes be tricky as they are usually not open to the street. Occasionally, you will have to ask a local. Grocery stores are a good place to access these machines because, as a foreigner, you have the protection of a crowd and a gun-wielding guard. You can usually withdraw US/CAN $500 per day from your account (as long as the cash is in there to begin with), more than enough for your daily travels.

CREDIT CARDS

Credit Cards are acceptable anywhere except at the tiniest food stall or market merchant. The most common are **Visa**, **MasterCard**, **Diner's Club Card** and **American Express**.

If you need money wired from home, contact **Money Gram**, www.moneygram.com, or **Western Union**, www.westernunion.com. Visit their websites to obtain local office numbers.

PLANNING EXPENSES

If you make all your own arrangements, your cheapest day could run about $50 per person. This would include a basic room with a fan, two meals in the market or one of the smaller restaurants and the entrance fee to one attraction, like a museum. Your main entertainment would be sunning on the beach and reading a book which you brought with you. Should you want to do more – whale watch, scuba dive or play golf – the price goes up substantially. A better hotel will cost another $50, and drinks with dinner raise the price quite a bit.

To go first class – enjoy a piña colada at your hotel while watching the sun set over the Pacific and rent a car – will run between $250 and $500 per day. Most people budget for somewhere

First-class hotels line Mexico's shores.

between the two extremes. There are, of course, a few places that offer even more than first class; prices at such resorts run around $1,000 a day.

HOTEL PRICE SCALES

For each hotel reviewed in this book, I give a price range rather than a fixed rate. The price for a single and double room is the same unless otherwise stated. Use these rates as a guideline only; always call and verify current prices.

HOTEL PRICE SCALE
Room price, in US $
$ . . . . up to $20
$$ . . . . $21-$50
$$$ $51-100
$$$$ . . . . $101-$150
$$$$$ $151-200

For each establishment, I give my personal impression, followed by a brief review. My impressions may have been influenced by whom I saw and how they treated me. Once you have used the book for a while, you will have an idea as to what events and experiences interest me and what level of service I expect.

TAXES & TIPPING

There is a 15% **Value Added Tax** (VAT) on everything for sale, except food purchased at a grocery store and medicines. Hotels have a 12% tax and you may also be charged 10% service charge over the quoted price for the room. Ask before booking.

Tipping is expected in restaurants and hotels. However, if a service charge is added to the bill, I fail to see why a tip would be expected; I don't tip. Taxi drivers appreciate a tip, although it isn't necessary. The average tip is between 10% and 15%, depending on the service.

DANGERS & ANNOYANCES

Some houses in Mexico are secured by high concrete walls that have glass shards or razor-wire cemented along the top and steel bars on the windows. Inside, there are either vicious guard dogs or security guards armed with machine guns. Banks, too, have armed guards, as do some of the high-end restaurants.

This high security is not an environment that nurtures a trusting personality. Instead, it produces a "get him before he gets me" attitude, which results in many rip-offs for the unsuspecting visitor. To help prevent this, always ask the price, especially if the item you want is not on the menu or if the taxi you are using has to wait while you check out of a room. If you are not comfortable with this kind of clarification, then you may want to book into an all-inclusive package and never venture into the streets. If this also is not what you want, then Mexico may not be for you.

Even with all my experience traveling in Latin American countries, I still get royally annoyed when I get taken. To avoid this, always clarify.

THEY GET A CHARGE OUT OF THIS

The latest scam is at the airports, particularly Puerto Vallarta and Acapulco. The workers at the security desks are now confiscating batteries, but only those still in packages. They tell the traveler that it is illegal to carry them on board. In fact, they are selling the batteries in the markets to supplement their incomes. You can take packaged batteries onto a plane.

AIRPORT SECURITY

Since 9-11, airport security has increased. Cameras and laptop computers are checked for explosives. People are asked to remove their shoes. I have even seen security guards demand that metal earrings be removed.

However, there are some things that most people would never think of. For an example, the explosive powders from firecrackers can set off alarms, as can the residue of explosives from those who have been at firing ranges or those who set off explosives for avalanche control. It is illegal to transport firecrackers and, if caught with them, you will be subject to a $25,000 fine and/or up to five years in prison. Fertilizer on the shoes of golfers and nitroglycerin for heart patients can also set off alarms. The most recent alarming substance is the glycerin in some hand lotions.

Doing your part in avoiding these substances before going to the airport will speed up your trip through the security monitors.

For those with a common last name, especially one like Garcia or Martinez, be aware that you may be stopped at

American immigration for questioning. The interrogations usually last no longer than 10 or 15 minutes, but they are irritating. Keep your humor and matters will be dealt with much quicker.

If you are a frequent flier you should get a letter from Customs declaring that you are not "the Garcia" or "Martinez" who has a criminal record or direct links to Osama.

■ COMMON-SENSE PRECAUTIONS

Every country in the world has robbers and petty thieves, whether you are in the polite society of Japan or the northern wilds of Canada. If you hang out in very poor sections of a city where you are unknown, if you are staggering drunk in a back alley, if you trust a stranger to hold your cash while you run to the washroom, you are going to have a sad tale to tell.

When out, be aware of what is around you. If it seems like you are being followed, go into a store or knock on someone's door. Make certain that expensive items like your camera or Rolex watch are out of sight.

Be inside at night and take a taxi back to your room if you have been out late. Don't be drunk in public. A drunk is a great target. Don't get mixed up in the dope trade. Save booze and dope for home. If you do get into trouble at home, you know the rules, you have friends to help and the prisons are far more comfortable than they are in Mexico.

Women should walk with confidence. If you appear frightened or lost, you are a target. Don't walk alone in non-populated places like jungles or secluded beaches. In the event that you are grabbed or accosted in any way, create a scene. Holler, scream, kick and fight with all your might. However, if you are approached by someone with a weapon, let them have it all. Being dead or seriously maimed isn't worth any possession you have, including your virginity.

■ TOILETS

Sewer systems are not like those in the US. Except for in the newer, up-market hotels, used toilet paper should be placed in a basket found beside the toilet. Please be sensitive to the needs of the Mexican Public Service Department and put your paper in the basket.

MEASUREMENTS

Mexico is metric, distance is given in kilometers, gas is sold in liters, and the temperature is read in Celsius (although, to accommodate the North American tourist, it is often quoted in Fahrenheit).

GENERAL MEASUREMENTS

1 kilometer	=	.6124 miles
1 mile	=	1.6093 kilometers
1 foot	=	.304 meters
1 inch	=	2.54 centimeters
1 square mile	=	2.59 square kilometers
1 pound	=	.4536 kilograms
1 ounce	=	28.35 grams
1 imperial gallon	=	4.5459 liters
1 US gallon	=	3.7854 liters
1 quart	=	.94635 liters

TEMPERATURE

For Fahrenheit: Multiply Centigrade figure by 1.8 and add 32.

For Centigrade: Subtract 32 from Fahrenheit figure and divide by 1.8.

Centigrade		Fahrenheit
40°	=	104°
35°	=	95°
30°	=	86°
25°	=	77°
20°	=	64°
15°	=	59°
10°	=	50°

Travel Information

TOURIST ASSISTANCE

POLICE & OTHER AGENCIES

Mexico has almost more types of police than it has beaches. There are the Federal Police and the Federal Traffic Police. The **Federal Police** have no jurisdiction over immigration documents or other tourist-type matters. If you are stopped and asked to show documents by these people, tell them to come to your hotel. Once there, have the manager call your consulate. Because of low wages, these police have a reputation of being corrupt.

The **Tourist Police**, on the other hand, patrol areas where tourists gather. To my knowledge, they are fairly good, and I never felt threatened or unsafe when dealing with them. If you are robbed or harmed in any way, report all instances to the Tourist Police (numbers are given at the start of each town section in this book).

Green Angels (Angeles Verdes) is Mexico's national road emergency service that is in place to help motorists on major highways. They have a fleet of 300 trucks that patrol fixed sections of major highways twice a day. Drivers

Green Angels truck.

speak both English and Spanish, can help with mechanical problems, have first aid, radio-telephone communications and can tow a brokcn-down vehicle into a garage. Although this is a free service, a tip is always appreciated. They can be reached at ☎ 800-903-9200.

The **Consumer Protection Service**, known as the Secreteria y Fomento Turistico (SEFOTUR), is in place for complaints about businesses in Mexico. They are located in all major centers. If you have problems with a merchant, report it to this agency.

COMMUNICATIONS

▨ TELEPHONE

Most public phones require a calling card. **Ladatel cards** are sold in 20 or 50 peso denominations and are available at stores, restaurants and automated machines at the airport and bus station.

To make international calls, you must dial the international access code (98), then dial the country code (1 for the US and Canada, 44 for England), the area code and the local number. To reach Mexico from overseas, you must use the country code (52), then the city code and the number you wish to reach.

Some common city codes are: Acapulco, 744; Guadalajara, 33; Oaxaca, 951; Puerto Vallarta, 322. Codes for cities not listed here are provided at www. telmex.com. There you can type in the name of the town and get the area code. If you are placing a city-to-city call, dial 01 (for long distance), the city code and then the number. No city code is needed when making a local call.

USEFUL PHONE NUMBERS
The following numbers are used throughout Mexico.
24-hour Tourist Assistance. . . . . ☎ 800-9-0392
Emergency Assistance . . . . ☎ 060
Operator-assisted international calls. ☎ 090
Operator-assisted national long distance . . . . ☎ 020
Automatic national long distance . . . . ☎ 01
Automatic long distance to Canada and the US . . . . ☎ 001
Information . . . . ☎ 040

To call a toll-free number from Mexico, dial, 01-8XX (numbers are usually 800, 888, 877, etc.) then the seven digits. You may find the following numbers useful.

Sprint, ☎ 01-800-877-8000

AT&T, ☎ 01-800-288-2872 or 01-800-112-2020 for Spanish.

Teleglobe Canada, ☎ 01-800-123-0200

You can also become a customer of companies like **World Wide Callback**, www.worldwidecallback.com, where you call a number that has been given to you by Callback from anywhere in the world. Once you hear the ring sound, you hang up and they call you back. From there you place your international calls. You are charged to a credit card at American rates. This system must be set up before you travel.

▨ MAIL

It is easy and safe to send and receive mail. It takes from five to seven days for a letter/postcard to reach the United States from anywhere in Mexico. The cost for a letter is about 40¢ for up to 20 grams. Parcels don't have to be inspected before being sent out of the country, so they can be wrapped before taking them to the post office. Insurance is highly recommended for parcels.

You can receive mail at the *post restante* in any town. You will need your passport for identification to pick up your mail.

International courier services are also available: **Federal Express**, ☎ 5-228-9904 (in Mexico) or 800-900-1100, www.fedex.com; **Airborne Express**, ☎ 5-203-6811; **Aeroflash**, ☎ 5-627-3030; **DHL**, ☎ 5-345-7000, www. dhl.com; **UPS**, ☎ 5-228-7900 or 800-902-9200, www. ups.com.

▨ MEXICAN NEWSPAPERS

English-language newspapers published for tourists are mentioned under the specific cities where they are published.

▨ *Reforma*, www.reforma.com, is in Spanish and covers both national and international news. You must subscribe to the paper before you can read anything but the headlines.

- *El Financiero*, www.elfinanciero.com.mx, gives a summary of the financial status of Mexican economics.

- *La Jornada*, www.jornada.unam.mx, seems to be a left-wing Spanish publication.

- *Excelsior*, www.excelsior.com.mx, is an on-line magazine that you must subscribe to. You can subscribe to only the sections that are of interest to you, be they TV information, articles or tidbits.

- *El Universal*, www.eluniversal.com.mx, is a mainline newspaper with everything from headlines to horoscopes.

- *Milenio*, www.milenio.com/mexico, has both national and international news, plus a good general interest section.

- *El Economista*, www.economista.com.mx, leans more toward finance than news and covers international finance too.

- *Cronica*, www.cronica.com.mx, offers general news daily.

- *El Norte*, www.elnorte.com, has full coverage daily.

- *Proceso*, www.proceso.com.mx, also has full coverage daily.

- *Expansion*, www.expansion.com.mx, makes American news a top priority.

INTERNET

The Internet is the best way to communicate; the country has over 3.5 million users. Internet cafés are almost as common as shoeshine boys. Prices are $1-2 an hour – the rate seems dependent on whether there is air conditioning in the café or not.

CULTURE SHOCK

PUBLIC AFFECTION

Once away from the beach resorts, you will find that Mexico is still a conservative country. Physical affection in public is not common. Holding hands seems to be okay, but passionate kissing, especially by same-sex couples, is still not acceptable. Mexico is a Catholic country where most people still follow the laws of the church. However, there is one nude beach at Zipolete, south of Acapulco, that the locals tolerate.

GAY & LESBIAN TRAVEL

There are numerous gay- and-lesbian-friendly bars and hotels along the coast. Cancún even held a gay festival. Although the possibility of finding a same-sex relationship with a Mexican exists, you must be careful not to think that because a Mexican has sex with you that she or he is gay. Some Mexicans look at having same-gender sex as entertainment, not a way of life.

The magazine **Ser Gay** is a good source of information for those who read Spanish. It can be found online at www. sergay.com.mx.

SPECIAL NEEDS TRAVELERS

Special needs persons are now considered in the tourist areas of Mexico and some hotels have wheelchair accessibility. The streets are still pretty shoddy in places, but taxis are plentiful. Taking a small wheelchair from a hotel to a restaurant that is on street level would be possible. Blind or deaf people should have an assistant.

FOOD

Mexican food needs no explaining to most people in North America and Europe because those countries have as many Mexican restaurants as they have hamburger and pizza joints. Mexican food is usually made up of onions, tomatoes, rice, beans, corn, eggs, cheese and *pollo* (chicken). These foods are accompanied by some kind of corn tortilla.

However, with the proliferation of tourism, today you can get any kind of food in Mexico, from Chinese to Japanese to Bavarian and Thai. Along the coast, of course, seafood or fish is the most popular meal. Be certain to try some ceviche, a raw fish or sea food pickled in lime juice, or *pescado* Veracruz, a fish smothered in fresh tomato and onion sauce.

Because you are in the tropics, seasonal fruits are abundant. Try guanabana, which has a slimy white substance that is succulent beyond belief. Taste some guava, especially if your stomach is a bit queasy as it is supposed to slow down peristaltic action

Guanabana fruit.

in the gut. Try the mango; when fresh there is nothing like it. Banana *con leche* (banana with milk) or fresh-squeezed orange or grapefruit juice will always refresh you when you are hot or tired. Other fruits to try are avocados, grapes, papayas (larger than those found in North America), peaches, fresh-picked peanuts, pears, pineapples, strawberries, watermelons and prickly pears.

FAVORITE DISHES

An **enchilada** is a tortilla stuffed with ground meat, beans and cheeses. A **tostada** is the same thing, only the tortilla is toasted and left flat on the plate.

Guacamole is made with avocado that is mashed and mixed with onion, tomato and lime juice. It is often served as an appetizer or included as one of the sauces for your meal.

FACT FILE: *Avocado is one of the few fruits that has a lot of calories.*

Mole de pollo or **mole poblano** is considered the national dish. It consists of *mole*, a tasty brown sauce, that is cooked with either chicken or turkey. However, the *mole* sauce can be served in many ways, including as a dark thick soup. The word "mole" comes from the Aztec word meaning "sauce." When you are offered a red mole with your chicken, you should ask how spicy it is. Chances are, it has a lot of red chilies. A brown mole will have a chocolate base and be less spicy.

Chilmole is occasionally called *relleno-negro*. It is made using a sauce that incorporates orange juice, chiles, cloves, allspice, black peppers, oregano, cumin and garlic. This is cooked with either chicken or turkey.

FACT FILE: *Prior to the arrival of the Spanish, the locals made tamales for the gods, as well as for themselves. Some were made in special designs like spirals, while others were huge, weighing up to a hundred pounds.*

Tamales are a feast dish that take hours to make and only minutes to devour. They are made with a corn flour paste filled with things like meat, chiles, fish, frogs, beans, turkey, squash seeds or any combination of these foods. Most are rolled into banana leaves and steamed or roasted.

CHEF'S SECRET

Should you decide to make your own tamales once you are back at home, the one secret I can pass on to you is that a tamale, no matter how much care is taken in the making, will not turn out unless the cook has music blaring in the background.

Quesadillas are made with wheat-flour tortillas and are the same as *tostadas*, except these have tons of melted cheese on top.

Frijoles refritos, or re-fried beans. In Mexico, it matters not if you are having breakfast, snack, meal of the day or beer – *frijoles* will appear. Served with sour cream, they are delicious and an excellent source of protein.

For a good glossary of Mexican foods, as well as recipes and interesting historical tidbits, go to the TexMex website at www.texmextogo.com.

BOOKING A ROOM

Many people book their accommodations over the Internet. This is okay, but be aware that not everything on the Web is true. Photos probably show only the best side of an establishment, and lighting plays a big part in making something look far more attractive than it is. You will not see the cockroaches in the corners or hear the bus terminal next door. Rates quoted may be off-season, with no indication of what in-season rates are, and taxes may not be mentioned. Ask some questions before turning over your credit card number.

- *Is there air conditioning or a fan?* In a thatched-roof hut, air conditioning is useless because the cold air goes out through the roof.

- *Is there hot water? How is it heated?* Water heated on the roof by the sun is far cooler than water heated in a gas water tank.

- *What does "all-inclusive" mean?* Is it rice and beans for three meals a day and a lawn chair around the pool, or does it include excursions around the area?

- *Do the prices include taxes and service charges?* Tax is an additional 25%; it makes a huge difference on your bill.

- *Does the hotel accept credit cards and do they add a fee for this?* Charging for this service is against their contract with the credit card companies, but some places add this anyway.

> ■ *How close to other places is the hotel? Will you be able to move around easily without having to pay for taxis?*

If you do book ahead, print out all correspondence and bring the documentation with you. Some proprietors have been known to offer one rate, but charge another after the customer has arrived. Make certain you read all the fine print.

If possible, book and pay for only a few days. That way, if you don't like the place, you can look around after your arrival and find another place.

See page 72 for a guideline to hotel prices.

GETTING HERE

There are many options. For a luxurious stay near the beach, you can have a tour agent from your own town book your flight and hotels so all you need to do is pack, grab your cash and credit cards, and get yourself to the airport. Or you may be on a long trip and arrive by traveling overland from the US, Guatemala or Belize. You may want to do nothing but visit one beach after another or stay on the same beach for the entire vacation. If you have specialized activities you would like to pursue, like kayaking or horseback riding, consider working with one of the companies that focuses on these activities. You may want to fly with a charter and return on a non-changeable date. These tickets are usually the best deal, especially if you can negotiate the flight without hotels. Be certain to confirm your return schedule at least 72 hours before departure.

The following airlines are the most common ones dropping into the west coast of Mexico. For more information about them, go to their websites or call them direct.

■ BY AIR

Aero California, ☎ *800-237-6225 (Mx), www.aerocali fornia.de,* flies from Los Angeles and Tucson to

Manzanillo, Mazatlan, Guadalajara, Puerto Vallarta, Colima and Tepic.

AeroMexico, ☎ *800-237-6639 (US), 800-021-4010 (Mx), www.aeromexico.com,* flies from Los Angeles, New York, Tucson, San Diego, Dallas-Ft. Worth, Atlanta and Miami in the States and Ontario in Canada. They have flights to Guadalajara, Mazatlan and Mexico City.

Alaska Airlines, ☎ *800-252-7522 (US), 800-468-2248 (US for packages), 55-5282-2484 (Mx), www.alaskaair. com,* serves 80 cities in the United States, Canada and Mexico, and has flights from Europe and Asia. I flew with them and found their prices the best, their planes full and their service exceptional, especially at the airport in Puerto Vallarta. I recommend this company.

American Airlines, ☎ *800-433-7300 (US), 800-904-6000 (Mx), www.aa.com,* was one of the first airlines to fly passengers and cargo into Mexico. They fly from Dallas-Ft. Worth, Miami and Los Angeles to Mexico City, Guadalajara, Puerto Vallarta and Acapulco. In my experience, Dallas-Ft. Worth airport is the easiest airport to get through in the United States. The security check is efficient, the greeters know where to send everyone, and the people manning the stations throughout the airport are friendly.

America West, ☎ *800-363-2597 (US), 800-235-9292 (Mx), www.americawest.com,* leaves from Phoenix and Las Vegas and flies to Acapulco, Ixtapa-Zihuatenejo, Puerto Vallarta and, through an affiliate, to Guaymas and Guadalajara.

Aviacsa, ☎ *800-735-5396 (US), 800-711-6733 (Mx), www. aviacsa.com.mx,* flies between Houston or Las Vegas and Mexico City. They also offer many flights inside Mexico.

British Airways, ☎ *800-AIRWAYS (US), 55-5387-0300 (Mx), www.ba.com,* offers three flights a week between London and Mexico City.

Continental Airlines, ☎ *800-231-0856 (US), 800-900-5000 (Mx), www.continental.com,* flies from Houston and Newark to 21 destinations in Mexico, including Manzanillo and Colima.

Delta, ☎ *800-241-4141 (US), 800-123-4710 (Mx), www. delta.com*, flies from many US areas, including Los Angeles, Dallas-Ft. Worth and Atlanta, to Mexico City, Acapulco, Puerto Vallarta and Guadalajara.

Frontier, ☎ *800-432-1359, www.frontierairlines.com*, flies from select US cities to Mazatlan, Puerto Vallarta and Ixtapa/Zihuatenejo.

Mexicana, ☎ *800-531-7921 (US), 800-509-8960 (Mx), www.mexicana.com*, leaves from Los Angeles, San José, San Francisco, Oakland, Chicago, San Antonio, Newark, Miami, Denver, Montreal and Toronto. There are numerous cities in Central and South America from which it operates. It flies to Mexico City, Puerto Vallarta, Guadalajara and Mazatlan. Mexicana has been in business since the 1930s and has a good safety record.

United Airlines, ☎ *800-538-2929 (US), 800-003-0777 (Mx), www.united.com,*flies from San Francisco, Chicago, Los Angeles, Washington, DC and Miami to Mexico City.

ARRIVING AT THE AIRPORT

When you fly into any Mexican airport, the procedure is simple. First, you go through Immigration, where you will receive a 90-day (usually) visitor's permit. You then pick up your bags and head for Customs inspection. You will be asked to push a button. If the light above the button turns green, you and your party are free to walk through. If it turns red, the inspectors will check your bags for any forbidden substances.

There are banks at the airports, along with some souvenir shops and places to eat, though the food is usually terrible.

To get to town, if you haven't arranged for a pick-up by one of the bigger hotels, you can take a taxi to the center. Fares are lower if you hop a cab from the street; taxis with ticket wickets at the airport are up to four times as expensive. When taking a taxi from the street, be certain to establish the price beforehand.

A bus is an option if you don't have too much luggage. Ask at the information booth in the airport which bus will take you where you want to go. Usually, the bus stops are just outside the airport, beyond the taxis on the street.

OVERLAND BY BUS

Buses from other countries do not cross the border into Mexico. They leave you at the border and you must either walk across or take a local bus or taxi to the nearest bus terminal and catch a Mexican bus.

Bus travel in Mexico can be first class, second class or peasant class. The first-class buses are roomy, air-conditioned vehicles that often come with an attendant to look after your needs. The 44 reclining seats on each bus are soft. Your lunch and a drink may be included in the price of the ticket and handed to you as you board the bus. There are toilets available and, often, you can even make yourself a tea or coffee. Videos are played, usually not too loud, and they are often fairly decent and in English. Some of the companies have private waiting rooms at the bus stations, where only their passengers may sit. These companies also offer bathrooms not used by the general public in the main terminal. Second-class bus service is almost as luxurious as first class, except you don't get lunch and the bus stops at some towns on the way to your destination. They are more like the buses found in North America. Peasant-class bus travel in Mexico is most interesting, although the least comfortable. You never get a lunch or an attendant and the buses stop at many towns. No matter what class service you use, no longer do buses go only when full and carry everything, including the chicken going to market.

Ticket prices run about $5 per hour of travel for the best class and drop to just over half that for second class (usually) and even less for peasant class. It is only the peasant-class tickets that do not have reserved seats. Bus drivers are the bosses of the road and of the bus. They know their job and do it well.

Bus stations are generally large buildings on the outskirts of bigger cities. You must pay a 25¢ tax if using buses from the terminals and occasionally your carry-on luggage will be searched by security. The following companies service travel from the US border down into central Mexico.

The Estrella Blanca (Elite), ☎ *221-0850, 290-1001 or 290-1014.* Buses leave for Guadalajara, Mexico City and all major stops in-between.

Primera Plus, ☎ *221-0095, www.flecha-amarilla.com.* The ticket price includes a sandwich and juice. The air-conditioned bus is a luxury liner and comes recommended for any trips in the area if their schedule is right for you. I traveled with them and was quite pleased.

ETN, ☎ *223-5665 or 223-5666, www.etn.com.mx,* has buses going to most major destinations. This, too, is a luxury liner, but I found them less-than caring about their passengers.

Transportes del Pacifico, ☎ *222-1015 or 222-5622,* has buses going around the country often, usually once every hour to major destinations.

TAP, ☎ *290-0119*, has buses going to 24 destinations around the country. I found the workers at the PV office helpful and honest. I would not hesitate traveling with them. TAP also covers many destinations to the north like Tijuana and Guaymas.

■ OVERLAND BY CAR OR RV

Before entering Mexico with a vehicle you must have an American, Canadian or international driver's license. At the border you must apply for a temporary **vehicle importation permit**. For this you need proof of ownership, registration, proof of citizenship and an affidavit from lien holders allowing this temporary importation. (If you take a rental car from the US or Belize into Mexico, the rental company will provide all necessary documents.) This permit is good for six months and can be used for multiple entries. The fee ($15) must be paid by Visa, MasterCard or American Express. The permit must be pasted onto the windshield. It proves that you paid to bring the vehicle in and shows the date when you must have the vehicle out of the country. If you overstay, your vehicle will be confiscated. RVs require an additional permit. It is illegal to leave your vehicle in Mexico unless you pay a 30% tax levied on the value of the vehicle.

The main roads between the American and Guatemalan border are all paved, double-lane highways. Secondary roads that follow the coast are also paved, but narrow and winding, with almost no shoulders. The speed limits, measured in kilometers, are reasonable (40-60 mph/65-100 kmh) and there are Green Angels around should you run into any mechanical problems (see page 76). Maps are accurate and signs well posted. RV parks are dotted along the coast; most allow tenting. Hotels often offer some sort of off-street parking, which is necessary if leaving the vehicle overnight.

If you have decided to bring your car, be certain it is in top shape, with good tires, a tuned-up motor, a recent carburetor overhaul, and so on. Paying for repairs at gringo prices would make this an expensive vacation. If taking a motor home, don't overload it. You can purchase anything you may want or need in Mexico and often the price will be less than at home.

INSURANCE

Mexican car insurance is essential. Foreign insurance is of no value. Offices of insurance companies line the borders for your convenience. There are two components to consider if you are involved in an accident. First, damage to the car, the property, the person, medical expenses and loss of wages. Then the moral damages are calculated. This is the pain and suffering incurred by the injured and, in Mexico, this is usually about one-third of what the actual damages are. You then have the choice of a civil or criminal case. In a criminal case, the victim receives an appointed lawyer and the liability is not limited like it is in civil cases. In the worst-case scenario, should you kill a person in an accident that you caused, you would have to pay for the damaged vehicle, the medical expenses incurred, funeral expenses and loss of wages. This would be calculated at the minimum daily wage of the person killed for a period determined by the courts. Moral damages would be added to all this. For an average person, $100,000 liability coverage should be adequate.

Travel Information

In the event of an accident, first and always, contact your insurance company. They know what to say and do. Do not sign anything or answer questions until you have a legal representative with you. This is your right as a driver in Mexico. If you are arrested, you have the right to be released on bail; the amount of bail is determined by a court official, not by the police. Should you be under the influence of drugs or alcohol, you may be detained for a long time.

Most of the car insurance information I used came from DriveMex.com (see below).

INSURANCE COMPANIES

There are numerous companies selling car insurance in Mexico. I recommend the following because they have built a good reputation. If you fall in with a fly-by-night company, you could lose some cash. Take the recommendations given here or those of a trusted friend.

International Insurance-Seguros, *1047 W. Madero, Mesa, AZ,* ☎ *480-345-0191, www.globalmedicalplans. com*, sells car, boat and medical insurance. They are responsive and knowledgeable. The company's owner, Patricia Romero Hamrick, is a Mexican lady with a lot of experience with insurance in Mexico. Patricia has many Mexican clients. Whenever I dealt with her, I was always satisfied. It is important to know that Mexican insurance claims can end up in court for years, whereas American claims are usually settled quickly. With this company, you can purchase insurance (dealing in English) before you head to Mexico and, since this is a Mexican company, the insurance is acceptable over the border. Their medical insurance includes emergency evacuation and reunion. That means a loved-one can join you should you be in hospital for a long time.

Sanborn's Insurance, ☎ *800-222-0158, www.sanborns insurance.com,* is a large company stationed in Mexico. It has been around for a long time.

Seguros Tepeyac, ☎ *800-837-3922,* was founded in 1944. It belongs to the MAPFRE system from Spain and operates in 26 countries.

DriveMex.com, ☎ *866-367-5053, www.drivemex.com,* is operated by Comerco Courtage Inc. I have worked with this company and I was pleased.

▨ BY SEA

You can come to Mexico by private boat, public ferry or cruise ship. If taking a cruise, your agent will look after all necessary documents. All you will need is this guidebook, clothing, some money and your passport. If going by ferry between La Paz, Baja California and Mazatlan, you may find that some boats offer poor service. The business has been privatized.

PRIVATE BOAT

If you are sailing your own vessel into Mexico, you will need to stop first at the Immigration office at the port of entry to get a **tourist visa** and a **temporary import permit** for your boat. You will need ownership papers proving the boat is yours or the lease agreement if the vessel is rented. You will need proof of citizenship so you can obtain a tourist visa and an arrival and departure clearance document. You must post a bond (for the value of the vessel, plus an added $10 processing fee) using a major credit card at the Banjercito bank.

You must then register your boat at a marina. If you plan to sail from one port to another, you must obtain a document specifying your arrival and departure clearances. For more specific information on sailing in Mexico, go to www.mexonline.com/boatmex.htm.

BOAT CHARTERS

Orca Sailing, *1017 15th St., Bellingham, WA,* ☎ *800-664-6049, www.orcasailing.com,* has a number of different yachts that can be rented by the week. They run between $14,000 per week for six people up to $175,000 for 12 people in a luxurious liner. The per-person cost is lower if you join a group, rather than hire the boat privately. With this company, once two people have confirmed their trip, the deal is a go. The prices include everything after you arrive at the boat's dock, even the wine with your gourmet dinners. You will be expected to help with the sailing by taking your share of the watch, monitoring weather,

getting cyclone updates, studying the ocean currents, using SSB & VHF radios and helping with chart selection. Your route can be tailored to your specs. Equipment for high-speed watersports is included. This is a great way to see Mexico.

Slow Dance is one of Orca's vessels that sails Mexican waters.

Cruise Ship Centers, ☎ 866-358-7285, 800-707-7327 (Canada) or 877-791-7676 (US), *www.cruiseshipcenters. com,* offers three- to eight-day cruises in the Pacific, stopping at places like Puerto Vallarta, Mazatlan and Acapulco. If you wish to have your every need catered to, eat more exotic foods than your encyclopedia could list, and still enjoy the best of Mexico, this is one option. The ships have a climbing wall, jogging tracks, mini golf, fitness and dance classes, spa facilities, pools and hot tubs, deck games, casinos, lounges, art auctions, duty-free shopping and facilities for children. The different restaurants are too many to name. The cost for one of these cruises starts at about $750 per person. I have worked with Carrol Johnson (cjohnson@cruiseshipcenters.com) for years and she has always managed to get me what I want, when I want it, for a price close to what I can afford.

Royal Caribbean, ☎ 800-511-4848, has a three-day trip to Ensenada where you can ride horse through the hills or just sit on the beach. The ship leaves from Los Angeles. Luxurious staterooms start at $530 a day, while regular rooms cost $220 a day. This is all-inclusive. The boat has two pools, nine bars, a cinema, a fitness center, a spa, a casino and children's facilities.

GETTING AROUND

BY PLANE

There are numerous companies working in Mexico. AeroMexico and Mexicana are the biggest. However, Alaska Air, Aviacsa and Aero California also offer service to many destinations at competitive prices.

Note that ticket changes are costly in Mexico, usually running 25% of the original fare. When traveling, arrive early as your seat could be sold to someone on the standby list. Carry on as much as possible. Lost luggage is not fun. I once had all my baggage lost and it took three days to be found. During that time the airline refused to supply even a toothbrush. It was an American couple listening to my arguments with the company representative who finally produced the needed items.

See *General Directory*, page 98, for airline contact information.

BY BUS

Unless you are in a hurry to get from one place to another, I suggest taking a bus. This way, you can watch the countryside, talk to locals and get to your destination feeling relaxed. Not that air travel is stressful, but bus travel is more comfortable in Mexico than it is in the US and Canada. After all, you did come to see the country.

Usually, you will find numerous bus companies going to your destination at different times during the day. If there is no direct bus, you may need to travel to the nearest city en route and connect to another bus going to your destination.

Tickets may be purchased in advance, in person. Bus companies do not take credit cards, but every bus station

Travel Information

except in the tiniest of villages has an ATM. Baggage is labeled when you hand it over and you get a ticket that you must present to get your bags back. It is customary to give the baggage handler a few pesos for his service when putting the bags on the bus. Occasionally, you will have to go through a wand-over-body security check. Theft of baggage is not a concern.

If traveling at night, buses are comfortable, children are quiet and there are no chickens in the carry-on baggage. You may find it easier to sleep on the right-hand side of the bus, without the glare of headlights from oncoming traffic.

■ BY CAR

For details about entering Mexico with your own car, see page 79. You can rent a vehicle from many of the main car rental companies in the US and Canada (see page 85). Privately owned companies are listed in the cities where they are located.

Mexican car insurance is essential (see page 89) and you must have a valid driver's license to rent. You must be 25 years of age or older and hold a major credit card. Remember, if you get into an accident, call the insurance company/car dealer before you answer questions or sign any papers.

> **AUTHOR EXPERIENCE:** *On my recent Mexico trip, I dealt with National, although I spoke with most other companies. I found that National was far more interested in telling me about the road conditions, things of which I must be aware and general information about driving in Mexico than they were in renting me a vehicle. They also gave me very good service.*

See *General Directory*, page 98, for car rental company contact information.

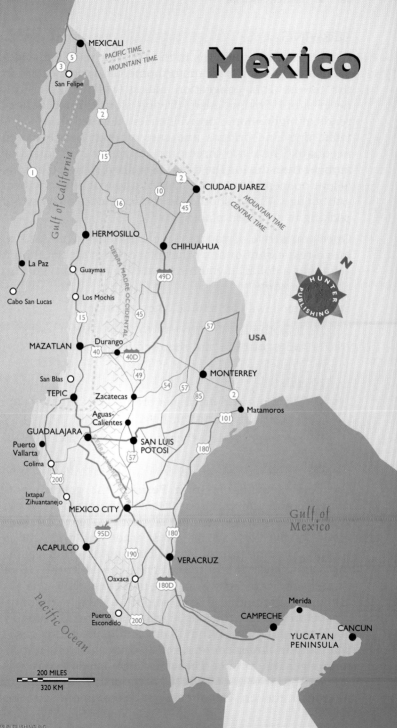

Mexico

PACIFIC TIME
MOUNTAIN TIME

MEXICALI

5

3
San Felipe

2

15

CIUDAD JUAREZ

2

10

16

45

MOUNTAIN TIME
CENTRAL TIME

1

HERMOSILLO

CHIHUAHUA

Gulf of California

La Paz

Guaymas

49D

Cabo San Lucas

Los Mochis

45

SIERRA MADRE OCCIDENTAL

15

57

USA

MAZATLAN

Durango

40

40D

49

57

MONTERREY

San Blas

TEPIC

Zacatecas

54

57

85

2

Matamoros

Aguas-
Calientes

101

GUADALAJARA

SAN LUIS
POTOSI

180

Puerto
Vallarta

Colima

57

Ixtapa/
Zihuantanejo

200

MEXICO CITY

Gulf of
Mexico

95D

180

ACAPULCO

190

VERACRUZ

Oaxaca

180D

Pacific Ocean

Puerto
Escondido

200

Merida

CAMPECHE

CANCUN

YUCATAN
PENINSULA

N

HUNTER
PUBLISHING

200 MILES

320 KM

007 HUNTER PUBLISHING, INC

DRIVING

Driving is on the right, as in the US. One problem, especially if you have a large motor home, is the congestion in the towns. This congestion makes walking a hazard, never mind driving. Also, driving along the secondary roads at night should be avoided as there are always animals, one-lane bridges and cars without headlights to negotiate. There are three times as many road fatalities at night than during the day. There are also speed bumps (silent policemen) at the entrance and exit of every town and village. These should be approached slowly. Avoid parking in secluded places.

Once you arrive, if you hire a car watcher while you go into a restaurant or any other place, the watcher should get about a dollar. If you hire a valet to park your car, tip about the same.

Some basic laws you should know include:

- It is the law for drivers to fasten their seat belts, but it is not required for passengers.
- Traveling in the back of a pickup truck is legal.
- Drinking and driving is prohibited, but passengers may drink in a vehicle.
- For motorcycles, there is no helmet law.

GAS

Gasoline is available from **Pemex**, the government-owned petroleum company. Some stations have a car wash and mini-mart and offer oil changes. They sell three grades of gas. Nova is the lowest grade and price and is sold from a blue pump. RVs should not use this gas as the octane level is less than anything sold in the US or Canada and can cause knocking in the motor. Magna sin is the mid-grade fuel that is sold from the green pump. The octane level of this gas is around 86 and is probably equal to regular gas in the US or Canada. Premium gas is sold only in larger centers and is the equivalent of premium gas anywhere. Diesel is also available and is praised by drivers of RVs, who claim it is superior to American fuel in cleanliness. It is commonly recommended that RVs have a pre-filter installed and fuel/water separators to protect their pumps and injectors. Gasoline costs about 65¢ a liter/$2.75 a gallon.

TOLL ROADS

Be aware that most motor homes and pick-up trucks are classified as two-axle vehicles. There is always an icon beside the term describing how many axles your vehicle has and those illiterate in the language of axles can make out what they will have to pay by matching their vehicle with the icon. If you are towing a trailer or a boat, you will be charged according to the number of axles. The cost for a car between Mazatlan and Culiacan is $31, and a motor home costs $35. The cost between Guadalajara and Tepic is about $35 for a car and $55 for a motor home. Go to www.mexperience.com/guide/essentials/toll_road_charges.htm and click on road charges for distances between places and the cost to travel on the toll highways. The site has other information, too. In my opinion, the amount one saves on gas, along with the savings in tranquilizers because of the better road conditions and the time saved, make the price of a toll highway well worth it.

POLICE/TICKETS

It was at one time common to pay the police a bribe and be on your way. This, with increased tourism, is changing. Now, if a police officer stops you and accuses you of a violation, ask for the fine. Usually, the police officer will leave you alone. If he does give you a ticket, chances are you are guilty of the crime. If you are, he will probably take your driver's license and give you a ticket. You can pay the ticket and retrieve your license at the nearest city hall. If you pay the ticket within 24 hours, it costs less than if you wait. If you are not guilty of a crime, the police officer will probably send you on your way with a warning not to do what he charged you with doing. Smile, say thank you, and be gone.

HITCHHIKING

Mexico is not a place to hitchhike. Although most Mexican families are friendly and willing to give you a ride, there is always the opportunist who will target a foreigner. Robbery or worse should always be considered. If for some reason you must hitchhike, go to a service station on the edge of town and ask for a ride from a family that is going in your direction.

AUTHOR'S TOP PICKS

1. Visit **Guadalajara**, where you can poke around the plazas and museums or take the Tequila Express tour. Page 189.

2. Bird at any of the sites around San Blas. Page 165.

3. Take the **Canopy Tour**. Page 127.

4. Eat and drink at the **Cliff** in Puerto Vallarta.

5. Sit on the **beach** all day with a beer in hand.

GENERAL DIRECTORY

■ MEDICAL & HEALTH CARE

Critical Air Ambulance . . . . ☎ 800-247-8326 (US); 800-010-0238 (Mx)
Sky Med . . . . ☎ 800-475-9633 (US); 866-805-9624 (Mx); www.skymed.com
Medic Alert . . . . ☎ 888-633-4298 (US); www.medicalert.org

■ CAR RENTAL COMPANIES

Avis. . . . . ☎ 800-288-8888 (US); 5-558-8888 (Mx); www.avis.com
Alamo . . . . ☎ 800-462-5266 (US); www.alamo.com
Budget . . . . ☎ 800-472-3325 (US); www.budget.com
Dollar. . . . . ☎ 800-800-3665 (US); www.dollar.com
Hertz. . . . . ☎ 800-654-3030 (US); www.hertz.com
National. . . . . ☎ 800-CAR-RENT (US); www.nationalcar.com
Thrifty . . . . ☎ 800-THRIFTY (US); www.thrifty.com

■ EMERGENCY CONTACTS

Tourist Assistance . . . . ☎ 800-9-0392
Emergency Assistance. . . . . ☎ 060

■ CONSULATES

For foreign consulates, see page 277, in the *Appendix*.

■ INSURANCE COMPANIES

International Insurance-Seguros .. ☎ 480-345-0191 (US); www.seguros-insurance.net
Global Travel Insurance ..... ☎ 800-232-9415 (US); www.globalmedicalplans.com

■ CREDIT CARD ASSISTANCE

NOTE: The telephone numbers listed here can, and do, change at any time. It is best to check the company's website for the latest contact details.

VISA .... ☎ 800-847-2911 (US & Mx); www.visa.com
MasterCard .. ☎ 800-MC-ASSIST (US); 800-307-7309 (Mx); www.mastercard.com
Diner's.......... ☎ 800-234-2377 (US); 5-258-3220 (Mx); www.dinersclub.com
American Express .... ☎ 800-992-3404 (US); 336-393-1111 (collect) .... wwww.americanexpress.com

■ AIRLINES

AeroMexico ... ☎ 800-237-6639 (US); 800-021-4010 (Mx); www.aeromexico.com
Alaska Airlines .... ☎ 800-252-7522 (US); 55-5282-2484 (Mx); www.alaskaair.com
America West . ☎ 800-363-2597 (US); 800-235-9292 (Mx); www.americawest.com
Aviasca .... ☎ 800-528-4227 (US); 800-711-6733 (Mx); www.aviasca.com.mx
Continental .... ☎ 800-231-0856 (US); 800-900-5000 (Mx); www.continental.com
Delta.............. ☎ 800-241-4141 (US); 800-123-4710 (Mx); www.delta.com
Frontier Air................. ☎ 800-432-1359 (US); www.frontierairlines.com
Mexicana........ ☎ 800-531-7921 (US); 800-509-8960 (Mx); www.mexicana.com

■ USEFUL WEBSITES

www.mexonline.com
www.visitmexico.com
www.mexico.com
www.go2mexico.com
www.mexconnect.com
www.elbalero.gob.mx_kids.html

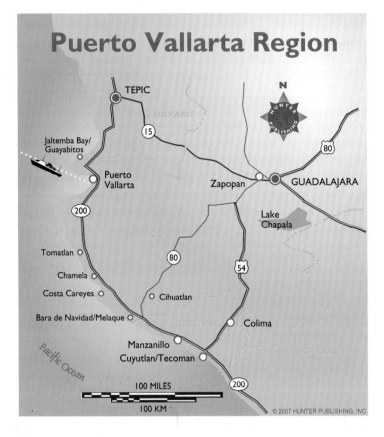

Puerto Vallarta Region

TEPIC

NAYARIT

15

Jaltemba Bay/
Guayabitos

Puerto
Vallarta

200

Tomatlan

Chamela

Costa Careyes

Bara de Navidad/Melaque

JALISCO

80

Cihuatlan

Manzanillo
Cuyutlan/Tecoman

Pacific Ocean

N

HUNTER PUBLISHING

80

Zapopan   GUADALAJARA

Lake
Chapala

54

COLIMA   Colima

MICHOACAN

200

100 MILES

100 KM

© 2007 HUNTER PUBLISHING, INC

Puerto Vallarta

■ BY PLANE

Numerous airlines serve Puerto Vallarta. If you are mobile (all your luggage in a big pack), you can hop on the city bus that goes to town. To get one, walk out the front door of the airport and turn to your left where you can see a pedestrian bridge. Buses stop under the bridge. Choose one that says "centro" on it and away you go. The cost is four pesos. Otherwise, you must hire a taxi.

Puerto Vallarta

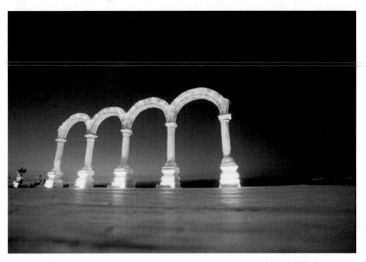

AIRLINE CONTACT INFORMATION

Aero California www.aerocalifornia.de	☎ 800-237-6225 (Mx)
AeroMexico www.aeromexico.com	☎ 800-237-6639 (US); 800-021-4010 (Mx)
Alaska Airlines www.alaskaair.com	☎ 800-252-7522 (US); 55-5282-2484 (Mx)
America West www.americawest.com	☎ 800-363-2597 (US); 800-235-9292 (Mx)
American Airlines www.aa.com	☎ 800-433-7300 (US); 800-904-6000 (Mx)
Continental www.continental.com	☎ 800-231-0856 (US); 800-900-5000 (Mx)
Delta Airlines www.delta-air.com	☎ 800-241-4141 (US); 800-123-4710 (Mx)
Mexicana Airlines www.mexicana.com	☎ 800-531-7921 (US); 800-509-8960 (Mx)

BY TAXI

Taxis from the bus station or airport to the center of PV cost about $5. There is a taxi booth at the airport that sells tickets for your destination (thus preventing any haggling over prices). However, these ticket stands charge up to four times as much as the drivers on the street. There are about a thousand taxis in town and they charge about $2 for trips around town. Always confirm the price before accepting the ride. Tips are not expected.

BY CAR

The big national chains are all here and, if you are going to leave the state, you should rent from one of these companies. That way, should you have a problem with the car, you can be serviced by one of their representatives wherever you are.

> **AUTHOR TIP:** *Always ask about taking a rental vehicle out of state, as some companies do not have insurance for their vehicles to leave the state.*

In order to rent a car you must have a major credit card, valid driver's license and recent photo ID. You must be at least 25 years old.

In low season, the average cost of a small car with air conditioning is between $23 and $35 a day. During high season, the cost goes to $40 or $50 a day for the same vehicle. This includes insurance and unlimited mileage.

Clover Car Rentals, *Villa Vallarta Shopping Center,* ☎ *322-224-0304 or 224-4910, cloverrentacar@prodigy. net.mx,* is a local company that charges $40 to $50 a day for a jeep, but you must stay within the state. The owner is honest and pleasant to deal with. His vehicles are in decent shape.

Thrifty, *Av Moctezuma # 3515,* ☎ *322-224-9280 or 224-0776, www.thrifty.com.mx,* is located at the airport. They will rent a VW beetle without air conditioning for $31 a day, including all mileage and insurance. In the event of an accident, Thrifty recommends that you call them for assistance before signing any papers.

Budget, *at the airport,* ☎ *322-224-2980,* offers a Chevy Pop for $175 a week, plus $12 a day for insurance and 15% tax. This works out to $286 a week. This is expensive for a small car. A Tsuru is $210, an Astra $245 and a jeep is $320, plus insurance and tax. A VW beetle is $140 plus.

BY BUS

Long-distance buses depart for stations around the country from the Medina Bus Station north of the airport. Local buses go to the national station. For long-distance, first-class trips, budget between $4 and $5 per hour of travel.

The Estrella Blanca (Elite), ☎ *322-221-0850, 290-1001 or 290-1014.* Buses leave for Guadalajara at 5:30, 7, 8:30, 10:30 am, noon and 5 pm. The cost is $29.20 per person. They also go to Mexico City in the afternoon and evening at 5:15, 6:15, 7:15 and 9 pm daily. The cost is $66.10 and the journey takes 12 hours.

Primera Plus, ☎ *322-221-0095, www.flecha-amarilla. com,* charges $29.20 for a bus to Guadalajara. The price includes a sandwich and juice. The air-conditioned bus is a luxury liner and comes recommended for any trips in the area if their schedule is right for you. I traveled with them and was quite pleased. Buses to Mexico City leave in the afternoon/evening at 5:15, 6:15, 7:15 and 9 pm. The cost is $66.10 per person. They also have buses going to numerous destinations around the country.

ETN, ☎ *322-223-5665 or 223-5666,* has buses going to Guadalajara at 12:30 am, 1:00 am, 8:45 am, 10:15 am, 11:45 am, 1:00 pm, 2:00 pm, 3:30 pm, and 5:00 pm. They have one bus a day leaving at 7 pm for Mexico City and one at 10 pm going to Leon. This, too, is a luxury liner, but I found they were totally indifferent to trying to help me. They have a downtown ticket office at Calle 31 de Octubre #89 (next to hotel Rosita).

Transportes del Pacifico, ☎ *322-222-1015 or 222-5622,* has buses going to Guadalajara every hour starting at 6 am until 1:45 am daily. The cost is $26.50 per person. Buses for Tijuana leave at 12:15 pm daily and cost $82. 30. This trip takes 34 hours. Buses to Mazatlan leave at 10:45 pm daily and cost $25.40. This trip takes seven hours. Buses to Tepic leave every 20 minutes starting at 4 am and take three hours. The cost is $11. Buses to Mexico City leave at 6 and 8 pm daily and take 12 hours. The cost is $66.10 per person.

TAP, ☎ *322-290-0119,* has buses going to 24 destinations around the country. I found the workers at the PV office helpful and honest. I would not hesitate to travel with TAP. They have buses going to Mazatlan at 8:10 am, 11:10 am, 1:10 pm, 3:10 pm and 5:10 pm. The trip takes seven hours and costs $25.70 per person. Buses for Mexico City leave at 5:10 and 7:10 pm daily. There is a one-/two-hour wait over in Tepic during this trip. The cost is $63.40. TAP also covers many destinations to the north, like Tijuana and Guaymas.

City buses cost four pesos per person, per ride. If you want to go from the center to the airport or bus station, take the bus labeled *Hotels* or *Aeropuerto*. If you want to go to the south end of town, take the bus labeled *Olas Altas*. This bus goes as far as Playa Muertos.

City bus.

The buses from the center going to Mismaloya cost 45¢ and depart from Basilio Badillo. Those going to Nuevo Vallarta and Punta de Mita leave from the Medina Bus station or at the bus stop across from the Sheriton Hotel. They cost $1 each way.

Remember, no area code is needed when making a local call.

■ BY WATER

Water Taxis, ☎ *322-297-1637, 209-5004 or 209-5092,* go to Yelapa, Las Animas, Quimixto and Mahujuitas daily from Los Muertos Pier at the south end of town. They leave at 10:30, 11 am and 11:30 am. For those wanting to stay overnight, there is a boat leaving at 4 pm. The round-trip costs $18.

SERVICES

The **Tourist Office**, *Calle Juarez and Ascencio #1712,* ☎ *322-223-2500, Monday to Friday, 8 am-4:30 pm.*

Puerto Vallarta Convention and Visitors Bureau is useful if you need more detailed information. It is near El Cid.

Post office, *Mina #188, Monday to Friday, 8 am-6 pm, Saturday until 1 pm.*

The **IAMAT Clinic**, *Calle Lucerna #48,* ☎ *322-222-5119,* is coordinated by Dr. Alfonso Rodriguez. English is spoken. A second one is at *Rio Nilo 132, #8,* ☎ *322-293-0036,* and the third is at *KB3 Blvd Francisco Medina Ascencio, Plaza Neptuno D-1,* ☎ *322-221-0023.*

Puerto Vallarta

Gold's Gym, *Av Fco. Medina Ascencio, half a block from the Calypso,* is the largest in the world. If a work-out is what you need and you like an inside air-conditioned gym, then I recommend trying Gold's. Known worldwide, their equipment is always in good repair.

Spa Puesto del Sol, ☎ *322-221-0770,* is a European health spa across from El Faro at the Tennis Club. It has a gym with 40 machines and a full line of weights. They also hold aerobics classes and massage services.

Aztec Massage, *Venustiano Carranza #307 (upstairs),* ☎ *322-222-4881,* offers therapeutic massages for pain relief and relaxation. They also do in-home service.

■ PUBLICATIONS

Vallarta Today is an English-language publication produced daily. It has the week's entertainment schedule featured on the second page. You'll find details about locally sponsored events, like the Vallarta Gourmet Festival that includes 23 participating restaurants, or the gourmet cooking classes offered by famous chefs and presented at the LANS Department store every Thursday.

The English-language magazine, **Vallarta Lifestyles**, has been around since 1990 and is sold at magazine stands for $2. This full-color, informative publication is directed at tourists. *Lifestyles* also puts out a free map and activity guide. **Vallarta Voice** is a free English-language publication that has news, events, reviews and profiles. It is published once a month from November to April.

The Times is an English-language newspaper that comes out on Friday. It offers local and national news (some US and Canadian news), as well as a crossword, horoscope and classified ads. This is a free publication.

Online, **www.virtualvallarta.com** has maps, photos and articles that offer the latest information about events in Puerto Vallarta.

SIGHTSEEING

Vallarta Cigar Factory, *two locations, Libertad #100-3, next to the flea market, or Vallarta #252 at 5 de Febrero,* ☎ *322-222-0300 (for either place), Monday to Saturday, 10 am-9 pm, Sunday 10 am-6 pm.* The factory welcomes visitors to watch cigars being made from Cuban, Nicaraguan, Mexican and Dominican tobaccos. The workers make three grades of cigars. The lowest grade includes the Corona, Robusto and the Churchill. These cost between $3 and $5 each. The next grade includes the Café, Rothchild, Doble Corona and Torpedo, which sell for $5 to $9 each. Then there are the Corona Gorda and the Campaña that sell for $12 and $13 each. This is an interesting tour.

Museum of Anthropology, *Isla Rio Cuale, no phone, Tuesday-Sunday, 10 am-2 pm and 4-7 pm, $2.* The director presents a free lecture in English every Tuesday at 10 am on topics relating to Mexican anthropology. This small museum has a few artifacts from Mesoamerica, but mostly items found in pre-Hispanic tombs in Jalisco, Nayarit and Colima states.

Manuel Lepe Museum/Gallery, *Juarez 533,* ☎ *322-222-5515, Monday to Saturday, 10 am-5 pm.* The gallery/museum is world renowned for the contemporary art of Manuel Lepe. His work includes tiny ceramic angels, boats, airplanes, papier mâché, jewelry, posters and lithographs of original works. The museum/gallery has some items for sale. Lepe is well known throughout the United States, Europe and Mexico for his Naif style of painting (miniatures). One of his exhibitions at the Sciences and Industries Museum in LA drew over a million people.

Museo Ernesto Muñoz Acosta, *Francisco I Madero #272,* ☎ *322-222-1970, daily, 10 am-7 pm.* This museum has works from contemporary artists, including some by Sergio Bustamante and Manuel Lepe. They also carry some traditional work from the Huichol people. The museum likes to carry pieces from promising regional artists. This, like the Lepe Museum is also a gallery.

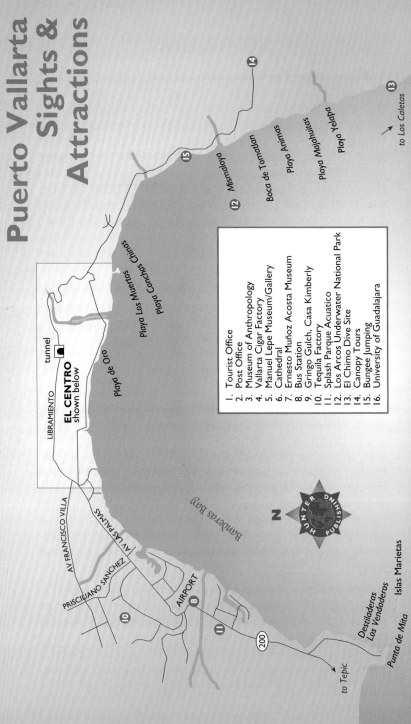

Puerto Vallarta Sights & Attractions

1. Tourist Office
2. Post Office
3. Museum of Anthropology
4. Vallarta Cigar Factory
5. Manuel Lepe Museum/Gallery
6. Cathedral
7. Ernesto Muñoz Acosta Museum
8. Bus Station
9. Gringo Gulch, Casa Kimberly
10. Tequila Factory
11. Splash Parque Acuatico
12. Los Arcos Underwater National Park
13. El Chimo Dive Site
14. Canopy Tours
15. Bungee Jumping
16. University of Guadalajara

EL CENTRO shown below

LIBRAMIENTO

tunnel

Playa de Oro

Playa Los Muertos

Playa Conchas Chinas

Mismaloya

Boca de Tomatlan

Playa Animas

Playa Majahuitas

Playa Yelapa

to Los Caletas

Banderas Bay

AV FRANCISCO VILLA

AV LAS PALMAS

PRISCILIANO SANCHEZ

AIRPORT

200

to Tepic

Destiladeras

Los Vendaderos

Punta de Mita

Islas Marietas

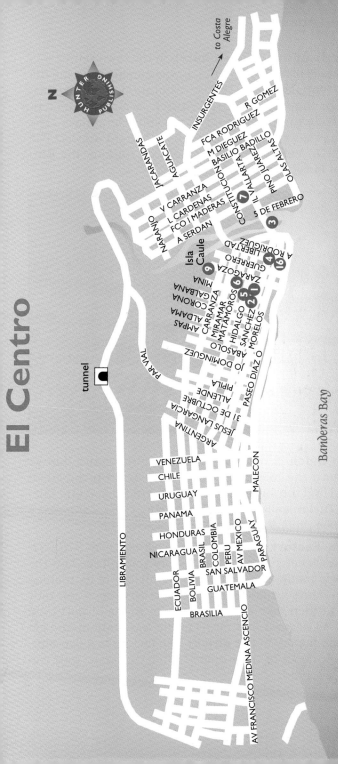

El Centro

to Costa Alegre

tunnel

Isla Caule

Banderas Bay

N

HUNTER PUBLISHING

INSURGENTES
R GOMEZ
FCA RODRIGUEZ
M DIEGUEZ
BASILIO BADILLO
IL VALLARTA
PINO JUAREZ
OLAS ALTAS
5 DE FEBRERO
A RODRIGUEZ
CONSTITUCION
LIBERTAD
GUERRERO
ZARAGOZA
MINA
CORONA
GALBANA
MIRAMAR
MATAMOROS
HIDALGO
SANCHEZ
MORELOS
ABASOLO
JO DOMINGUEZ
PASEO DIAZ O
PIPILA
ALLENDE
31 DE OCTUBRE
JESUS LANGARCIA
ARGENTINA
MALECON
VENEZUELA
CHILE
URUGUAY
PANAMA
HONDURAS
NICARAGUA
SAN SALVADOR
GUATEMALA
BRASILIA

JACARANDAS
AGUACATE
NARANJO
V CARRANZA
L CARDENAS
FCO I MADERAS
A SERDAN
CARRANZA
ALDAMA
AMPAS

ECUADOR
BOLIVIA
BRASIL
COLOMBIA
PERU
AV MEXICO
PARAGUAY

PAR VIAL

LIBRAMIENTO

AV FRANCISCO MEDINA ASCENCIO

7
3
4
9
6
8
2
1

© 2007 HUNTER PUBLISHING, INC

The **Virgin of Guadalupe Church** in the town center was built between 1929 and 1939. It was damaged during the last earthquake in the 1990s; restoration is in progress. Although the interior of the church is not exceptional, the outside tower is the city's crowning landmark. The tower has a wrought-iron crown with eight angels. The crown is a replica of the one worn by Carlota, the Empress of Mexico from 1864 to 1867.

Gringo Gulch is reached by climbing the stairs that go up toward the hills from the main plaza. Up the gulch you will find the former home of Richard Burton and Elizabeth Taylor called **Casa Kimberly**, *Calle Zaragoza # 445, open daily 9 am-6 pm, $6.*

Tequila Factory, *Carretera Tepic, Km 12,* ☎ *322-221-2543, open noon-3 pm.* At the factory you will see how the tequila is made, learn some of the history of its making and, of course, taste a bit. Make reservations for your tour and then take a bus to Tepic or to the airport from the center of town (not far from the bus station) and get off at the factory or the airport (the factory is a five-minute walk north of the airport). After you taste, you can purchase. I did.

THE GREAT LOVE STORY

Isolated beaches rimmed with palm trees lured John Huston here in the 1960s to film *Night of the Iguana*. His cast included Elizabeth Taylor and Richard Burton, and the two fell in love. Richard bought Elizabeth a 24,000 square-foot house for her 32nd birthday. It was similar to his own that overlooked Bandera Bay. The houses were across the road from each other. The couple then built a pink and white walkway, called "the love bridge," between the two homes so they could visit each other more discreetly. Elizabeth left Eddie Fisher, her husband at the time, and married Burton. Their story became one of the great love stories of our century. She owned the house for 26 years and, when she sold it in 1990, left nearly all of the possessions in the house. While on tour, you see posters, the original furniture, mementos and photos.

ADVENTURES ON FOOT

■ HIKING & WALKING

The **malecón**, the walkway along the beach, was first constructed in the 1950s using tons of cement, stones and rocks. Most of the rock used was taken from the Cuale River. With the rock not holding the earth back along the riverbed, there was tremendous soil loss during rains. The silt that was washed into the bay was filtered by sea cucumbers that hung out around the mouth of the river. For a time, the

Statue along the malecón.

over-harvest of sea cucumbers created a problem with murky water being in the bay. However, present conservation practices now forbid the harvest so we again have clean water in the bay near the river and the cucumber population is increasing.

The *malecón* is formed by a series of retaining walls. During construction of the walls, roads were built to access the oceanfront area. The major construction road, beside the *malecón*, is now used as the main road.

The *malecón* is about three miles/five km long. Starting on the north side of the river, the bay stretches all the way around to Punta Mita. It is lined with restaurants, hotels, shops and people.

■ GOLF

There are seven courses in PV, some designed by world-class golfers such as Jack Nicklaus, Tom Weiskopf and Robert von Hagge. To date, Hagge has designed 11 courses in Mexico.

> **FACT FILE:** *Because of the quality of its courses, PV was chosen to host the EMC World Golf Cup in 2002, and the 2001 Ford Collegiate Championships and USGA Junior Girls' Tournament.*

In addition to the world cup, Puerto Vallarta sponsors its own golf cup competition each year in mid-November. This is a high-profile event that lasts for three days and, so far, has included 120 amateur competitors from all over North America.

Flamingos Golf Club, *Tepic Highway #145, www. flamingosgolf.com.mx*, was designed by Percy J. Clifford and has 18 holes. It is a ways from town so they provide a shuttle bus from the Sheraton Hotel at 8 and 10 am; return trips are at 2 and 4 pm. You must reserve for pickup. This is a par 72, 6,452-yard course where the challenge lies in chipping, although the landing areas are about 40 yards wide on average. Low-season greens costs start at $115 per day.

LOCAL GOLF CHAMP

Lorena Ochoa, a young gal from Guadalajara, is often seen playing on the courses in PV. Lorena became a professional golfer in 2002 and has already earned close to $350,000 in prize money. Besides money, this champ has a list of awards that are longer than a child's Christmas wish list. Among them is the National Sports Award (presented by President Vincente Fox), Player of the Year Award and the Golfstat Cup. She has managed to achieve a seven-tournament winning streak. This record has been beat only by Byron Nelson, who had an 11-game winning streak. Also, in 2001 Lorena had the nation's lowest average score of 71.71.

Four Seasons *at Punta Mita on the Four Season's Resort property, www.fshr.com, no phone,* was designed by Jack Nicklaus. This 18 hole, par 72 course has one hole sitting on an island about 175 yards offshore. It is surrounded by the largest water hazard in the world and is the only natural-island green. If the water is too rough, or the tide too high for the little boat to take you to the island, an alternative green can be played. This is a semi-private course intended for hotel guests. The cost during mid-season is about $230 per person. Club rentals cost $35 and shoes $15. Caddies are not available on this course.

The course at the Four Seasons.

Marina Vallarta, *Paseo de la Marina, www.foremexico. com*, is within walking distance of most hotels. It was designed by Joe Finger and is a 6,700-yard, par 71 course. The obstacles are palms, tropical plants, wildlife and water fountains. There is a driving range, golf shop, chipping/putting green and a full-service clubhouse. The property is owned and operated by the Club Corp International from Dallas. It is rumored that they have nearly $2 billion in assets and are considered the world's leader in operating country clubs and golf resorts. The cost to play is $120 a day and this covers the cart rental. Clubs can be rented for $20 a day. There is a discount for frequent players.

La Vista, *Circuito Universidad #653,* ☎ *322-221-0073, www.vistavallarta- golf.com,* has two courses. One is a par 72 course that sits on 478 acres of palm grove dotted with tiny creeks. It is located on the higher grounds of the property. This course was designed by Jack Nicklaus. The second course, opened in 2001, was designed by Tom Weiskopf. The course runs through natural jungle, deep gorges and swift rivers. Both courses have 18 holes and are designed with challenges for both the amateur and the professional. The clubhouse includes practice facilities, restaurant, bar and golf shop. On-course beverage service is offered.

El Tigre, *Paradise Village, Av Paraiso, Km 800,* ☎ *322-297-0773, www.paradise- mexico.com,* was designed by Robert von Vagge and Rick Baril. The course is an 18-hole, par 72, 7,239-yard run with 12 holes featuring water. The designers incorporated five or six tees per hole, extra-wide fairways, beach bunkers and lots of water. The clubhouse is huge and there is a 300-yard driving range and a putting green. Inside the club is a restaurant, bar, spa and golf apparel shop. The cost is $130 a game during high season and there is a special "twilight" price of $85 for those starting after 2 pm. Club rentals run $45 and shoes are $15.

Mayan Palace, *Av Paseo de las Moras, www.mayanpalace.com.mx,* is now open to the general public. If you think you can get past the time-share salesmen, you may like this course. It was designed by Jim Lipe and has 18 holes with water and sand hazards. The water hazards alone consist of seven lakes, one river and the ocean. The cost is about $130 for the 18 holes, and a caddy ($15, plus tip) is mandatory.

ADVENTURES ON WATER

BEACHES

PV has 40 beaches open to the public. Those at the north end of the bay have soft white sand and shallow water, while those at the south tend to have coarser sand and deeper water. However, the south has many little coves hidden between the rocks where you can spend the entire day alone. To save confusion, the beaches have general names that were given to them years ago. As the city developed, smaller stretches of beach within the larger beaches have been named. This is to make directions more specific.

Puerto Vallarta beach.

BEACH DANGER FLAG SYSTEM

There is a system of red, yellow and white flags that indicates possible dangers in the water.

- RED – The undercurrent is dangerous to swimmers and under no circumstances should you go into the area between the two red flags. Undertow is not to be ignored; it has caused many deaths.

- YELLOW – Jellyfish are in the area. To avoid being stung, do not go into the water between the two yellow flags.
- WHITE – The white flags mean there is some soft surf, but have fun.

Las Animas, Quimixto and **Yelapa beaches** can be reached only by boat. Las Animas, "Beach of the Souls," is strictly for snorkeling, sunning and eating. If it wasn't for its beauty, it would be almost boring. Food and drink are available along the beach at some of the palapa-hut establishments or from local ladies selling their home-made goods. Quimixto is a little village surrounded by reefs that divers can enjoy. Yelapa is another isolated village that has some rustic cabins, lots of birds and is quiet. To get here, take the water taxi in PV, hire a private boat at the docks, or use a tour company. Boats at Boca (see below) can also take you here.

Playas Conchas Chinas is a series of rocky coves south of Los Muertos. The name describes the spiraled shells found on this beach. To get here, take buses marked *Mismaloya* or *Boca* and get off where the sand looks good. **Mismaloya** is good for birding and it is also where you can see the movie set used in the filming of *Night of the*

Mismaloya beach.

Iguanas. Once at the beach and hotel of the same name, walk south, past the hotel to where the Horcones River flows toward the ocean. Continue past the beachside restaurants to the set. The building behind is where stars lived while working. **Boca de Tomatlan** is the last beach going south that is accessible by bus/car. It is eight miles/13 km south of the town center. Boca is far more isolated than all the other beaches in the area and the swimming here is safe. *Pangas* (small boats) are available to take you to Yelapa, Las Animas or Quimixto beaches (see above). There are numerous little huts selling food and drink. The last bus returns to town at about 7:30 pm. These beaches are for surfing, sunning or fishing.

Los Muertos Beach starts south of the river and stretches for a mile or so. It is a favorite for swimming and wading as there is no undertow. Jet Skiing and parasailing are popular pastimes also. The banana boat ride here is fun and  should be tried at least once. Equipment can be rented from any of the hotels along this section of the beach. **Los Muertos Pier** is also along this beach.

Playa de Oro is a long stretch of beach with a few rocky areas north of Los Muertos. The strip of beach includes Playa Camarones, Las Glorias and Los Tules. The sand is moderate to fine and the surf gets stronger the farther north one goes.

Punta de Mita is best for surfing. It is at the very north end of the bay.

Los Venaderos is also to the north and offers good snorkeling and windsurfing. It is close to Las Marietas Island, a bird sanctuary and good snorkeling area. Boats can be rented from locals living around this beach.

Destiladeras is, like Los Venaderos, close to Las Marietas Island and offers good windsurfing or snorkeling. To get here, take a bus going to Punta de Mita and, again, get off wherever the sand looks good. You will need to bring your own equipment.

WATER PARKS

Splash Parque Acuatico, *Km 156 on the Tepic Highway,* ☎ *322-297-0708, www.splashvallarta.com,* is a family-oriented water park that features 12 slides, all different speed levels, a river zone for the quieter splashers, and a children's pool. You can also swim with dolphins (advance reservations required). There are dolphin/sea lion

© Splash Parque Acuatico

shows, diving exhibitions and bird shows offered on an ongoing basis starting at 10:30 am; the last show starts at 5:30 pm. Check with the tourist office for times of specific shows. The cost to enter the park for the day is $10 per person.

Swim with Dolphins, ☎ *322-297-1252,* is a program offered by Vallarta Adventures. You can go to the pool and learn about dolphin physiology, anatomy, history, husbandry and training. Once in the water, you can feel a dolphin's skin and maybe even get towed by one. You can

have a video made of your encounter. Life jackets are provided. Children must be five or older to swim with the animals. The cost is $130 to swim, $60 for an encounter and $240 for a full-day program.

BOATING

A trip aboard **_La Marigalante_**, ☎ *322-223-0875, www. marigalante.com.mx,* costs $60 per person. This old-styled boat seen crossing the bay every day was built in

Veracruz by the Asociacion Mar, Hombre y Paz (Association of Sea, Man and Peace) to commemorate the 500th anniversary of the discovery of America by Columbus.

A DEBT REPAID

When Columbus was sailing the *Niña, Pinta* and *Santa Maria*, he offered 10,000 gold pieces to the first man who spotted land. Rodrigo Detriana (whose real name was Juan Rodriguez Bermejo) saw the land and let Columbus know, but was never paid his reward. The organizers of the Marigalante collected money from 33 American countries and took a 52,000 nautical-mile journey around the world, eventually landing in Seville, Spain. The ship carried the money owed to Rodriguez and had it placed in his name in the cathedral. During the journey, the crew collected enough memorabilia to stock four museums, one of which is on board the ship.

You can take a daytime cruise on the ship or an evening dinner cruise. The evening cruise starts with a mariachi band, has a rope-twirling demonstration and dinner, which includes shrimp brochettes, filet mignon and red or white wine. This is followed by a sound and light show that finishes with a firework display. The daytime cruise leaves in the early morning and includes a Mexican breakfast of eggs, refried beans, fresh fruit and juice. The show has a pirate theme that starts with the weighing of anchors and proceeds to a naval battle that uses water-filled balloons as artillery. The show ends with a pirate torture contest and a few sword fights that could involve a passenger or two. Lunch is barbequed chicken and ribs, rice, salad and corn. There is an open bar and part of the day is spent at one of the beaches along the bay.

To go on this ship you can book with any tour office (it is not possible to book direct). Or (I don't recommend this) you can go to a time-share event where you listen to the blurb about buying a chunk of paradise and, as a reward; you get the tour.

Puerto Vallarta

You can **learn to sail** with Vallarta Adventures (see page 130, www.vallarta-adventures.com). They offer basic training and allow you to be as interactive as you choose. If you find that you don't like it, the crew on board will  take over and you can relax instead. There is also a sunset cruise that includes wine and cheese, seafood hors d'oeuvres and an open bar. The boat is available every day.

■ SCUBA DIVING

Scuba diving is popular in PV mostly because of Los Arcos Underwater National Park that is just half an hour from the dock. There are two companies who can take you diving and the costs are comparable. They are **Ecotours Vallarta de Mexico**, *Ignacio Vallarta 243,* ☎ *322-222-6606 or 223-3130*; and **Chicos Dive Shop**, *Av. Diaz Ordaz # 772,* ☎ *322-222-1895, www.chicos-*

 *diveshop.com.* You must have your PADI certification with you or you will be required to take an in-pool session before the guides will take you down. Divers who have not been underwater during the last 12 months are required to take a refresher course.

Those not certified can take pool sessions taught by PADI certified instructors at the Sheraton, Canto del Sol, Velas, Crown Paradise, Vista Club, Mayan Palace, Melia, Nautilus, Westin, Las Palmas, Holiday Inn, Villa del Palmar or Embarcadero hotels. The lessons are offered daily from 10 am-5 pm. Courses include home study, classroom sessions, pool training and one ocean dive.

> **WARNING:** Be aware that not everyone who claims to have PADI certification does, in fact, have it. Just as the dive masters must see your PADI card, you should check theirs as well.

Los Arcos Underwater National Park, off Playa Mismaloya, has dives from 12 feet/four meters down to 60 feet/20 meters. There are granite arches, caves and a wall that goes down about 1,800 feet/600 meters. The continental platform where the wall begins is located near the main arch. Numerous crags and crevices hide the black coral forest that is rejuvenating itself now that harvesting is illegal. Common wildlife includes rays, eels, morays, octopus and lob-

ster. It takes half an hour by boat to reach the park. Night dives are done near the "Shallows of Christ" close to here, where lobster and octopus are said to be abundant. A number of small islands offer push-off points for snorkeling. Because underwater currents force plankton up near the surface, the number of fish feeding on them is enormous.

The **Marietas Islands**, often called the Galapagos of Mexico, are 21 miles/32 km or one hour by boat from the mainland. You can dive around caves, coral reefs and drop-offs, where there are mantas, turtles, dolphins and humpbacks (in season December to March). You can also combine diving with bird watching. Blue-footed boobies are known to hang out here. It is common to play with dolphins while in this area.

El Morro, just beyond the protected waters of the bay's north end, is four miles/six km past the Marietas and 1½ hours from PV by boat. This area is famous for its pinnacles that rise from the ocean floor and harbor sea life such as mantas, turtles, skipjacks and eels. This is a dive for experienced divers only.

El Sequial is also for experienced divers only. This impressive spot has sea sponges, groupers, snappers, mantas and sharks swimming around pinnacles and caves.

El Chimo is an hour from PV by boat at the south end of the bay. Here you will find eagle rays, damsels, sea fans and even some black coral. The ocean floor has a large plateau with a series of pinnacles, some of which form columns like those in a church. This, too, is a dive for the experienced only.

Corbeteña is two hours north of PV. It is often called "The Rock" and is considered one of the best dives in the entire country. In addition to the steep walls, caves and

arches, wildlife attractions include giant mantas, sharks and (in season) whale sharks. Moderate currents and a dive depth of about 120 feet/40 meters make this a good spot for small groups of experienced divers.

■ SNORKELING

Majahuitas Beach is less than an hour from town on the south side of the bay. It is regarded as one of the most beautiful beaches in the PV area. Because of the wildlife sanctuaries along this coast that cause a spillover effect, the wildlife here is abundant. Large schools of tropical fish swim alongside turtles, dolphins and mantas.

Los Caletas has some drop-offs for diving, but it is better for snorkeling in the shallows where you may spot manta rays, turtles and a variety of fish. The beach area was first used by John Huston for his private beach. You can hike or kayak in the bay, read a book while swinging on a hammock or visit the spa and have a body massage or facial. However, everyone I spoke to who came here with a tour operator did not feel they got their money's worth. They said that the ride out takes an hour, the water for snorkeling is rough and the food is so-so. The scenery is beautiful, but you can get that at other places for much less money.

ADVENTURES IN NATURE

BIRDING

Birding is good along the rivers that run from the mountains down to the ocean. You can go as far as the village of El Nogalito or Tomatlan at the south end of the bay or walk along the bay and follow any path going inland. There has been 355 species of birds recorded in the area. These include macaws, parakeets, trogons, magpies, jays, boobies, frigates, egrets and herons (shown at right). For real birders, Ecotours (page 131) offers day trips, four-day trips and six-day trips to birding areas. They know exactly where the birds are.

■ TURTLE-WATCHING

The Olive Ridley sea turtle arrives at Bandera Bay around the beginning of July each year to lay her eggs. This wonder continues until the end of November. Once the eggs are laid it takes six weeks for them to hatch. This means that you can possibly see turtles laying their eggs between July and November and see the hatchlings between mid-September to mid-February. It is a thrill to sit on the sand and watch the little heads poke out of the shells. Then, no matter what obstacles stand in their path, they make their way to the ocean. Sometimes there are only a few turtles hatching, but if you are lucky you will be able to see hundreds.

For the best luck you should join a group that is involved in turtle preservation. These people know where the turtles are and when the hatchlings will start to break out of their shells. They also know what to do to keep them safe.

> **AUTHOR NOTE:** *Bounce, a static remover used in clothes dryers, tucked into your belt loop or buttonhole will prevent bees and mosquitoes from attacking.*

■ WHALE-WATCHING

Whale-watching tours are offered by many companies in PV. Check to see which ones are most involved in the study and preservation of the whales before booking. At a minimum, choose so that some of your tour dollar ends up helping conservation. Whale season here is December to March.

WATCHING THE RULES

The government has set rules for observation of whales. Your boat must not be closer than 250 feet/80 meters to an animal and you must not be in the water (you must be in the boat) when approaching one. You must not obstruct a whale's passage in any way or touch one. Jet Skis, kayaks or boats with motors running are not permitted in the area while observing the animals. Your time in the area should not exceed 30 minutes and, if it is a pod that you spot, observation time is dropped to 10 minutes.

It is the responsibility of the paying tourist to see that these rules are implemented. Often, a tour company will want to please its clients by bending a rule or two just to be guaranteed the business and praise. Do not permit this.

For more information on the whales and how to help with their conservation, go to www.ine.gob. mx, or write to Direction General de Vida Silvestre, Av Revolucion #1425, Nivel 1, Col. Tlacopacm, San Angel, CP 01040 Mexico DF, ☎ 55-624-3655.

Humpback and gray whales can be spotted around Punta Mita at the north end of the bay and near the Marieta Islands. During the early part of the season, around mid-December, you may spot the whales doing their courting rituals where they swim side by side, bumping and rubbing each other, thus stimulating the hormones needed for reproduction. Later in the season you will see moms and kids floating around enjoying each other. Some tour companies carry an underwater microphone so you can hear whale sounds. The great gray whale spends its summers in the cool waters off the shores of Alaska in the Bering Strait. In September it starts its journey south to the warmer waters of Baja California and the mainland near PV. Once in the warm waters, the whales mate and the females give birth.

MEXICAN WHALE RESERVES

In 1948 Mexico signed an international agreement for the regulation of the hunting of whales in its waters. However, the agreement did little to actually stop whale hunting. It was not until 1972 that preserves were established. The first was **Laguna Ojo de Libre**. In 1979, **Laguna San Ignacio** was added to the preserve list and, in 1980, **Laguans Guerrero Negro** and **Manuela** were also declared preserves. These saltwater lagoons are all near the west coast.

Since most whales spend time around Baja California that is where most of the preserves were established. However, it was soon realized that many of the whale pods liked to hang around the PV area so that area also became a preserve. In 1993, the waters around PV were declared a UNESCO site.

ADVENTURES ON HORSEBACK

Rancho El Charro, ☎ *322-224-0114, www.ranchoel charro.com,* offers rides ($60) through the jungle to a waterfall that is near a canyon.

Rancho Capomo, *Gorion #172,* ☎ *322-224-0450,* offers five-hour rides into the jungle that start at 9 am. There are bilingual guides and breakfast or lunch can be included. The ranch is in the mountains and the ride goes to a waterfall (there are many in the PV area) and back to the ranch. Rates are not advertised because they change regularly.

Rancho Ojo de Agua, *Cerra Cardenal # 227,* ☎ *322-224-8240,* also offers trips into the jungle and they do longer rides of up to four days. Stop by any tour office in town to book these trips or call them direct. See *Tour Operators*, below, for more details.

ADVENTURES IN THE AIR

■ CANOPY TOURS

© Canopy Tours

There are two canopy tours in the PV area that offer the opportunity to swing from cables strung across the jungle at heights of up to 350 feet/110 meters.

The first tour is offered at Los Palmas in the Sierra Madre Mountains on private property owned by Vallarta Adventures. There are 14 observation platforms for wildlife observation. To get from station to station, you are harnessed into mountain climbing gear and sent across the cables. Some platforms are as far as 375 feet/120 meters from each other. This is not a tour for anyone afraid of heights. Macho men may want to try the optional extreme game where you swing to a platform, climb a net and then crawl across a rope ladder back to the starting platform. At the end of the tour, you must rappel down 55 feet/18 meters to the ground.

The price ($60 for the day) includes transportation to and from the site, plus all climbing gear. You should wear either shorts or pants and running shoes, although strap-on sandals are acceptable. You are allowed to bring a small pack with water in it, but cameras are not permitted for safety reasons.

You must be able to walk uphill for 15 minutes and have enough strength to climb a 15-foot/five-meter ladder. You must also be able to stand on a platform that is 3x3 feet/1x1 meter in size without hyperventilating, vomiting or fainting. Pregnant woman or anyone with heart trouble, seizures, no balance, or back, neck or shoulder disabilities should not join this tour. Children must be eight years or older to participate.

The second canopy tour goes through the treetops and across a river gorge 350 feet/110 meters below. It uses 1½ miles/two km of cable in a series of 10 zip lines that run between stations. Crossing the gorge is a real rush. The longest cable run is 1,000 feet/350 meters. After you have done this run, go down to the rock-lined river and swim in one of the natural pools or sit on a tiny sand beach.

The minimum age limit for either tour is eight years. To reach the second canopy site, catch a bus from La Jolla de Mismaloya at the south end of town. Buses depart at 8:30, 10 and 11:30 am, then 1 and 2:30 pm. Allow some extra time for travel, as occasionally they run late. See tour agents (page 132).

Pacific Bungee Jumping, ☎ *322-228-0670*, is south on the coastal highway toward Mismaloya, about a quarter-mile past the President Intercontinental Hotel at Km 9.2. Past the hotel, you'll see the bungee crane over the water. Jumping the 120 feet/40 meters toward the water can be fun and, since 1993 when the jump was established, there has not been a death. You have the choice of a full body or ankle harness. The jump is open 10 am-6 pm daily and reservations are not required. If you let them know ahead of time, they will supply you with an "I did it" certificate. This company also rents dune buggies to rod around in the sand. If taking a public bus from PV, go to the stop on the corner of Basilo Badillo and Insurgentes and take a bus marked *Boca* or *Mismaloya*. Ask the driver to stop at the bungee.

ADVENTURES OF THE BRAIN

University of Guadalajara, *Libertad #105-1*, ☎ *322-223-2082, www.cepe.udg.mx,* has specialized courses for survival Spanish and for advanced levels. You can go for a few hours a day for one week, two weeks and four weeks. There are special children's classes from elementary to senior levels. There is also an immersion program where you can stay with a Mexican family. Intense, long-term courses are about $8 per hour, while the shorter-term, two hours a day for a week courses run $10 an hour.

OUTFITTERS/TOUR OPERATORS

Rancho El Charro, ☎ *322-224-0114, www.rancho elcharro.com*, offers rides through the jungle to a water-fall that is near a canyon. The guides are bilingual and the saddles cushioned. They take only small groups and welcome children. Trips can be anywhere from three hours to eight, although the five-hour trip is the most common. An all-day trip with guides and food costs about $100 per person. Otherwise, the cost is about $15 per hour, with guide. For real horse lovers, they also offer a full week of riding, camping out, staying in colonial ha-ciendas and exploring mountains. This adven-ture runs just over $100 per day. El Charro has special pick-up points in PV and they will deliver you to your hotel at the end of the ride. You can book ahead via their website; they will respond with a confirmation. I found this company coop-erative and quick to re-spond to anything I wanted.

Rancho Ojo de Agua, *Cerrada de Cardenal # 227*, ☎ *322-224-0607*, offers the same ride as above and they also do longer rides of up to four days. Prices for these rides should be negotiated. Tropical jungle rides depart 10 am or 3 pm and return at 1 pm or 6 pm. The shorter ride costs $47 and the longer ride costs $60, including lunch. They also have a sunset ride from 4:30-7:30 pm, dinner included, for $52. A long ride with an overnight costs $185, including meals. There is free transportation from town out to the ranch. Contact them to make arrangements.

Rancho Capomo, *Gorion #172, no phone*, has five-hour rides into the jungle that leave at 9 am from their ranch in the mountains. There are bilingual guides and breakfast or lunch can be included. The ride goes to a waterfall (there are many in the PV area) and back to the ranch. The cost is about $55.

Carnival Tours, ☎ *322-222-5174, www.carnival.com*, has a catamaran that goes to Los Arcos, Quimixto or Las Animas. The tour includes breakfast, open bar (for national drinks), snorkeling equipment, music and lunch (on the beach) that is either grilled fish, chicken in sauce, hamburgers or quesadillas. Their tours leave from the marina at 9 am and you should be there half an hour early to purchase your ticket. This company specializes in tours for the cruise ship crowd.

Vallarta Adventures, *Calle Mastil, Marina Vallarta and at Paseo Las Palmas #39-A, in Nuevo Vallarta,* ☎ *322-224-*

8354 or 226-3732, www.vallarta- adventures.com, offers tours to some of the outlying villages, cultural tours to Huichol villages, whale-watching, scuba diving, snorkeling and a canopy adventure. They also have a variety of wildlife excursions where you can watch turtle hatching/egg laying (June-Sept., $60), watch for dolphins ($65, four hours), visit a crocodile rejuvenation program run by the University of Guadalajara ($32) or take a hike and look for birds in the jungle ($45, five hours). They also rent plastic, non-tip kayaks at a cost of $65 for six hours.

Mex Bike Adventures, *Calle Guerrero # 361,* ☎ *322-223-1834 or 322-223-1680 from Canada or the US,* run hiking and biking tours for all experience levels. Their 12-mile/20-km bike trip up the Cuale River takes three to four hours and costs $44 per person. This includes bike, helmet and refreshments. The bikes are 24-gear, front-suspension mountain bikes. Mex Bike will go with a minimum of three people.

Ecotours Vallarta de Mexico, *Ignacio Vallarta 243,* ☎ *322-222-6606 or 223-3130, www.ecotoursvallarta.com* has been offering tours since 1991. Ecotours is owned by Astrid Frisch, a biologist, and Karel Beets, a specialist in sustainable development. Their excellent reputation in conservation has led them to work with the World Wildlife Fund, the American Museum of Natural History in New York, the St. Louis Zoo and the National Wildlife Federation. Ecotours offers diving, snorkeling, bird watching, hiking and kayaking, and is involved in the Humpback Whale Photo-identification project and in the Sea Turtle Conservation Program. Astrid is also involved in the inter-

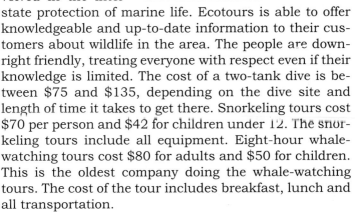

© Ecotours Vallarta

state protection of marine life. Ecotours is able to offer knowledgeable and up-to-date information to their customers about wildlife in the area. The people are downright friendly, treating everyone with respect even if their knowledge is limited. The cost of a two-tank dive is between $75 and $135, depending on the dive site and length of time it takes to get there. Snorkeling tours cost $70 per person and $42 for children under 12. The snorkeling tours include all equipment. Eight-hour whale-watching tours cost $80 for adults and $50 for children. This is the oldest company doing the whale-watching tours. The cost of the tour includes breakfast, lunch and all transportation.

Ocean Friendly Tours, *Paseo del Marlin #510,* ☎ *322-225-3774, www.oceanfriendly.com,* runs whale-watching tours during the winter and nature photography all year long. Whale trips run from 9 am-2 pm between mid-December and the end of March. This tour has an ocean specialist along as guide. They also have professional photos of ocean wildlife for sale.

Exotic Tours, *Av Diaz Ordaz #652, on the malecón next to the Hard Rock Café,* ☎ *322-222-8653, exotictours@ hotmail.com,* has a showroom with videos, brochures, photos and a simulation of the ocean and jungle. Watch the TV monitors to see what can be done on each tour – beside a large papier mâché whale, a whale-watching video is playing, and among the jungle vegetation is another video about the canopy tour. A tremendous amount of work has gone into this showroom and seeing it will give you a good idea of what to expect. I highly recommend stopping in here. This company co-ordinates a lot of tours for other companies.

Open Air Expeditions, *Guerrero #339,* ☎ *322-222-3310, www.vallartawhales.com,* offers numerous tours, including a whale-watching trip in Banderas Bay ($75, four hours); turtle watching on the bay ($65, four hours); and spotting crocodiles at the University of Guadalajara Research Station ($32, four hours). You can also take a river trail hike ($55, five hours) or a kayak trip in a non-tip kayak ($65, six hours).

Canopy Tours, *Los Juntas de los Veranos,* ☎ *322-223-6060, www.canopytours-vallarta.com,* offers canopy tours that go over a canyon. A bus runs five times a day out to the site. Transportation, soda and insect repellent are included in the price, $60 for the day. They accept direct-reservations only – that means either you book by telephone or online – up to one month in advance.

Chicos Dive Shop, *Av Diaz Ordaz # 772,* ☎ *322-222-1895, www.chicos-diveshop.com,* has been around since 1968 offering diving and snorkeling tours, diving courses and jungle tours. They know all the spots, and offer nitox tanks, night dives and custom trips. They also have a wide variety of rentals for those not carrying any gear. Pathfinders, a subsidiary company, offers dune-buggy trips twice a day (9 am-noon and 2-5 pm), every day except Sunday. The trip follows the Bay of Banderas and then goes along some jungle rivers and into the foothills. The cost for machine, helmet and water is $25 for the half-day.

Natura Expeditions, *Terminal Maritima*, ☎ *322-224-0410, www.naturaexpeditions.com,* runs hiking, biking and horseback riding trips into the mountains. Their hiking tour ($35, five hours) begins at a ranch in the mountains and you hike for three hours through the forest and jungle with an English-speaking guide who can point out different plants and their uses. Birders will find this a good walk. You will stop at a hot spring for a short dip midway during the hike. The trip includes transportation to trailhead, fruit, water, guide and shot of tequila at the end of the day. You should wear either hiking boots or good running shoes. Those not into walking can ride a sure-footed and well-trained horse ($45, five hours) along the Mascota River where the vegetation is lush and the bird life abundant. You will pass mango and banana plantations en route to the hot springs. Back at the ranch, you will be invited to feed the ostrich. This trip includes two hours travel time. The price includes transportation, horse, guide and water. Bikers travel off-road past plantations and small towns on a 21-gear, full-suspension bike. Along the way, wildlife will be spotted. The cost for this is $35, including your bike, water, equipment and guide. Add a dinner of barbequed ribs to any of the above trips for just 10 bucks. Natura also has a trimaran called *Simbad* that can carry 17 people. You can hire the boat fully equipped with a full bar and lunch or just the boat. The cost is $220 for an eight-hour day without the bar and lunch. This is a good deal.

B-B-Bobby's Bikes, *Miramar #399 at Iturbide,* ☎ *322-223-0008,* has bikes for rent to take either on your own or with a guide for the day or a week. They use the RACE brand of bike and supply helmets, gloves, shorts and water.

Rainbow Dancer Cruises, *Francia #487,* ☎ *322-299-0936, www.rainbowdancer.com, or go to the Main Marina, off Av Escuela Naval Marina, across from San Javier Hospital.* The boat leaves the port every day except Sunday at 9:30 am. There is a $1 charge to enter the port and you can purchase tickets for the catamaran boat trip at the dock. The cost is $40 per person and half price for kids. This includes all meals and drinks on board ship. You

Puerto Vallarta

start with breakfast on board as you travel to Los Arcos where you can snorkel. Lunch is in Quimixto at a local restaurant and the meal is included, although the drinks are not. Those wanting to ride a horse will pay an additional $13. The *Rainbow Dancer* caters to a gay/lesbian crowd.

Santa Maria Catamaran, *Los Muertos Pier,* leaves every day at 9:30 am and 10:15 am, and returns at 6 pm. Included in the price is a continental breakfast, fruits, lunch, open bar on board, snorkeling gear, kayaks, fishing gear, music to dance by and air conditioning in the bathrooms (how about that?). This boat visits Los Arcos, Las Animas and Quimixto. It is a wild time.

AnclaTur, *Cerrada de Playas #2, Nuevo Vallarta,* ☎ 322-221-2244 or 322-278-2606 (cell), has a 38-foot/12-meter catamaran called *Eleganz* that can hold 23 passengers.

> **FACT FILE:** *Eleganz was built in 2000 by Beneteau of France, one of the world's leading boat builders.*

On board is radar, weather fax, water maker, GPS, echo sounder, auto pilot, auto life raft, VHF radio and satellite phone. For entertainment there is a CD stereo player, TV, VCR and video games for the kids (big and small). Watersports include a kayak, snorkeling equipment and fishing tackle. You can opt for the full meal plan which includes continental breakfast, snacks, lunch of tacos, quesadillas or enchiladas, and national alcoholic beverages for $30 a day, plus tax. The luxury plan, $48 per day, includes everything that is in the above plan, plus a beach lunch of shrimp or lobster (in season) or an entire fish and an imported bottle of wine. The boat, totally equipped with a full crew and experienced captain costs $5,000 a week.

DAY TRIPS

Las Juntas village is 14 miles/22 km south of PV and can be visited as a day trip by using a local bus, your own vehicle or a taxi. Once there, you can do a horse trip up the river, swim for a while, hike up the river and/or eat and drink in the restaurant. There are two restaurants, one upstream from the other. **Chico's Paradise Restaurant**, ☎ *322-473-0413, www.chicosparadise.com.mx, open 10 am-6 pm,* is surrounded by jungle vegetation. Chico works with the local indigenous people so a lot of the profits go to them. The best dish is the beef brochette, served with rice, beans, French fries and salsa for $11. For dessert, try the caramel custard (flan). Chico's has the Santa Lucia waterfall at its side and is next to La Tuito stream that has swimming holes. I have no details on the second restaurant.

A run to Las Juntas should be done as a day trip from PV as there is no place to stay at Las Juntas. This is a popular destination.

SHOPPING

Huichol Collection, *Paseo Diaz Ordaz #732,* ☎ *322-223-0661 and Morelos #490,* ☎ *322-223-2141,* are retail outlets carrying the best in Huichol art. The stores are run by locals who ensure that some of the profits return to the communities where the art originated. One of the newer styles of art is being represented by the solid beaded pieces that come in every size and shape imaginable.

Libros Libros Bookstore, *31 de Octubre (just south of Hidalgo Park),* has both Spanish- and English-language books.

Shop in PV.

HUICHOL SYMBOLS

- The **Iguana** is the adviser of the future and the eyes of the spirit.
- The **bird** is the symbol of freedom and messenger of good.
- **Turtles** help the rain goddess and are considered good luck.
- **Corn** indicates health and prosperity.
- The **scorpion** is the protector of the peyote and the people.
- **Snakes** are intermediaries between humans and the spirit world.
- **Butterfly** is the symbol of good luck.

Indigera, *Juarez # 628,* ☎ *322-222-3007, five blocks north of the main plaza,* specializes in "Day of the Dead" art, but they also carry some exceptional crystal that has been decorated with 23kt gold leaf. They have some exquisite Huichol Indian art and unique masks. Because quality is good, prices are fairly high.

Shop in PV.

La Bohemia, *Constitución and Basilio Badillo,* ☎ *322-222-3164,* has a collection of unique resort-wear (clothes that look great in Mexico, but the pits once home). They also carry a line of jewelry and accessories that is quite exquisite. Prices are fairly high. La Bohemia sponsors a fashion show every Thursday at 1 pm at the Camino Real.

The **Flea Market** by the Rio Cuale Bridge holds numerous shops and *tiendas* selling everything from seashells to fine art. Prices have to be bartered here and you would be wise to look at other shops to have an idea of where to start (or end).

Habanos, *Calle Aldama #170,* carry the best Cuban cigars, including Cohibas, Montecristo, Cuaba, La Gloria, Cubana, Ramon Allones, Partagas, Upmann, Romeo y Julieta, Punch, Bolivar, Hoyo de Monterrey, Fonseca and La Flor de Cano.

CIGAR SAVVY

Some of the things to look for that guarantee Cuban quality are the red serial number of the Republic of Cuba on the cigar and, on the bottom of the box, the factory code (several letters). It must have the brand of Cuba on it saying "Hecho a Mano."

PLACES TO STAY

There are 111 hotels registered with the tourist office in Puerto Vallarta. They vary in quality from zero to five stars and include luxury timeshares to unregistered places that are often smaller and less expensive. It is beyond the scope of this book to list them all. Some are all-inclusive, which means, meals, entertainment and local booze is part of the package. The web page, www.puertovallarta.net, lists most of the hotels and gives a brief description. If you want specific things like golf courses, tennis courts or child-care that aren't included in this book, look on the net.

HOTEL PRICE SCALE
Room price, in US $
$ . . . . up to $20
$$ . . . . $21-$50
$$$ $51-100
$$$$ . . . . $101-$150
$$$$$ $151-200

Puerto Vallarta

> **WARNING:** When booking online, be aware that photos never show the cockroaches in the corner or the paint peeling from the ceilings. Never pay for your entire stay up front, just in case the real thing doesn't meet your expectations. If the place looks too good for the price, it may well be. Check www.tripadvisor.com for reviews about places you are considering. Some of the postings are obviously put there by staff, but others are legitimate and helpful.

Timeshare hawkers will drive you bonkers in PV. If you are genuinely interested in purchasing, be careful. Timeshares are not always what they are made out to be. Give yourself at least 48 hours cooling-down time from when you are wined and dined by the salesman until you sign a contract. The Mayan Palace is about the largest timeshare in the area (and has the most hawkers).

Remember, no area code is needed when making a local call.

■ LAP OF LUXURY HOTELS

The luxury places usually have a couple of pools, air conditioning, and a disco/bar and restaurant. They are big, sometimes with more than 500 rooms. Some are timeshares and all are above average as far as hotels go, especially when it comes to entertainment. Below are a few.

Camino Real, *Km 3.5 Barra de Navidad Hwy,* ☎ *322-221-5000*, $140-$550 per night, 337 rooms.

Four Seasons, *Punta Mita,* ☎ *322-291-6000,* $390-$790 per night, 140 rooms.

Hacienda Cora, *Calle Pelicanos #311,* ☎ *322-221-0800,* rates start at $177 per night, 67 rooms.

Hotelito Desconocido, *Carreterra A Mismaloya #479,* ☎ *322-298-5209,* $200-$280 per night, 27 rooms.

La Jolla de Mismaloya, *Km 11-5 Zona Hotelera Sur,* ☎ *322-226-0660,* standard rooms are $252-$282 a night, 303 rooms.

Marriott Casa Magna, *Av Paseo de la Marina #5,* ☎ *322-221-0004,* $90+ per night in low season, 433 rooms.

Melia Pto. Vallarta, *Paseo de la Marina Sur, #H7,* ☎ *322-226-3000,* has rooms as low as $110 per night, 357 rooms.

Premiere Buenaventura, *Calle San Salvador #117,* ☎ *322-226-7001,* $160-$290 per night, 83 rooms.

Sheraton Buganvilias, *Blvd Fr. Medina Ascencio 999,* ☎ *322-226-0404,* $80-$275 per night, 684 rooms.

Sunterra Vallarta Torre, *Paseo de las Garzas,* ☎ *322-224-0366*, no prices available, 66 rooms.

■ TO SUIT ALL BUDGETS

Hotel Belmar, *Insurgentes #161,* ☎ *322-222-0572 or 223-1872, $,* offers rooms at $13.50 per person without air conditioning. With air conditioning, the cost is a bit higher. This is a tiny hotel just 500 meters from the Playa de Los Muertos and three blocks from the *malecón.* Rooms are basic but okay.

Hotel Hortencia, *Calle Francisco Madero #336,* ☎ *322-223-3221, www.hotelhortencia.com, $,* has rooms with bathroom and fan. The hotel is in a colonial styled building and is clean. Part of the attractiveness of this hotel is its bright white walls. It also has rooms with air conditioning but the cost is $35 for a double and for that price you can get a lot better in one of the fancier hotels.

Hotel Azteca, *Calle Francisco Madero #473,* ☎ *322-222-2750, $,* has 40 rooms that are fairly bright considering the windows open onto a central courtyard rather than the street. There are two desks and nightstands in each room, plus fans. The place is hospital clean, the staff is

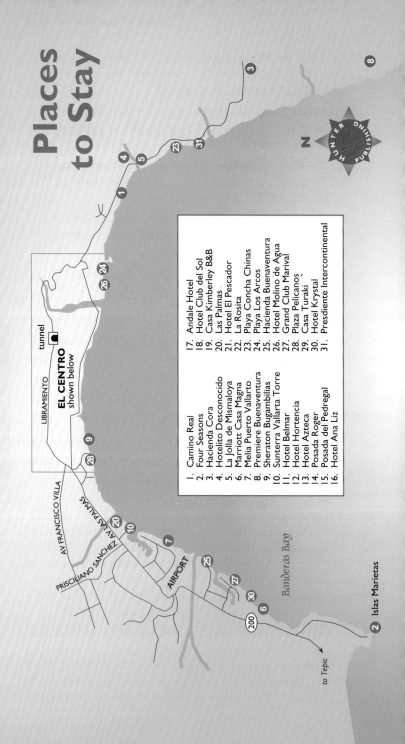

Places to Stay

EL CENTRO
shown below

LIBRAMIENTO
tunnel

AV FRANCISCO VILLA

AV LAS PALMAS

PRISCILIANO SANCHEZ

AIRPORT

Banderas Bay

to Tepic

200

2 Islas Marietas

N

HUNTER PUBLISHING

1. Camino Real
2. Four Seasons
3. Hacienda Cora
4. Hotelito Desconocido
5. La Jolla de Mismaloya
6. Marriott Casa Magna
7. Melia Puerto Vallarto
8. Premiere Buenaventura
9. Sheraton Bugambilias
10. Sunterra Vallarta Torre
11. Hotel Belmar
12. Hotel Hortencia
13. Hotel Azteca
14. Posada Roger
15. Posada del Pedregal
16. Hotel Ana Liz

17. Andale Hotel
18. Hotel Club del Sol
19. Casa Kimberley B&B
20. Las Palmas
21. Hotel El Pescador
22. La Rosita
23. Playa Concha Chinas
24. Playa Los Arcos
25. Hacienda Buenaventura
26. Hotel Molino de Agua
27. Grand Club Marival
28. Plaza Pelicanos
29. Casa Turaki
30. Hotel Krystal
31. Presdiente Intercontinental

El Centro

to Costa
Alegre

INSURGENTES

R GOMEZ

FCA RODRIGUEZ

M DIEGUEZ

JACARANDAS

BASILIO BADILLO

AGUACATE

OLAS ALTAS

PINO JUAREZ

IL VALLARTA

14

V CARRANZA

CONST.

12 13

16

MADERAS

L CARDENAS

11

S DE FEBRERO

A SERDAN

A RODRIGUEZ

LIBERTAD

15

Isla
Caule

GUERRERO

ZARAGOZA

19

MINA

GALBANA

CORONA

CARRANZA

ALDAMA

MIRAMAR

AMPAS

MATAMOROS

HIDALGO

22

SANCHEZ

ABASOLO

MORELOS

JO DOMINGUEZ

21

PASEO DIAZ O

PIPILA

ALLENDE

PAR VAL

31 DE OCTUBRE

JESUS LANGARICA

tunnel

ARGENTINA

VENEZUELA

CHILE

URUGUAY

PANAMA

MALECON

HONDURAS

NICARAGUA

BRASIL

COLOMBIA

PERU

AV MEXICO

PARAGUAY

SAN SALVADOR

ECUADOR

BOLIVIA

GUATEMALA

LIBRAMIENTO

BRASILIA

18

AV FRANCISCO MEDINA ASCENCIO

20

N

Banderas Bay

friendly and it is quiet. Some rooms have kitchenettes. What more can one want for $18 a night?

Posada Roger, *Basilio Badillo #237,* ☎ *322-222-0836, profiled on www.puerto-vallarta.com, $$,* has 48 rooms decorated with heavy Mexican furniture. Each room has a private bathroom, cable TV, telephone, air conditioning and a fan. The hotel features a rooftop pool, surrounding gardens, currency exchange and safe-deposit boxes.

Posada del Pedregal, *Agustin Rodriguez #267,* ☎ *322-222-0604, www.mexonline.com/pedregal.htm, $$,* is a small hotel that has clean large rooms at reasonable prices. During low season, the owner will barter a little. The cost of a room with private bathroom and hot water is $30 for two people sharing a bed. You must pay for your room in advance.

Hotel Ana Liz, *Calle Francisco Madero # 429,* ☎ *322-222-1757, $$,* has small clean rooms with fans. Each room has its own bathroom. This place is a family run establishment and often has repeat customers. It is just a block from the beach, on the south side of the river.

Andale Hotel, *Olas Altas #425,* ☎ *322-223-2622, $$,* is above the Andale Restaurant in the center of town and has seven standard rooms and two, two-bedroom suites. The rooms have tiled floors, brick walls with iron-bared windows, closets, double beds, small reading lamps and tables. This is a very nice place to stay, not fancy but certainly fun.

FACT FILE: *In 1980, José Peña and his burros helped build the Andale Hotel. The burros, treated like prized pets, were trained to carry sand from the river up the stairs to the second level of the building.*

Hotel Club del Sol, *Blvd Francisco Medina Ascencio, Km 15,* ☎ *322-222-2188, www.hotelesclubdelsol.com.mx, $$$,* is an average hotel with friendly staff. Their 103 rooms come with or without kitchenettes. All have air conditioning and fans, fridges, two beds, telephones and cable TV. There is a restaurant and sports bar on the property and a 180-foot/60-meter water slide. Prices are not bad at this middle-of-the-road place.

Casa Kimberley B&B, *Calle Zaragoza 445,* ☎ *322-222-1336, www.casakimberley.com, $$$,* is in the home previously owned by Richard Burton and Elizabeth Taylor. The nine bedrooms/suites in the Burton side of the house are named after some of the movies in which he starred. Just to be near the place where these two romantics lived is fun. There is a pool, bar and dining area, and you get to use the walkway over to the Elizabeth side where the museum is located. The rooms are luxurious, with tiled floors, private bathrooms, night tables, sitting areas and area rugs.

Las Palmas, *Paseo de la Marina # 161,* ☎ *322-224-0650, $$$,* has 221 rooms, each with private bathroom and balcony, cable TV, air conditioning and tiled floors. Some rooms have kitchenettes and the views are either of the ocean or their garden. This beachside hotel has two pools, a tennis court, a bar and four restaurants. There is laundry service available, beach and pool towels are provided and safe deposit boxes can be used.

Hotel El Pescador, *Paraguay # 1117,* ☎ *322-222-2169, $$$,* has 100 rooms in a large nondescript building on the beach. Most rooms have a balcony and they all have tiled floors, lamp, a nice closet area, air conditioning or fan and a private bathroom. There is a pool, lounge chairs (little shade) and a nice dining area. For a moderately priced hotel, this is a good choice. It is right down town and is the sister hotel to La Rosita.

La Rosita, *Paseo Diaz Ordaz #901,* ☎ *800-297-0144 from US (no local number), $$$,* has been around since long before my first visit to PV more than 20 years ago and has been consistent in the quality and service offered to its customers. It has over a hundred rooms, all clean and comfortable with rustic Mexican furniture, soft beds, tiled bathrooms, TVs (no cable) and fans. Some rooms overlook the ocean. There is a pool and restaurant and the price of the room includes breakfast. The central location is always a draw.

Playa Concha Chinas, *Carretera Barra de Navidad, Km 2.5,* ☎ *322-221-5763, $$$/$$$$,* is a tiny place with just 17 rooms, each a little different. They are done in tile and have small bathrooms, but some have a Jacuzzi on the balcony. There is air conditioning, safe deposit boxes and cable TV. Some of the edges are a bit worn, but not badly. By this I mean that there are chips in the paint, a few dustballs in the corners and maybe a spot or two on the window or shower door. The hotel is a little way from the center so it is quiet, yet it is easy to get into town if you need to. The beach is rocky and the jungle behind is close. The pool is not large and overlooks the ocean. There is a restaurant and laundry service.

> **AUTHOR NOTE:** *You can also purchase a 9,000-square-foot villa at the Real de Concha Chinas (different than the Playa Concha Chinas). The cost is just a million and a half (more or less). If interested, contact a real estate agent when in PV.*

Playa Los Arcos, *Olas Altas #380,* ☎ *322-222-1583, www.playalosarcos.com, $$$/$$$$,* has 185 rooms mostly decorated in Mexican motif with tiled floors, skylights and balconies in some rooms. But some rooms are small and dingy. All bathrooms are minuscule and all the reports that I got said the beds were hard as cement. The staff is fine and the hotel is on the beach in the old section of town. Their breakfast, offered with some package

deals, is good. Although they offer an all-inclusive package, I seldom recommend these because they limit your experience of the real Mexico.

Hacienda Buenaventura, *Francisco Madina Ascencio # 2699,* ☎ *322-224-6667, $$$/$$$$,* has 155 rooms that show a bit of wear. This is not a five-star, nor is it on the beach, but it is not a bad deal. The rooms are large with Mexican décor, balconies and telephones. There is air conditioning, an outdoor pool, cable TV, tour desk, money exchange, laundry service, bar and restaurant. Guests may use the facilities at their other hotel called, simply, The Buenaventura. It is in the hotel zone.

Hotel Molino de Agua, *Ignacio L. Vallarta # 130,* ☎ *322-222-1957, www.molinodeagua.com, $$$/$$$$,* has guest cabins and rooms. The grounds have two pools, as well as parrot and monkey houses. The cages for the monkeys are not very big, and the animals don't look comfortable. There is also a problem with school kids using the pools and making the grounds noisy. However, the rooms are large and comfortable, though the beds are a bit hard. There are no TVs, which I sometimes regard as a plus. The hotel is in the very center of town, but because the grounds are large and walled, it is not noisy from street traffic. The staff is exceptionally accommodating.

Grand Club Marival, *Paseo Cocoteros, no phone, www. gomarival.com, $$$/$$$$,* is in Nuevo Vallarta about half an hour (eight miles/12 km) from the center. Its 650 rooms, each with private bathroom, cable TV and air conditioning, run from $65 to $350 a night. There are six restaurants, seven bars, four pools, numerous tennis courts, a fitness center, an outdoor Jacuzzi, a games room, an arcade and a business center. Professional entertainers present each evening in one of the restaurants. Although the building was built in 1983, it has been renovated recently. This hotel is a long way from the center.

Plaza Pelicanos, *Calle Diego Rivera #120,* ☎ *322-224-4444, $$$$,* has over 400 recently renovated rooms with air conditioning, private bathroom, telephone and cable TV. Each is well decorated. There is a children's pool and an adult pool, a Jacuzzi, a games room and a babysitting service. This hotel offers many different packages with lures like free beach craft and night shows. However, I suggest

© Plaza Pelicanos

you take only the room and maybe breakfast. It is far more fun to explore, unless you have just a few days and need an exotic place to crash.

Casa Tukari, *Calle España #316,* ☎ *322-224-7177, www. tukari.com, $$$/$$$$ (rates change according to the season),* is in a Mexican colonial-style house that has all the modern conveniences. All four rooms have a view of the garden, which has guava, lime and banana trees, plus a small pool. Each room has a telephone, ceiling fan and a fridge. There is also a Jacuzzi. A massage can be ordered from an on-site therapist who practices the Reiki technique, magnet therapy, light and sound therapy and aromatherapy. PV has been awarded the title of "the most friendly city in the world," and Casa Tukari certainly falls into the same friendly classification.

Hotel Krystal, *Av La Garzas Sur,* ☎ *322-224-0202, $$$$$,* has 405 rooms that cost between $170 and $500 each. The Moorish-style building is moderate in luxury

© Hotel Krystal

and rooms have mini-bars, air conditioning, satellite TV and daily maid service. They have a pool, safe deposit boxes, bar, lounge, restaurants, tennis, racquetball, hot tub and fitness center. The breakfast buffet is good and lasts until 11 am. There is also an authentic show called "Fiesta" starting every evening at 7 pm.

Presidente Intercontinental, *Carretera Barra de Navidad, Km 8.5,* ☎ *322-228-0191 or 228-0191, www. ichotelsgroup.com. $$$$$,* has 120 rooms with an ocean view and 97 rooms without. Fourteen suites have private Jacuzzis, five of them indoors. The three master suites have two bedrooms each, both with balconies and Jacuzzis on each balcony. The presidential suite has all this and a private pool. Services offered include a travel agency, a gift/magazine shop, a business center, a gymnasium, a tennis court and two restaurants. However, the hotel does not have a good reputation. It has a lack of security, a very small pool, and is often full of locals who really want to party on their vacation. The place is a bit tattered in places and needs a facelift. It is more than an hour's walk into town; taxis are generally used.

PLACES TO EAT

PV has all the franchise restaurants like Hooters, Hard Rock Café, Dairy Queen, MacDonalds, Planet Hollywood and Señor Frog's. These are all familiar and safe and I fall back on them occasionally. But I much prefer to patronize the locally owned establishments.

There are so many choices in PV that it is hard for me to make much more than a random selection and give my preferences. Explore on your own and find some of the gems I haven't yet been to.

GOURMET FEST

A 10-day gourmet festival held in mid-November is sponsored by 23 of the area's most prestigious restaurants. The fair starts with a reception cocktail party where you can schmooze with the chefs. It closes with a banquet that could only be called a food orgy. The festival also offers events like cooking classes and seminars directed at learning about foods, especially cheeses and wines. If you're in town during this time, check at the tourist office or at your hotel for times of events.

Este Café, *Libertad #336* ☎ *322-222-4261*, is a tiny place that has good fresh-baked bread, along with fruit, yogurt and granola, cakes, frappés, shakes or smoothies. The bagels are ordinary and the coffee is something like watered-down espresso. A coffee and pastry runs $4.50 – fairly expensive.

Al Taurino, *Paseo Diaz Ordaz #868,* ☎ *322-223-2817,* is an attractive, middle-of-the-road restaurant that has a good seafood stew ($8) cooked with lots of chilies. Portions are moderate.

La Piazzetta, *Olas Altas and Rodolfo Gomez #143,* ☎ *322-222-0650*, is open Monday to Saturday 1 pm-midnight.

Pizza cooked over a wood fire is their specialty, but their veal scallopini is not to be overlooked.

Beanz American Café, *Olas Altas 490-7*, is open 8 am-midnight. Although they guarantee good coffee, they can't seem to guarantee good service. I waited by the counter for quite a while but couldn't get the attention of the waitress, even when I spoke to her. I went elsewhere.

Café Due Espresso Bar, *Commercial Center Villa Vallarta on Francisco Medina Ascencio*, ☎ *322-224-6567*, has excellent bread and good bagels. This is a good spot for a sandwich or breakfast with juice.

Pie in the Sky Coffee Shop, *I.L. Vallarta #150 at Aquiles Serdan*, ☎ *322-222-8411*, serves good specialty coffees and pastries in its air-conditioned restaurant. They also sell cookies, Italian ice cream, carrot cake, cheesecake and bagels. The pastry is excellent. A piece of apple pie (made with real apples) and a coffee was $4. This was my favorite afternoon coffee spot.

Calypso Café, *Av Francisco Medina Ascencio #1939*, ☎ *322-225-4870*, is open every day and serves excellent coffee and pastries. The owner is a fellow from Pheonix who married a Mexican woman and decided to make PV his home. The place is air-conditioned, which is a draw during the hot muggy days. The computers are fast and cost around $2 per hour.

Ruben's Hamburgers, *Olas Altas #463*, ☎ *322-223-1445*, is the Mexican version of Burger King. The service is excellent, the meals large and the prices low. The deep-fried banana with ice cream is recommended, as is the baked potato. The hamburgers are served with lots of sliced onions – always a favorite with me – for just under $5. The restaurant is located on two floors. The bathrooms are spotless but, when I was there, they were missing toilet seats.

The RiverWay Restaurant, *Calle Morelos #101*, ☎ *322-222-6873*, has an excellent location near the beach, down by the flea market. Open for breakfast, lunch and dinner, this place has good food at low prices. Lunch is about $4 per meal. They often offer a second drink free if you have supper. Reservations are recommended during high season.

Mickey's No Name Café, *Morelos #460,* ☎ *322-223-2508, nonamecafe@prodigy.net,* is a sports bar that specializes in barbeque ribs and chicken. The meat is good, but the portions are small and the prices are high. A two-for-the-price-of-one beer costs double what it would cost in some other restaurants. The service, however, is good and friendly.

Santa Barbara, *Olas Altas #351,* ☎ *322-222-4477,* offers Mexican and American food and their menu sports such dishes as a Reuben on rye, liver and onions, chicken mole and fajitas. They have a good selection of wines and, if you have room, homemade desserts are available. The prices are less than $20 a plate.

Planeta Vegetariano, *Iturbide # 270, just above Avenida Hidalgo,* ☎ *322-222-3073,* is open 8 am-10 pm. The breakfast buffet offers fresh fruit, oatmeal, tofu omelette, soy milk and hotcakes made without eggs or milk. There is also yogurt, fruit drinks and the best coffee in town. You get all you can eat for $3.50. Lunch or dinner starts at 11:30 and is served until 10 pm. For $5.50 you have the choice of five main dishes that include soup, salad bar, fruit drinks, tea, coffee and dessert. This is one of the best places in Vallarta. The restaurant holds about five or six tables, so go early, or just off regular meal times, so you can get a seat.

El Torito, *Ignacio L. Vallarta #290,* ☎ *322-222-3784,* has world-famous barbequed ribs and chicken, plus a choice of over 100 liquors and wines. This is a large sports bar that has 25 television sets, all set at a different sport. El Torito has been in business since 1982, so they are doing something well.

Outback Steakhouse, *Francisco Medina Ascencio #4690,* ☎ *322-225-4906,* offers steaks done Australian style and served with a bonzer salad. For the seafood lover, they also have a catch of the day special that is superb. To finish your meal, try their "Chocolate Thunder from Down Under."

Places to Eat

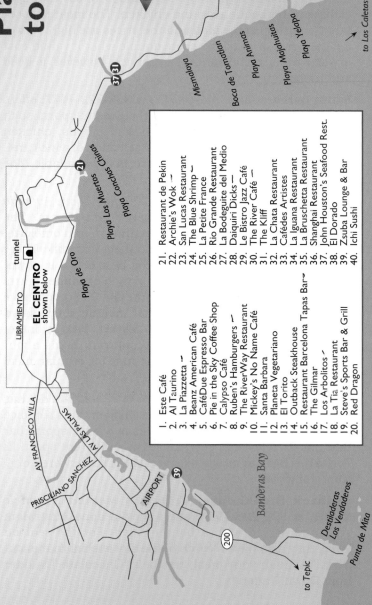

1. Este Café
2. Al Taurino
3. La Piazzetta ✓
4. Beanz American Café
5. CaféDue Espresso Bar
6. Pie in the Sky Coffee Shop
7. Calypso Café
8. Ruben's Hamburgers ✓
9. The RiverWay Restaurant
10. Mickey's No Name Café
11. Santa Barbara
12. Planeta Vegetariano
13. El Torito
14. Outback Steakhouse
15. Restaurant Barcelona Tapas Bar ✓
16. The Gilmar
17. Los Arbolitos ✓
18. La Tia Restaurant
19. Steve's Sports Bar & Grill
20. Red Dragon

21. Restaurant de Pekin
22. Archie's Wok ✓
23. San Lucas Restaurant
24. The Blue Shrimp ✓
25. La Petite France
26. Rio Grande Restaurant
27. La Bodeguite del Medio
28. Daiquiri Dicks ✓
29. Le Bistro Jazz Café
30. The River Café ✓
31. The Kliff
32. La Chata Restaurant
33. Cafédes Artistes
34. La Iguana Restaurant
35. La Bruschetta Restaurant
36. Shanghai Restaurant
37. John Houston's Seafood Rest.
38. El Dorado
39. Zsuba Lounge & Bar
40. Ichi Sushi

LIBRAMIENTO

EL CENTRO
shown below

tunnel

AV FRANCISCO VILLA

AV LAS PALMAS

PRISCILIANO SANCHEZ

AIRPORT

Playa de Oro

Playa Los Muertos Chinas

Playa Conchas Chinas

Mismaloya

Boca de Tomatlan

Playa Animas

Playa Majahuitas

Playa Yelapa

to Los Caletas

Banderas Bay

Destiladeras
Los Vendaderos

Punta de Mita

to Tepic

200

39

21

37 31

N

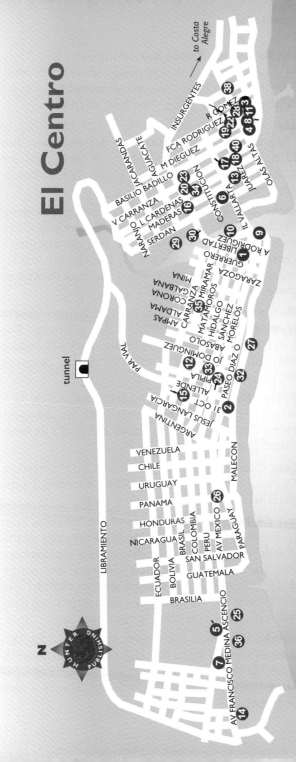

El Centro

to Costa Alegre

tunnel

Banderas Bay

N

HUNTER PUBLISHING

© 2007 HUNTER PUBLISHING, INC.

LIBRAMIENTO

PAR VIAL

INSURGENTES
R GOMEZ
FCA RODRIGUEZ
M DIEGUEZ
JACARANDAS
AGUACATE
BASILIO BADILLO
V CARRANZA
L CARDENAS
NARANJO
MADERAS
SERDAN
CONSTITUCION
I VALLARTA
JUAREZ
OLAS ALTAS
LIBERTAD
GUERRERO
A RODRIGUEZ
ZARAGOZA
MINA
GALEANA
CORONA
ALDAMA
MATAMOROS
HIDALGO
SANCHEZ
MORELOS
ABASOLO
PASEO DIAZ O
PIPILA
ALLENDE
31 OCT
JESUS LANGARICA
ARGENTINA
VENEZUELA
CHILE
URUGUAY
PANAMA
HONDURAS
NICARAGUA
COLOMBIA
BRASIL
PERU
SAN SALVADOR
GUATEMALA
BRASILIA
AV FRANCISCO MEDINA ASCENCIO
AV MEXICO
PARAGUAY
MALECON
ECUADOR
BOLIVIA
AMPAS
CARRANZA
JO DOMINGUEZ
MIRAMAR
BASILIO
O L CARDENAS
FCA RODRIGUEZ

Restaurant Barcelona Tapas Bar, *Matamoros and 31 de Octubre,* ☎ *322-222-0510,* is open daily from 5 pm-midnight. If you like to sip fruit-flavored wine and munch on appetizers, then try this place. The food is good.

The Gilmar, *Francisco Madero #418,* ☎ *322-222-3923*, is between Aguacate and Jacarandas, across from the Bernal Hotel in the old part of town. A good spot for breakfast, it is open daily, 8 am-11 pm. The coffee is fairly strong.

Los Arbolitos, *Lazaro Cardenas and Camino de la Ribera # 184,* ☎ *322-223-1050,* is open 11 am-11 pm daily. Try the onion soup for under $4 – it will fill you up. They also have flan (caramel custard) for $3.50, but the serving isn't big enough to satisfy me. See if you can talk them into a bigger piece.

La Tia Restaurant, *Pino Suarez #240 and Lazaro Cardenas,* ☎ *322-223-0667,* is open 8 am-10 pm. For breakfast, the French toast ($2) is great. They also make a fruit plate with yogurt and granola for $2.50. Suppers run between $7 and $21.

Steve's Sports Bar & Grill, *Basilio Badillo #286,* ☎ *322-222-0256,* is a fish and chip joint that sells the cheapest beer in town. It is open daily 11 am-1 am and has both American and Canadian satellite TV.

Red Dragon, *Insurgentes # 323,* ☎ *322-222-0175*, makes the best Cantonese food in the city. They are open 1 pm-midnight and will even deliver to your hotel.

Restaurant de Pekin, *Olas Altas and Los Muertos Pier,* ☎ *322-222-8609*, is open noon-midnight every day of the week. The Pekin has been renovated so the atmosphere is exquisite. The menu has seven appetizers, five soups and two dozen main dishes. Their pineapple shrimp and Kung Pao chicken are spiced just right; anything with peanut sauce is good. The price is right, too.

Archie's Wok, *Francisca Rodriguez # 130,* ☎ *322-222-0411*, has been around since film director John Huston's day when Archie was Huston's personal chef. They specialize in Thai, Chinese and Filipino foods. This is a very good place to eat.

San Lucas Restaurant, *Cardenas and Insurgentes,* ☎ *322-222-3126,* is a pleasant eatery that overlooks the street from its second-floor location. It is open noon-10 pm and specializes in seafood and steak.

The Blue Shrimp, *Morelos #779,* ☎ *322-222-4246, www. theblueshrimp.com.mx,* is open noon-1 am daily. The décor includes relics of ancient ships and the walls are made to look like reefs. There are fish tanks interspersed around other sea-styled items and the room is lit with a blue light that adds to the underwater ambiance. Even the bathrooms are shaped like shells, the men's like a snail and the women's like a conch. The food is shrimp of every size prepared in almost any exotic style. I liked the coconut shrimp in a batter, covered in a coconut-milk sauce. There are so many varieties of shrimp, served in so many ways – the owners even managed to make a shrimp popcorn. Although there are other dishes, such as mahi mahi and tuna, shrimp is the real draw. This restaurant also has an excellent salad bar. They have the largest percentage of return customers in PV.

La Petite France, *Francisco Medina Ascencio Km 2.5,* ☎ *322-293-0900,* open 8 am-midnight daily. La Petite is a must for those who love French food, French wine, French décor and French service. The breakfast omelets, served in the garden, are a huge draw. I also liked the filet de poisson à la Petite France, a white fish with shallots, white wine and hollandaise sauce, all for $12.

Rio Grande Restaurant, *Av Mexico # 1175,* ☎ *322-222-0095,* open 8 am-11 pm, specializes in jumbo shrimp, red snapper and whatever the catch of the day may be. They have been in business since 1984, have air conditioning and offer the second drink free when you order one of the main dishes. For something special, try the crabmeat tacos.

La Bodeguita del Medio, *Malecón, Paseo Diaz Ordaz #858,* ☎ *322-223-1585,* will take you back to the 1940s in Havana with live Cuban music and delicious Cuban food cooked by a Cuban chef. The specialty is beans, rice and pork, spiced with hot chilies. Compliment this with a *mojito,* the drink of Hemingway, made with Cuban rum and lemon juice. Top all this off with a Cuban cigar, also available at La Bodeguita, and you'll go home to write your own version of *The Old Man and the Sea.*

Daiquiri Dick's, *Olas Altas #314,* ☎ 322-222-0566, is open every day except Wednesday from 10:30 am-midnight. This is one of the restaurants that partakes in the Gourmet Festival each year (see above). It started as a small beachside hut and transformed over a period of 18 years into the gourmet establishment you see today. They serve dishes like filet of tuna in a sesame crust over ginger-braised spinach and sukiyaki sauce, or chunks of lobster sautéed with serrano chili pepper, tomato and asparagus. They have come a long way in 18 years. This is one of the best places to eat in PV.

Le Bistro Jazz Café, *on the island on Rio Cuale,* ☎ 322-222-0283, is open every day except Sunday from 9 am-midnight. It offers some of the better wines available in PV. It is a romantic spot, especially when the jazz players are working. My favorite meal here is the coconut tempura shrimp royal served with a hot curry sauce. However, my husband had the filet mignon with mushrooms and baked potato and still says this was the best meal he ever had. (He says this a lot.)

The River Café, *Isla Rio Cuale #4,* ☎ 322-223-0788, *www.rivercafe.com.mx,* is open noon to 11 pm daily and has live jazz music Thursday through Sunday evenings. The café hires the best chefs to cook your meals, which are served along the riverside walkway. This is a romantic spot and the food is very good. My waiter was eager to give me exactly what I wanted, yet he never hovered. The calamari is a specialty, but if you are tired of seafood, how about rack of lamb done with garlic and rosemary sauce? During high season, reservations are recommended.

Le Kliff, ☎ *322-228-0666 or 224-0976, www.lekliff.com,* is the classiest restaurant in town. Meals are served under the largest palapa roof in the world and the restaurant overlooks the ocean. It is most romantic to go before sunset and watch as the sun sinks into the ocean. The Kliff offers a huge variety of foods, all first class, for about $25 a dish. The house specialty is the fresh filet le Kliff, but I liked the tequila jumbo shrimps. The after-dinner coffees are an act in themselves. It takes two waiters to prepare one, as alcohol-laden liquid is poured from one decanter to another in a display of agility. It is good entertainment for the guests. Once mixed, the coffee is brought flaming to your table. This is a treat that should not be missed. They also have non-intrusive live entertainment.

La Chata Restaurant, *Paseo Diaz Ordaz #708*, ☎ *322-222-4790*, is a clean, tastefully decorated restaurant. The upstairs room overlooks the bay, which makes it a good place to take in the sunset while enjoying a meal. Prices are better than most along the *malecón* and the portions, although not large, are big enough for an average appetite. I had the ceviche, but it was not exceptional.

Café des Artistes, *G. Sanchez # 740*, ☎ *322-222-3228*, *www.cafedesartistes.com/artistes*, is open 6-11:30 pm daily. It is owned and operated by international prize-winning chef Thierry Blouet, whose creations are legendary. How about a prawn carpaccio with caviar sauce? Or honey-glazed roasted duck with a green lime sauce and pumpkin risotto? This is not for the diet-conscious. The restaurant has original art, an indoor stream and lush gardens. For all this you will pay about $20 a plate.

La Iguana Restaurant, *Lazaro Cardenas #311*, ☎ *322-222-0105*, is open daily (except Monday), 11:30 am-1 am. This moderately-priced Mexican restaurant offers all the standard Mexican dishes, but it is the seafood that is really good. Try the shrimp in a Mexican sauce served with rice. On weekends, they have a mariachi band and often host events such as a folklore show, cockfight exhibition (I'm not certain what this is, but I believe cockfights are now illegal) and fireworks. During the week there is no cover charge and there is live music for dancing.

La Bruschetta Restaurant, *Calle Corona #172*, ☎ *322-223-1177*, is a cozy little Italian restaurant that does not have a hawker at the door trying to lure you in. That was a big draw for me. I had the Caesar salad and some lasagna. The meal was delicious, but it barely qualified as an appetizer. I left hungry and unsatisfied. The cost for a salad and spaghetti was about $15.

Shanghai Restaurant, *Francisco Medina Ascencio, Km 2,* ☎ *322-224-1961,* is a first-class establishment that serves foods made closer to the Hong Kong style than the American "Chinese" style. Their shrimp in black bean sauce is delicious. A meal in this air-conditioned restaurant runs less than $10.

John Houston's Seafood Restaurant, *in the Jolla de Mismaloya Hotel, Hotel Zone South at Km 11.5,* ☎ *322-226-0660,* is a true seafood place that serves seafood appetizers, snacks, salads, soups and main dishes. Steak is on the menu, but the choices are limited. The octopus cocktails, done in a tomato sauce, were exceptional. Meals run about $15.

El Dorado, *Pulpito # 102,* ☎ *322-222-1511,* is open 9 am-9 pm and has been in business since 1961. Their specialties are seafood and Mexican dishes. Try the fried dorado. Meals are large and prices are just under $10 per serving.

Zsuba Lounge and Bar, *Paseo de la Marina #245 (near the faro),* ☎ *322-221-0669,* is open 1-11:30 pm. They serve traditional Japanese cuisine from sake and Sapporo beer to sushi, but you can also get a prime rib. This is a quiet place for a pleasant dinner. A meal costs between $10 and $15.

Ichi Sushi, *Juarez #797,* ☎ *322-222-6100*, offers Japanese meals that can be delivered to your hotel or eaten at the restaurant. They carry foods like makisushi, nigiri sushi, teppanyaki, temaki, teriyaki, yakitori, tempura, sweet-and-sour dishes and special combos. The meals run about $5 per serving.

NIGHTLIFE

The nightlife in PV is extensive and offers everything from quiet piano bars to rowdy discos. If candlelit dining is your thing, you have tons of options.

You can get live entertainment, too; there are many folk shows. Walking the *malecón* is a favorite pastime, especially for locals. There is often a free show near the arches along the *malecón* and you can watch a light show on the old boat, *La Marigalante*.

Tequila bar.

For drinking, dancing and carousing, go to any bar near your hotel. Bars in areas near the hotels tend to be patronized by ex-pats and tourists, rather than locals.

■ MOVIE THEATERS

> **AUTHOR NOTE:** *English-language movies always have Spanish subtitles in Mexico. Most films are North American productions.*

Cine Bahia, *Insurgentes # 63*, ☎ *322-222-1717*, has five screens featuring American- and Spanish-language films. They have three showings for each screen and the matinee is usually at 4:30 pm.

Cine Luz Maria, *Calle Mexico # 27*, ☎ *322-222-0705*, has two screens with three showings for each screen. They often have a low-cost matinee during the week.

Cine Versalles, *Av Francisco Villa # 799*, ☎ *322-225-8764*, has five screens with three showings for each screen.

Cine Colonial, *Calle Bolivia 141*, ☎ *322-222-1675*, has two screens with two showings every day except Sunday, when they have three and four showings, the first one starting at noon.

■ MUSIC SCENE

PV is developing an international music scene that is worth taking in. Go to the tourist office for updated information on who is in town and where they are performing. Violinist **Willie Royal** and guitarist **Wolfgang Lobo Fink** started playing here in 1990 and even though they now do world tours, they still come back once a year to perform. The Mayor of Margaritaville, **Richard Kaplan**, has performed with his two Macaws for 22 years in PV. The venue is the Playa de Oro Resort and he offers a blend of Jimmy Buffett, Willie Nelson and Kenny Loggins. **Antonio LeComte** is an award-winning pianist who plays new-age music. He was nominated by the Theatre Journalists Association for best original score in 1993. He is accompanied by **Bob Tansen**, and the two of them usually play at the Café des Artistes (see above). Other performers who come here include **Jethro Tull**, who plays the blues; **Alberto Perez**, who has been performing jazz for 15 years; and **Righoberto**, who plays classical guitar and is accompanied by singer, harpist and flautist **d'Rachel**. The best of the jazz artists are **Beverly and Willow**. **Ron Doering** directs the **Sweet Life** quartet and they often play at La Dolce Vita. Ron plays rhythm guitar and sings blues. There are more. Be sure to take in a few.

Kalhua Bar, *on the* malecón *just north of the plaza, no phone,* is a popular place to put up your feet on the windowsill, have a tall drink and watch the sun fall into the ocean.

La Dolce Vita Restaurant, *Paseo Diaz Ordanz # 674,* ☎ *322-222-3852,* has live jazz every weekend starting at 9 pm and going till midnight. You can enjoy an excellent Italian dinner (about $12) here before the jazz starts.

Discoteca Valdez, *Guerrero #179, no phone,* is just off the main plaza and is a great hopping place for a dance or two.

Wild Coyotes Bar and Grill, *Venustiano Carranza #208,* ☎ *322-222-8324,* suggests that you should not only get drunk but get wild. This does not interest me, but the place is popular. It is located in the older part of town just two blocks from the beach.

North from Puerto Vallarta

San Blas

he Bells of San Blas was written by Henry Wadsworth Longfellow. It was his last creation before he died on March 24, 1882.

> *What say the Bells of San Blas*
> *To the ships that southward pass*
> *From the harbor of Mazatlan*
> *To them it is nothing more*
> *Than the sound of surf on the shore,*
> *Nothing more to master or man.*
> *But to me, a dreamer of dreams*
> *To whom what is and what seems*
> *Are often one and the same,*
> *The Bells of San Bas to me*
> *Have a strange, wild melody,*
> *And are something more than a name*
> *For bells are the voice of the church*
> *They have tones that touch and search*
> *The hearts of young and old*
> *One sound to all yet each*
> *Lends a meaning to their speech*
> *And the meaning is manifold.*

This is the newest and, so far as I can tell, the most beautiful beach in all of Mexico. The 50 miles/80 km of sand and surf is dotted with a few estuaries and undisturbed by huge hotels. But that will change rapidly and my guess is that in 10 years my comments about the place and the hotels will be history. The town is a tiny fishing village of about 12,000 people and is surrounded by rainforests and mangrove swamps. At present those stretches of beach hold surfing waves, ruins from the early Spanish explorers, turtle sanctuaries and wildlife-riddled estuaries.

> **AUTHOR NOTE:** *The only drawback to visiting San Blas are the* **mosquitoes** *and the insects referred to as a* **sand fleas**, *no-see-ums or jejenes (hay-HAY-nays). Avon's Skin so Soft is good for the jejenes and for your skin. Long shirt-sleeves and long pants are also a help. Insect repellent is a must. The reason there are so many insects is because there are mangrove swamps nearby. Don't let the insects stop you from coming; just come prepared.*

GETTING HERE

Buses from Puerto Vallarta cost about $12 and take 2½ hours on a first-class bus. San Blas is two hours by bus from Tepic and four from Guadalajara.

The closest **airports** are in Puerto Vallarta, Tepic and Guadalajara.

HISTORY

San Blas, founded in 1768, became an important port for the Spanish. It was **Manuel Rivero y Cordero** who, under command of Carlos II, made San Blas the port for Spanish ships sailing along the California coast. The Customs House was the first one built in the New World and served as both a tax collection place for incoming goods and as a defense fort. It was also from here that **Fray Junipero Serra**, a Franciscan missionary, ruled the 15 missions along the coast. He arrived in San

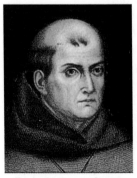
Fray Junipero Serra.

Blas on April 1, 1768 and, using two ships that had just been built in the harbor, started colonization of the area. Fray Junipero Serra died in San Carlos Barromeo de Carmelo on August 28, 1784.

MISSIONS ESTABLISHED BY SERRA

1769 – San Fernando de Velicata and San Diego de Alcala

1770 – San Carlos Barromeo de Carmelo

1771 – San Gabriel Arcangel and San Antonio de Padua

1772 – San Luis Obispo de Tolsa

1776 – San Juan Capistrano

1776 – San Francisco de Asis

1777 – Santa Clara de Asis

1782 – San Buenaventura

SERVICES

The **Tourist Office**, *Calle Mercado, Monday to Friday, 8:30 am-5 pm, Saturday until 1 pm*, has maps, a guide-book and pamphlets about the area. The staff speaks English and is quite helpful. They sell used paperbacks written in English.

Police, *Calle Sonola, across from the bus station*, ☎ *323-285-0028.*

People at the **Health Center**, *Calle Campeche and Batallion*, ☎ *323-285-0232*, speak only Spanish.

Post office, *Calle Sonora and Echeverria*, ☎ *323-285-0295, Monday to Friday, 8 am-2 pm.*

ADVENTURES ON FOOT

The Mafia Hotel is not a place you will want to stay, but it is interesting to walk around and have a look at what may have been had nature not intervened. The luxurious stone structure, located on the beach, has over 150 rooms overlooking the ocean. On the opening night, when even the president was there, an army of sand fleas (*jejenes*) attacked, sending the guests back to their homes in the city. Now the building is falling apart. Obviously, the owners had not heard of Skin so Soft by Avon – a sure-fire protection from the pesky biting bugs.

The Ruins, on Cerro de San Basilio at the northeast end of town above the cemetery, include the remains of La Nuestra Señora del Rosario Church and the Contadura, the counting house. The church was built in 1769 and was used until the late 1800s. The counting house was built with large stones and held together with little mortar. It had arched doorways. The old cannons around the building were used to keep British pirates away. During the 18th century, José Maria Mercado used this fortification to successfully keep invaders out.

> **FACT FILE:** *The first ship to arrive and be taxed here was the Chinese Nao coming from the East with silks and spices.*

Although restoration was being done at the ruins, a recent hurricane took out a lot of the work. There is a $1 entry fee. There is a bathroom at the gate. Open daily from 10 am to 6 pm.

The old **Customs House** is located across the river from the docks. It is constructed of brick that is now crumbling. Next to the ruins is a new, rather nondescript Customs House but it, too, is not in use.

Isla del Rey is on the bay and is actually part of the peninsula, rather than an island. It is the sacred lands of the Huichol Indians and has a pilgrimage trail. The Indians came to this site every spring to worship the sea goddess, Aramara. Today they still come, dressed in traditional costume, to enjoy their spring celebrations. You must cross the estuary by boat to get here (50¢). The dock is across from Tesoro Bungalows.

Cerro Vigia, near ceremonial grounds of Isla del Rey, holds El Faro, the red-and-white striped lighthouse where you can get good views of San Blas. A trail from the dock passes scrub and the Huichol ceremonial ground before heading up the hill. You must cross the estuary by boat to get here (50¢). The dock is across from Tesoro Bungalows.

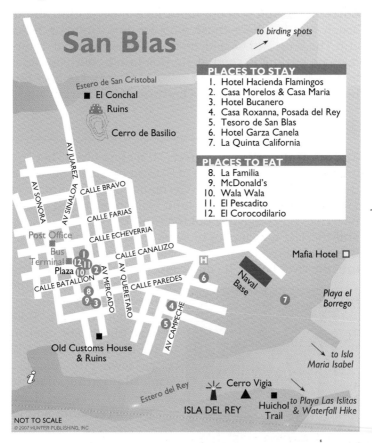

San Blas

to birding spots

Estero de San Cristobal

■ El Conchal

Ruins

Cerro de Basilio

PLACES TO STAY
1. Hotel Hacienda Flamingos
2. Casa Morelos & Casa Maria
3. Hotel Bucanero
4. Casa Roxanna, Posada del Rey
5. Tesoro de San Blas
6. Hotel Garza Canela
7. La Quinta California

PLACES TO EAT
8. La Familia
9. McDonald's
10. Wala Wala
11. El Pescadito
12. El Corocodilario

AV JUAREZ

AV SONORA

AV SINALOA

CALLE BRAVO

CALLE FARIAS

Post Office

CALLE ECHEVERRIA

Bus Terminal

CALLE CANALIZO

Plaza

CALLE BATALLION

AV MERCADO

AV QUERETARO

CALLE PAREDES

AV CAMPECHE

Old Customs House & Ruins

H

Naval Base

Mafia Hotel □

Playa el Borrego

to Isla Maria Isabel

Estero del Rey

Cerro Vigia

ISLA DEL REY

Huichol Trail

to Playa Las Islitas & Waterfall Hike

NOT TO SCALE
© 2007 HUNTER PUBLISHING, INC

ADVENTURES ON WATER

BEACHES

La Islitas Beach has the longest wave in the world, according to the Guinness Book of World Records. This wave is supposed to be about 20 feet long (six meters) and can carry the skilled surfer for a mile or more before petering out. The beach is five miles/eight km south of San Blas and buses pass by every half-hour. There are a number of beachside restaurants, some with hammocks where you can relax, read and enjoy a beer. You can be certain there will be many experienced surfers talking the talk and waiting for the "Big One".

Borrengo Beach is about half a mile down (south) on the beach and is where those who are into camping hang out. The bugs can be bad, so repellent is essential. Intermediate surfing is good along this beach, but you must bring your own equipment. Boogie boards are also fun here. Snorkeling is not good because of the murky water.

■ WATERFALLS

El Cora Waterfalls are 30 feet/10 meters high. They are located just out of the town of El Cora on an old hacienda that was once owned by Germans. The revolution of 1910-1914 resulted in the land being confiscated by the new rulers. Petroglyphs dot the trail. The walk is not long and there is a cool pool to swim in at the bottom of the falls. The tiny stream that forms the waterfall empties into the river below. It can be crossed below the pool and

a grunt up the side of the cliff will take you to another pool and falls. Take a bus (the white one) or drive from San Blas to El Cora town (10 miles/16 km) along the road to Santa Cruz/Tepic. Turn south at Tecuitata and go five miles/eight km to a loading platform where you can leave your vehicle. Follow the creek downstream. The final bit is steep, so hiking boots are recommended. Bring your bathing suit.

Tecuitata Waterfalls are near the village of the same name. Go the same way as to El Cora, only half a mile past the village of Santa Cruz get off the bus or turn downhill along a dirt road where the sign indicates

Balneario Nuevo Chapultepec. At the bottom of the hill there is a waterslide, a restaurant and a small pool. Walk upstream through the jungle to the Arroyo Campsite and the waterfall. This waterfall is not as spectacular as El Cora, but certainly easier to reach.

ADVENTURES IN NATURE

■ BIRDING

According to the Audubon Society, San Blas is second only to Panama for having the largest number of bird species. There are many habitats – mangroves, mud flats, lagoons and offshore islands with thorn scrub and pine/oak woodlands – where you might spot rare and exotic birds.

Military macaws.

BIRD WATCH: *More common Mexican birds, like the blue bunting, the yellow-winged cacique and the mangrove cuckoo, will be easy to find. However, avid birders should keep a lookout for bare-throated tiger herons, lesser roadrunners, boat-billed herons, Colima pygmy-owls (these are so cute!), Rufous-necked wood-rails, rosy-thrush tanagers and military macaws.*

Most birders log over 200 species in a week. If you don't have a bird book with you, purchase the one at the tourist office, *Where to Find Birds in San Blas*. This book tells you of other places around town where birds can be seen. A spotting scope or binoculars is essential. Bring insect repellent.

Where to Find Birds in San Blas, by Soalind Novick and Lan Sing Wu, is available by mail (178 Myrtle Court Arcata, CA 95521, US $4.50) or you can purchase it at one of the hotels/shops in town.

San Cristobal and **El Pozo Estuaries** are birder specialty places, but they are also rich with turtles, iguanas and crocodiles. The vegetation includes vines and giant ferns. Fresh springs run through the estuaries. The boat ride through this area goes for several miles, and San Cristobal estuary connects to the freshwater lake of La Tovara. The El Pazo inlet is where the annual fishing derby starts each year. Boats can be hired either at your hotel or at the dock. **Chencho**, ☎ *323-285-0716*, takes morning trips to San Cristobal and the cost, depending on duration, is $50 for up to five people. He takes you up the river to the lake. You need not go all the way if you are interested in seeing the wildlife in the estuary. This must be negotiated with the boatman.

La Tovara Lagoon is reached by traveling through the jungle and mangrove swamp up the estuary where crocodiles are wild and protected. Because there are so many, seeing them will almost become ho-hum by the end of the trip. However it is the Northern potoos, a bird that likes to be out after dark, that is the big draw. Green kingfishers and great black hawks are also common. Along the way you'll see vines, bromeliads, mangroves and flowering plants. At the right time of year, large hordes of butterflies gather here. An interesting spot on your river journey is an old movie set with huts on stilts set along the water's edge. The trip goes to a spring where you can swim in cool waters and then have a drink or a snack at the restaurant near the dock. The pool is large and the water clear. The spring provides drinking water for San Blas residents. There are fish in the water. **Chencho** (see above), the famous river guide, has an evening trip to the pool that costs $40 for up to four people. He is at the dock midday taking reservations and may group you with other people to make a load of four. You leave around 4 pm and return after dark. It is a thrill to travel through the jungle after dark. The sounds are eerie. Birders Novick and Wu suggest you hire **Oscar Partida**, who speaks English and knows his birds very well. He can be contacted by phone, ☎ 323-285-0324, or at Las Brisas Hotel.

You'll see many crocs as you cruise this area.

AUTHOR TIP: *During peak seasons, when private boats are busy, the tourist office will put on a boat that is much cheaper than a private boat but also more crowded. See them at the office for details.*

Roca Elephante is a tiny island (a rock) just offshore to the northwest of the town that has both the blue- and brown-footed boobies as well as red-billed tropicbirds nesting. You will need to hire a boat at the dock to take you there. As you approach the island, swarms of frigate birds will cloud the skies. Peregrine falcons and pelicans also reside on Roca Elephante. You can't go onto the rock, but the boat will circle a number of times until you have had your visual fill.

North from Puerto Vallarta

Singayta Inlet is a jungle environment where El Manglar Environmental Center has built a traditional Nayarit village with a palapa hut that is used as an information center. Their objective is to protect the 260 species of birds in the surrounding forest. The organic nursery has prized orchids, some of which have taken four years to establish themselves. Near the huts are some Aztec petroglyphs. Boats are available to take people into the mangroves and lakes. To get here from San Blas, take the bus to Singayta (on the inlet and where El Manglar Environmental Center is located) from the plaza for a dollar each way. This is one of the most popular birding spots in all of western Mexico, even with the lush population of mosquitoes and sand fleas.

MEPG

The Mangrove Environmental Protection Group in San Blas was started in 1993 to protect the mangroves and surrounding land from mega-tourism and shrimp farms. Their main concern is education and enforcing the laws that have been passed. The president is Juan Garcia, a local businessman. Among other things, the group developed a bicycle path that leads from the entrance of town at Conchal Bridge, all the way to the bay and along the beach to Los Cocos. The most frequent users of this path are the oyster fishers.

Parque Nacional Isla Isabel is a bird and underwater sanctuary 52 miles/70 km from San Blas. It is a narrow volcanic island, one mile/1.6 km long that has a deciduous forest starting to cover the lava base. The island was formed about 3.5 million years ago and has evidence of nine separate volcanoes. There are bare rocks, cliffs and sandy beaches surrounding the small coral reefs just offshore. In the center is a crater lake with water 18 times saltier than the ocean. The landscape is unmatched and the island is often called the Galapagos of Mexico. It is also a birder's paradise, with numerous seabirds; blue- and brown-footed boobies nest here.

> **FACT FILE:** *The interesting thing about boobies is the sibling rivalry. The oldest bird will often kill its nest-mates if food is scarce.*

There was at one time a huge colony of sooty terns on the island, but cats almost made them extinct. The cats were removed and the terns are recovering. Alongside the many endangered birds, Isla Isabel has a healthy community of amphibians, including the fake coral snake and the brown and green iguana. A research station operates for five months of every year, and visitors are welcome to camp as long as they bring all their supplies, including water. The researchers rely on local fishers and the navy to bring in water and supplies. **Ancla Tours** in Nuevo Vallarta, ☎ *322-297-1464*, takes people to the island. In San Blas, **Tony Aguayo**, ☎ *323-285-0364, at the end of Calle Juarez,* is a recommended guide. He charges about $200 per person (based on two people going) for a full-day island trip. His boat will hold about six people.

Cerro de San Juan Ecological Reserve, ☎ *311-213-1423,* is 6,200 feet/2,000 meters high and is another good hiking/birding area between San Blas and Tepic. It's about 15 miles/25 km from San Blas. The area has pine and oak forests.

> **BIRD WATCH:** *Rare birds have been spotted in the San Juan reserve, including Mexican wood nymphs and Rufous-crowned motmots. Although not seen, the eared-poorwills have been heard. There are also yellow grossbeaks, woodcreepers, redstarts and buntings.*

There is a ranch-style lodge at the top of the mountain. To get to the reserve, you must take a bus from the center of town. On the way you can stop at El Mirador del Aguila and look for military macaws.

■ CROCS

Ejido de la Palma Crocodile Farm is three miles/five km south of Matanchen Village, near Las Islitas Beach (see page 163). These crocs are in captivity. There is a freshwater lake on the site and the surrounding jungle houses butterflies, turtles and lizards. There is an entrance fee of $2 per person – the money goes toward the protection of the crocs.

OUTFITTERS/TOUR OPERATORS

Bird Treks, *115 Peach Bottom Village, Peach Bottom, PA,* ☎ *717-548-3303 (US), 800-224-5399 (Mx), www.bird treks.com,* offers a tour that starts in Puerto Vallarta. It takes half a day traveling to San Blas where you set up home base in one of the better hotels. The next seven nights are spent sleeping at the hotel, while the days are spent hunting birds with expert birders (who are also the tour leaders). The cost is $2,200 for an all-inclusive package from PV to San Blas and back. This does not include booze, personal supplies (such as mosquito repellent) or tips.

Wings Birding Tours, ☎ *888-293-6443, www.wings birds.com,* offers birding trips all over the world. I have worked with them in Bolivia and I know they are first class. Their website has a bird list that is far too long to put in here. The tour starts and ends in Puerto Vallarta, with most of the time spent in the San Blas area. This is a nine-day, eight-night tour that includes everything except the pen to tick off the birds seen. The cost is $2,450 per person for double occupancy. Wings allows only 12 people in a group, plus the leader.

PLACES TO STAY

Casa Morelos, *Calle Heroico Batallion # 108,* ☎ *323-285-0820, $,* is between town and the beach and two blocks from the bus station. The guesthouse has clean rooms without private bathrooms and is owned by the same family who owns **Casa Maria**, just around

HOTEL PRICE SCALE	
Room price, in US $	
$ . . . . up to $20	
$$ . . . . $21-$50	
$$$ $51-100	
$$$$ . . . . $101-$150	
$$$$$ $151-200	

the corner (same phone number). Both have communal cooking areas and gardens in which to sit. These are friendly Mexican establishments that are comfortable but simple.

La Quinta California, *halfway between town and the beach,* ☎ *323-285-0603, $,* has bungalows around a common courtyard that is thickly vegetated with every plant imaginable, including a strangler fig tree. The rooms are not big, but the kitchens are fully equipped with small stove and fridge. Each comfortable two-bedroom bungalow has enough beds to accommodate four people. Prices are reasonable. However, you can get weekly and monthly rates that are even more attractive. There is no daily maid service.

Rafael's Apartments, *Calle Campeche and Calle Hidalgo, $$,* has clean apartments that surround an enclosed garden that is second only to La Quinta's. The kitchens have full stoves (ovens included). The place is clean, safe and economical, but there is no phone or e-mail address so you have to take your chances. Hit town and head over here.

Casa Roxanna, *Callejon el Rey #1, www.sanblasmexico. com/casaroxanna/, $$,* is a very neat and tidy little place that has a pool with an adjacent bar, and rooms with air conditioning, cupboards and cable TV. The kitchens are fully supplied with fridge and stove and have an apartment-sized working area. The décor is tasteful, the floors tile. The sitting area is large and there is laundry service and secured parking. The large bungalows sleep up to five people and the small up to three. This is a real gem and, as a birder, I could stay here for a month with no problem. The gardens are lush.

© Casa Roxanna

Bungalows Conny, *Calle Chiapis #26,* ☎ *323-285-0986, www.bungalowsconny.com, $$,* is a Mexican hacienda-style hotel that is comfortable and clean. The rooms have

North from Puerto Vallarta

air conditioning, television, two double beds, private bathrooms and hot water. Laundry service is offered. This place is a good find and just four blocks from the main plaza.

Hotel Bucanero, *Av Juarez #75*, ☎ *323-285-0101, $$,* is older and with a décor that is more interesting than most in town. In the garden is an anchor and a couple of stuffed crocs. The rooms have high ceilings and are cool, but dingy. There is a pool, but no restaurant. Note that the disco next door could keep you awake on weekends.

Posada del Rey, *Av Campeche #10,* ☎ *323-285-0123, $$/$$$, www.sanblasmexico.com/posadadelrey.* Some of the dozen rooms have air conditioning, but none of the

© Posada del Rey

private bathrooms has separate shower stalls. There is a small pool with a poolside bar, a beach-supply shop and a restaurant. The owners are friendly and will arrange tours for you. They speak English, French and Spanish.

Tesoro de San Blas, *Calle Campeche and Hidalgo,* ☎ *323-285-0537, www.geocities.com/dougcb68/tsb.htm, $$,* features rustic, three-room bungalows that have hot-water showers in the bathrooms, gas hot plates and refrigerators in the kitchens and a comfortable sitting space in the living rooms. The cabins are kept clean. There is a large maintained garden full of exotic plants like mango, banana and papaya. There is also off-street parking. One small room in the house is available for rent. The cabins are on the estuary so the view of the lighthouse adds to the sunsets. Birders like to use this as a home base because they can walk around the estuary when bird activity is high.

Hotel Hacienda Flamingos, *Calle Juarez # 105,* ☎ *323-285-0930 or 285-0485 (no English spoken), www. sanblas.com.mx, $$$,* is right in town close to the plaza. This is the restored German import house, first built in 1883 to receive goods from the orient. It was then called

Casa Delius. The last officer to work at the Customs House was displaced in 1932 and had to find other work. His grandson purchased the building out of nostalgia in 1990 and started restoration that has been done to perfection. Photos of the family remain in the hallways that still have the original tiles. There is a pool, a fountain that works all the time and a lush garden. The eight rooms are as beautifully finished as the rest of the building and come with private bathrooms, air conditioning and coffee makers (coffee is supplied).

Hotel Garza Canela, *Calle Paredes # 106 South,* ☎ *323-285-0112, www.garzacanela.com/acommodations.htm, $$$,* has 45 large rooms with tiled floors, air conditioning and fans, satellite TV, safe deposit boxes and private bathrooms with all the amenities. Some larger rooms have a fully supplied kitchenette with fridge and stove. There is also a pool surrounded by a well-tended garden, private parking, laundry service, souvenir shop, travel agent and a babysitting service. Your breakfast and purified water is included in the price. The restaurant is open beam, with linen tablecloths, good service and homemade foods. This is a family-run establishment and their pride in excellence is obvious. The owners are friendly, helpful and knowledgeable about the area. They speak English and some German.

Miramar Paraiso Hotel, *Km 18 on the highway between San Blas and Puerto Vallarta,* ☎ *323-254-9030, www.sanblasyogaretreats.com, $$$,* is 20 minutes by bus from San Blas. This restored colonial mansion overlooks the ocean and has a path leading to the beach about 200 yards away. Two pools and palapa huts dots the lush grounds. There are six different styles of rooms, some with a balcony, some with extra-large windows and some that hold up to four people. All rooms have a private bathroom and shower. The Miramar is also a yoga

© San Blas Yoga Retreats

retreat. Two yoga classes are offered daily: the morning class is more strenuous, while the evening class focuses on meditation and relaxation. They also offer a jungle survival course that would be of interest to anyone planning on hiking in the tropics in the future. Between classes you can do some exploring. The food is vegetarian and the lifestyle conducive to losing weight. They encourage daily hiking, Kombucha mushroom therapy and cleansing fasts. The lady who does the mushroom therapy also teaches dance, surfing and aerobics. Massage therapy is available. The owner does Huichol beadwork and will give lessons. Seven nights here, including meals and one excursion per day (minimum of four people) is about $1,200.

■ CAMPING

Los Cocos Trailer Park, *Batallon Rd, (1.5 km from Zocalo),* ☎ *323-285-0055, $,* has 120 trailer pads with hookups, plus an area designated for tenting, all tucked into a coconut grove. There are hot showers and the popular Coco Loco Bar.

PLACES TO EAT

El Delfin, *at Hotel Garza Canela,* ☎ *323-285-0610, 1-9 pm,* is extremely clean and the water is safe to drink. The cost for a dinner is about $10 per serving. This is a first-class restaurant and should be tried at least once – for that special night out. If you are tired of seafood, the steak here is excellent.

La Familia, *Calle Batallon #18,* ☎ *323-285-0258*, is best for dinner. Their seafood is famous – try their fried snapper. The décor is totally Mexican and the service is down-home friendly.

McDonald's, *Calle Juarez #35, 7 am-10 pm*, offers hamburgers that are nothing like the US chain version. These actually have tons of meat in them. Other meals are offered, too, but nothing that stands out. This is a popular place, which means the food is tasty and nobody gets sick from eating it.

Wala Wala, *Juarez #29, 8 am-10 pm daily except Sunday.* People come here for the fresh uncooked vegetables (they are safe to eat as they are washed in purified water). This, too, is a popular place, in part because of its simplicity and sparkling cleanliness. Meals cost under $10.

El Pescadito, *Calle Juarez and Canalizo,* is on the plaza. It comes highly recommended, although I didn't try it.

El Cocodrilario, *Calle Juarez and Canalizo, 8 am-10 pm.* The specialty here is spaghetti for $8 per serving. They have large servings and good service.

The Bakery, *Calle Cuauhtemoc,* around the corner from Posada del Rey, is the place to try great Mexican chocolate that has been baked into interesting cakes, cookies and tarts.

Jaltemba Bay

Jaltemba Bay is a wide palm-dotted bay that has four villages around it and one scenic island. The villages start at Punta Raza, a rocky point that serves as the southern tip of the bay. From south to north, they are **Los Ayala, Rincon de Guayabitos, La Peñita** and **La Colina**. The island, visible from all villages, is **Isla Peña**. The town of La Peñita is joined by a bridge to Rincon de Guayabitos two miles/three km away. La Piñita has one traffic light, so "laid back" is what you can expect here among the 8,000 residents. The most restful places are in Rincon de Guayabitos, although there are some splendid spots in busier La Peñita.

North from Puerto Vallarta

It is best to have your own transportation if you want to explore along the coast. If you haven't got a car, a guide with a vehicle can be hired. There is an informative web page sponsored by those from Casa Libertad. Key in www.members5.boardhost.com/CasaLibertad/msg/9216.html.

GETTING HERE

From the center of Puerto Vallarta, you can take a local, second-class **bus** for the hour-long (a bit longer if traffic is thick) trip to Jaltemba Bay.

You can also take a **taxi** for about $50.

> **AUTHOR NOTE:** *Note that some of the hotels offer free transportation from the PV airport to their hotel.*

If flying to Puerto Vallarta, take a taxi from the airport to the first-class bus station just five minutes away and take a bus from there to La Peñita. The cost is about $5 one way; buses leave every half hour. Local buses run between the other spots along the bay.

SERVICES

Tourist Office, *near the main highway on Av del Sol Nuevo*, ☎ *327-274-0693, Monday to Friday, 9 am-7 pm.*

Post office, downtown, *Monday to Friday, 9 am-1 pm, 3-6 pm.*

Clinica Renteria, *Calle Valle de Acapulco*, ☎ *327-274-0140.*

Caturera's Farmacia, *Av del Sol Nuevo and Tabachines*, not only dispenses medicines but also sells stamps, has a fax and gives tourist information not found on the web or at your hotel.

There are no **police** on Jaltemba Bay, which says a lot for the community.

FIESTAS

The Virgin of Talpa is celebrated every May and the party lasts for about two weeks. The pedestrian walkway where most of the celebrations occur is decorated in palm fronds. There are fireworks, dances, elaborate costumes and special foods for sale along the walkway. Contact the Tourist Office for more information. Since this is low season, hotel reservations are not necessary.

© Paulprescott/Dreamstime

ADVENTURES ON FOOT

GOLF

El Monteon Course, ☎ *327-303-2929,* is located in El Monteon village. It is a nine-hole, par-three (per hole) course that costs $30 to play, including transportation to and from your hotel in Jaltemba Bay or Guayabitos, your clubs, one set of balls and tees, lunch and a drink. What a deal! This information was given to me by Charlie and Mona Bryant of Casa de Ensueños.

ADVENTURES ON WATER

Isla Islote is visible from anywhere around the bay. The island is a wildlife sanctuary. To get here, take one of the glass-bottomed boats found along the beach that cost $5 per person. The abundant sea life is spectacular and easy to see because the water is so clear and the waves so gentle. On the island are nesting birds such as terns, boobies and frigates. Snorkeling is good, too.

Catamaran *Fanta-sea*, Freddy's Tours, ☎ *327-274-9559 or 274-0248,* will take you on a tour/party for four unfor-

North from Puerto Vallarta

gettable hours. On the boat, you can dance, drink and sing or just take photos to show others how much fun people can be. There are seats in the sun and in the shade, two bathrooms, a bar, safety equipment and lots of music. The cost is $60, including dinner.

■ BEACHES

The south end of the beach starts at the rocky point and curves around to the little cove of Guayabitos, where there are palapa hut restaurants and fishing boats. Two miles farther north the beach becomes wider and offers good swimming and body surfing possibilities. People also windsurf along this stretch. Past La Peñita is more of the same, except the surf is a bit stronger so intermediate surfers can have some fun.

Take the road to the village of **Los Ayala** and, from the village, go down a dirt road to the beach. The water is calm and the swimming is excellent. There are places to eat and have a beer and, farther in, there are a few places to stay. If you walk south back toward La Peñita you will pass a cemetery that goes all the way to the water; the name of the beach is Playa los Muertos, or Beach of the Dead. Locals don't like cars along the beach so they have tried to block passage. However, you can walk around that. If you continue walking north, maneuvering around the coves, you will come to a turtle nesting area called **Playa Punta Raza**. Here, locals are trying to protect the creatures. If you are conservation minded and give them a hand, they may tell you when the turtles are due to hatch and let you come to watch. Seeing one of these giants of the sea ramble onto land, dig a hole and lay some eggs is a thrill, but even more thrilling is watching the little ones hatch and find their way into the water. The jungle behind the beach is lush and has numerous trails to get you up to the road (if you have a vehicle there). The beach is not good for swimming as there is a riptide here.

Playa Platanitos is north of Las Varas. It is a small cove with a white sand beach that stretches for 12 miles/18 km north and has a gentle slope. The beach is good for swimming as the surf is gentle. Parts of the cove have vegetation coming right to the water. This is a fishing village with a few palapa-hut restaurants along the beach that serve fresh fish for less than $5 a meal. To get here, take the bus toward San Blas from Las Varas and get off at Platanitos. From there you can walk to the beach a little more than a half-mile away. This is a good destination for a day trip.

© CSP/Dreamstime

Along this beach is **Villas Exotica**, *$$$$$,* which offers two-bedroom, two-bathroom villas. The villas have full kitchens, huge decks, air conditioning, satellite TV, hair dryers, microwaves, toasters and VCRs. There is a swimming pool, a Jacuzzi and a business office with Internet service. Kayaks and canoes are available, and there is even a telescope for those who want to stargaze. You can arrange for all meals to be included in the price.

ADVENTURES IN NATURE

Walking south toward Puerto Vallarta will always net you some birds that can be added to your list.

> **BIRD WATCH:** *Birds found in this area include rough-winged swallows, cowbirds, crows, grackles, anis, orioles, frigate birds, pelicans, vultures, boobies,*

hummingbirds, egrets, bitterns, coots, woodpeckers, gnatcatchers and king-fishers. Birders with a car should also visit **Compostela**, **Santa Maria del Oro** *and* **Tepic***. The birds you can expect to see in those places are ant-tanagers, scrub euphonias, blackbirds, moorhens, gross beaks, buntings, cedar waxwings, peewees, flycatchers and great-horned owls.*

ADVENTURES ON HORSEBACK

Horse tours are possible at the stables next door to Cocos, **Retorno Las Palmas**, in Rincon de Guayabitos. Make reservations with Chorro at the stables (no phone). Rental is not expensive and the horses are gentle. On the other side of Cocos is a stall that rents Jet Skis.

OUTFITTERS/TOUR OPERATORS

© Marcoregalia/Dreamstime

Bob Howell *at Mi Casa es Su Casa,* ☎ *327-274-0312,* offers wildlife-viewing trips that end at hidden waterfalls, old villages, coffee planta-tions or hot springs. He will also take you bik-ing, fishing, snorkeling or hiking to an active volcano. Lunch, pre-pared by Vicky, Bob's business partner, is in-cluded. If you stay at their house for more than a week, pick-up and delivery at the PV airport is included. Trip costs vary depending on where you go and how long you are gone. A half-day hike with transportation to the trailhead should run $45.

Freddy Tours, ☎ *327-274-0453 or 274-0248,* offers two-hour whale-watching or sightseeing tours on the bay. They begin at 2 pm and last until 6 pm, just after dark. They also have snorkeling ($45 for half a day), waterskiing ($25 per hour) and nature tours ($10-$45, depending on what you do). Their boats are well equipped with safety equipment like vests, radios and shade. Fishing charters with a local fisher can also be arranged by Freddy's at a cost of $170 for two and $10 more for each additional person. All gear is supplied, but you must bring your own grub. There is a limit of two beers per person allowed on this excursion.

Aquatic Adventures, *Rincon de Guayabitos,* ☎ *327-294-1283*, has diving and fishing trips available for an hour or two or all day long.

DAY TRIPS

Boca de Chila is 28 miles/45 miles north toward San Blas along Highway 200. Drive through Las Varas and, two miles/three km after that town, is a roadside *tienda*. This is the village of El Conchal – there is no other sign. The road going west (left) leads to the beach. You will need a four-wheel-drive vehicle or you must walk to get there. After about a mile or two, you will cross a cement bridge and then follow the stream for a bit before breaking out onto the sandy beach with an estuary at the one end. The beach is six miles/nine km from El Conchal and has nothing on it but a few anglers looking for a restful day rather than a catch. There is often someone around with a panga who can pole you up the estuary for $10 or so. The estuary will take four or five hours to travel and is similar to Tovara out of San Blas. The other thing that you can do is look for Spanish coins along the beach and near the estuary. Apparently, pirates used to hole out here while waiting for Spanish galleons to show themselves. There are crocs and iguanas in the estuary.

> **BIRD WATCH:** *Birds are ubiquitous in the estuary area and include such species as the kingbird, sandpiper, stilt, egret, cormorant, hummingbird, heron, flycatcher.*

Information about this trip to Boca de Chila was from Bob Howell's website, http://members5.boardhost.com/CasaLibertad/?poll.

Zacualpan, also north of Las Varas (six miles/nine km) and accessible by public bus, has an outdoor museum near the Pemex Station in the center of town, four blocks from the plaza. The museum has numerous petroglyphs, some similar to those at Alta Vista. These were found when the road was being built. Some have faces, others have symbols, some are round with flat surfaces and one is about two feet wide. A selection of the glyphs has been placed in the museums in Las Varas and Tepic. Those ones were found in two tombs six feet/two meters deep. After the stones were removed, the tombs were covered. Today, no one knows their location.

SHOPPING

The local **Thursday Market** starts at about 7 am and lasts until 2 pm. It is located next to the church in La Peñita. The market features indigenous art (huichol), local wares and produce, jewelry and an assortment of novelty items. This is an excellent place to purchase souvenirs.

PLACES TO STAY

Andreas Bungalows, *Calle Retorno Gaviotas #2, $, www.geocities.com/andreasbungalows/mypage,* has five units, each with kitchenette, bedroom with one single and two double beds and a bathroom with a shower. The floors are tiled, the décor includes local hand-painted murals, and the furniture is chunky Spanish design. Rooms are set around a central courtyard and the building is barely five minutes from the beach. The bungalows are very clean and affordable. The owner, Irene Lopez Vences, is super-friendly, which makes this place better than home.

HOTEL PRICE SCALE	
Room price, in US $	
$ . . . . up to $20	
$$ . . . . $21-$50	
$$$ $51-100	
$$$$ . . . . $101-$150	
$$$$$ $151-200	

Bungalows Alexa, *Playa Los Ayala, no phone, listed on www. guayabitos.com, $$,* has motel-style rooms with kitchenettes that are plain but clean. The kitchens have a stove and fridge, there is a sitting area and the floors are tiled. For the price and seclusion, this isn't too bad a deal.

Posada del Sol, *Calle Andando Huanacaxtle,* ☎ *327-274-0043, $$,* is spartan and spotless. Each unit has a full kitchen, private bathroom with shower, bedroom with ceiling fan, and some of the best pillows in Mexico. There is a nice patio. The *posada* is half a block from the main street.

Posada la Mision, *Retorno Tabachines #6, in Guayabitos,* ☎ *327-274-0357, $$,* is on the beach. The 20 clean rooms, located on two floors, are spaced around a pool in a central courtyard. They have tiled floors and archways that create a feel of old Spain, especially when the slow-moving ceiling fans are whirring. Units have a private bathroom, cable TV and hot water. There is a restaurant and private parking, but the big draw is the lush garden area with rubber trees and a huge old strangler fig.

Posada Real Hotel, *Av Sol Nuevo and Huanacaxtle, in Rincon de Guayabitos,* ☎ *327-274-0177, $$,* has rooms and bungalows. The bungalows are set around a verdant courtyard that has birds playing in the fruit trees. The rooms, at the front of the complex, have private bathrooms. There is a small pool, a children's pool with a water slide, a racquetball court and off-street parking.

Bungalows El Delfin, *Retorno Ceiba and Cocoteros,* ☎ *327-274-0385, www.bungalowseldelfin.com, $$,* has rooms with kitchenettes that include fridges, stoves, ceiling fans and purified water. They also have 15 bungalows that are much more comfortable than the rooms and suitable up to for four people. The pool is surrounded by greenery. Off-street parking is available. This is one of the more popular middle-of-the-range places available in Guayabitos.

Casa Libertad, *Calle Circuito Libertad #7, $$$, www. home.gci.net/~casalibertad/,* is a Spanish-styled bungalow that has white stucco and a red-tiled roof. There is bougainvillea around the new outside fence and the covered porch has red tile on the floor, arched wooden windows, rattan furniture and potted plants. There is also bright lighting and fans. The rooms have arched windows, open-beam ceilings, space galore and comfortable Mexican furniture. The walls have some art. A large upper terrace offers an expansive view of the bay. If the bougainvillea doesn't have enough color for you, the rose garden may. The gardens are under the care of the resident manager who lives in an apartment on the property. The rates change according to the number of days you are here. If you stay for six weeks, the rate drops to half ($42 per day). The owners are active in the community and work hard to make guests happy. The photos you see on the Internet don't begin to show the beauty and comfort of this place. The owners live in Alaska and you can contact them at 11000 Snowline Dr. Anchorage, AK 99507, ☎ 907-344-0986, e-mail casalibertad@ak.net. Their bulletin board is a great resource. If the web page listed above doesn't work for you, do a search for Casa Libertad and follow the links.

Mi Casa es Su Casa, *Flamingo 14 and Av. Sol Nuevo,* ☎ *327-274-0312, $$$,* is owned by Bob Howell and his business partner, Vicky, a character loved by everyone. Their two-story Mexican home is near the beach and across from a small rainforest. The two clean, comfortable bedrooms have balconies, night tables and tiled floors. The bathrooms (also clean) have lots of warm water. One room has an adjoining bathroom, while the other has a bathroom just outside the door. Breakfast is included, and the coffee is made from beans roasted and ground fresh every day. There is satellite TV in the common living room. There is a minimum two-night stay. Happy hour is held between 5 pm-6 pm and a margarita during this time is included in the price of the room.

They also have for rent a 400-sq-ft bungalow with a second-level patio of the same size. The bungalow has a living room, bedroom, bathroom and fully equipped kitchen. The floors in the kitchen and bathroom are all tiled. The bungalow comes totally furnished and includes microwave, electric stove, fridge, TV, dishes, toaster and blender, as well as air conditioning and satellite TV. Bicycles, beach gear and tennis courts are also available. Rental is $600 a month, including utilities. For those staying longer than a month in the bungalow or more than a week in the B & B, Bob includes an orientation visit to three villages.

Casa de Ensueños B&B, *Calle Golondrinas #19, ☎ 327-274-1230, www.casadeensuenos.com, $$$*, has five spacious rooms overlooking the bay. They have king-sized beds, private bathrooms, bedside tables and ceiling fans. One room is wheelchair-accessible. The floors are tiled. The place is cleaned to a sparkle. Amenities include satellite TV, volleyball court, beach chairs and umbrellas, nooks around the property to hide in with a book, bikes

(complimentary use) and a barbeque, making it as comfortable outside as it is inside. A complimentary sunset beverage is served each evening. The breakfast consists of fresh baked rolls, fruit and coffee and is served on the outside terrace overlooking the bay.

If arriving by car or walking from town, the following directions are from the entrance to the town at the highway. When you come to the T in the road at the tourist office, turn right. Follow Av Sol Nuevo and turn left on Pavo Real, right onto Flamingos and then left onto Golondrinas. The owners, Charlie and Mona Bryant, also have two large houses and two bungalows on the north end of the beach, next door to the trailer park. To see them go to www.oasisinmexico.com; if you are interested, you will have to e-mail the Bryants for information and rate details.

Decameron Los Cocos, *Retorno Las Palmas, Rincon de Guayabitos,* ☎ *327-274-0190, www.decameron.com, $$$,* is a great resort, but stay out of building #2 as it is dungeon-like. The 240 rooms have air conditioning, satellite TV, phones, a bathroom with shower and one king-sized

© Cameron

or two double beds. There are four pools, three bars, three restaurants, a gift shop, a disco (usually not too swinging), laundry service, a massage parlor and tennis courts. This is a quiet place where nightlife is not the main

draw, but you can rent bikes, kayaks, boogie boards and pedal boats to have fun all day.

Villa Corona del Mar, *Retorno Gaviotas #15,* ☎ *327-274-0015, www.villacoronadelmar.com, $$$/$$$$,* has seven rooms in the main house, each with a private balcony,

© Villa Corona del Mar

overlooking the ocean. They have private bathrooms, rustic Mexican furniture, king-sized beds, night tables with bright lamps, purified water, fans and large closets. There are also two bungalows for rent that have living rooms,

kitchenettes with dining areas and beds enough to sleep four. The bungalows that hold up to six people cost $129 per night. The property has a pool with a poolside bar, a Jacuzzi, and a tennis court. The outdoor kitchen is where your continental breakfast will be served each morning. There is also a restaurant.

Casa de los Amigos, *Calle Mirador #3,* ☎ *327-274-0713 or 888-434-4673 in the US, $$$$, www.casadelos amigosmx.com,* is a Moorish-styled villa built in 1986 and designed by the famous architect Salvador Cache Perez. There are three guest rooms available, all with private bathroom and balcony overlooking the ocean. Breakfast is served on another balcony (not your private one) and includes fresh juice, fruits and buns. The house also offers a complimentary cocktail at about 5

© Casa de los Amigos

pm. They have a Jacuzzi on the terrace, surrounded by a well-maintained garden, and there is purified water in your room. Should you wish, an in-room masseuse can be hired. *La Casa* offers airport pick-up in PV at no extra cost. The minimum stay is one week. The hospitality of this place is exceptional.

La Peñita de Jaltemba, *Calle Lazaro Cardenas #36,* ☎ *327-274-0776, www.casitadelapenita.ws, $$$$,* has seven suites located on two levels around a pool. They each have a living room, fully supplied kitchen with microwave and stove, private tiled bathroom and separate bedroom. The price includes pick-up from PV airport. The seven suites are all a different size and hold between two and six people. There is parking and a Jacuzzi. The gardens are well tended, with tiled patios and barbeque pits.

© Casita de la Peñita

Villas Buena Vida, *Retorno Laureles #2,* ☎ *327-274-0756, www.villasbuenavida.com, $$$$,* has large, luxurious rooms furnished with traditional Mexican furniture. The suites have kitchens and some are wheelchair-accessible. There is also a pool. This is a large complex with white buildings that sparkle in the sun.

North from Puerto Vallarta

PLACES TO EAT

Vendors at the western end of La Avenida have excellent food at excellent prices. If there is a crowd around the stall, you can rest assured that the food is delicious, safe and clean. Otherwise, walking along the beach and deciding on a place is often the best way to go. I can list only a few of the many possibilities.

Esmeralda's, *at Villas Buena Vida, Retorno Laureles #2,* ☎ *327,274-0756,* known as Victor's place by the locals, often has live entertainment such as jazz bands. The food has been recommended by a number of people and the specialty is a fish dish, known as *sarandeado*, that uses the freshest fish available. The entertainment, along with the food, makes this a very special place. Meals cost between $8 and $12.

Nina and Pedros Restaurant, *on the beach in Rincon de Guayabitos,* is excellent for lobster when it is in season. The cost is about $9 per serving with all the trimmings.

Rincon Mexicano, *Hotel San Carlos, Retorno Ceiba #2,* ☎ *327-274-0155,* offers authentic Mexican seafood at a cost of less than $10 per serving.

Piña Colada Bar and Grill, *Av Guayabitos #15,* ☎ *327-274-1211*, has the best fajitas in town. A full meal costs about $10. The roadside atmosphere is fun and very Mexican. They also cook up a mean steak if you are extra hungry.

Tukan Restaurant, *Carretera Federal # 200,* ☎ *327-274-0427,* serves local fresh shrimp, but is best known for its *milanesa*, a veal or pork steak pounded, breaded and fried (similar to Wienerschnitzel, served in Germany). For me, *milanesa* is like a fast-food meal, except it is really good. Each meal will cost $6 or $7.

Besa del Sol Restaurant, *on the beach in Guayabitos,* is considered the finest restaurant in the area. The tables are well spaced; you don't have to listen to your neighbor breathe. The place is clean, the kitchen newly renovated. A steak done to perfection costs $7.50. They also serve any exotic drink you could possibly want.

Jaqueline, *Retorno Cedro #4,* ☎ *327-274-0913,* has good Mexican food. It is on the beach in Guayabitos in the hotel of the same name. A meal seldom costs more than $8.

Hinde & Jaime's, *on the main street in Guayabitos*, should be called the Canadian Bar as there are more Canadians there than Mexicans. The atmosphere is saloon complete with a pool table. The food is also good – a supper of hamburger and fries runs about $6.

Restaurant Campañario, *Hotel Posada la Mision, Retorno Tabachines #6, in Guayabitos,* ☎ *327-274-0357,* has been a favorite for as long as there have been visitors to Guayabito. The Mexican-styled shrimp is good as are the burgers. A meal runs anywhere from $7.50 to $10 per person.

Cristobal, *on the beach in Guayabitos just down from Campañario,* is another favorite. Seafood is the specialty – if you want steak you will have to go to Besa del Sol.

NIGHTLIFE

Nightlife is not wild on this bay. The best I can muster up for you is the **Fanta-sea catamaran tour** offered by Freddy's. But new bars and discos open all the time, so ask other travelers.

Guadalajara

Guadalajara is the second-largest city in Mexico, with more than three million people. If the heat from the beaches is getting to you, a few days in Guadalajara and Laguna Chapala, just 30 miles/45 km from the center of the city, will give you a refreshing break. With the city sitting at about 5,000 feet/1,600 meters, the temperature averages at 22°C/72°F year-round. If this is still too hot, the lake always has a cooling breeze coming off the water.

Guadalajara is a sprawling city and the long-distance bus station is located a long way from the center, through the industrial area. In the center, plazas and parks are bordered by historical buildings as well as restaurants and shops. Because of its lovely parks and gardens, the city is often called the City of Roses. It is also credited with being the birthplace of the mariachi bands and the Mexican Hat Dance.

Guadalajara is easy to get around. Public transportation is abundant and hotels are found in all areas of the city. The restaurants are a little harder to find, but they are excellent. If you're looking for a little bit of home, you can always stop at one of the franchises, like Dunkin Donuts, Pizza Hut and McDonald's.

GETTING HERE & AROUND

■ BY PLANE

The airport for Guadalajara is halfway between the city center and the lake. Buses and taxis commute between the center and the airport. The cost for a taxi is about $15.

■ BY BUS

The long-distance bus station is new, large and well organized. Some of the better bus companies have private lounges in the terminal, reserved for their customers; you can't get into those areas until you have purchased a ticket.

To get into the city from the station, go out the door and behind the station to the main road where buses stop.

> **AUTHOR NOTE:** *Do not cross the parking lot to catch a bus that runs along the main road. Those buses make their way to the city only after they go in and out of numerous subdivisions.*

The best bus to take is TUR (blue in color and found at a separate stop from regular city buses). The city buses take longer and don't go directly to the plazas. However, to get on a TUR bus you must go to one of their specially designated stops. I often could not find one, so I just hopped onto a city bus.

A taxi to the center from the bus station runs about $10, well worth the fare if you have baggage.

First-class bus service goes to most places in Mexico almost every hour, although some may go to Mexico City before connecting with places like Oaxaca or Vera Cruz. Buses to Mazatlan go every hour from 5 am-9 pm daily; the trip takes seven hours. The cost is $31.50 one-way on a first-class, air-conditioned bus. Your ticket may include a sandwich and juice. Unfortunately, for confirmed readers like me, these buses also offer videos.

BY CAR

Driving in downtown Guadalajara is for those extremely skilled at stockcar racing, or for locals. However, the large eight-lane highways around the city are easy to drive.

The airport has all the international car rental companies like Hertz, Avis and Budget. To book in advance, do so online at www.rentalcarmomma.com/cities/guadalajara.htm. I have no phone numbers for the companies at the airport. The companies listed below are all off the airport compound.

Buelah Rent a Car, *Av Niños Heroes #968,* ☎ *333-614-1135,* has compact vehicles at competitive prices. This is a local company.

Alamo, *Av Niños Heroes #982*, is open 8 am-8 pm. A small Chevy standard will cost $270 a week, including insurance; a Venture Van, automatic, will cost $700, with unlimited mileage. Extra insurance is not included. To get coverage for collision you must pay an extra $15 per day.

Arrasa Rent a Car, *Av Lopez Mateos #62,* ☎ *333-615-0522,* has locations at Hotel Presidente and the airport. They have standard vehicles and suburbans ($750 a week). This is a local company.

North from Puerto Vallarta

BY SUBWAY

The subway, Tren Lingero, is an efficient and reliable way to get around. There are two lines; one going north and south and the other going east and west. Look for a subway sign (stairs going down) and, once downstairs, purchase your token from a machine beside the gates. The cost is $1 for a two-train trip. You will need correct change (a 10 peso coin). The trains don't operate after 10 pm.

SERVICES

The **Tourist Office**, *Av Morelos just off the Plaza de Liberacion,* ☎ *333-614-0123, www.mexperience.com/ guide/majorcity/guadalajara.htm, setujal@jalysco.gob. mx.* Although they don't have a huge amount of pamphlets for visitors, they are cheerful and helpful. The best map of the city is put out by the Direcion General de Turismo y Promocion Economica and costs 50¢. It is available at the tourist office. In the event of an emergency, call their 24-hour hotline, ☎ 55-250-0123 or 800-903-9200.

The **post office**, *Independencia and V. Carranza, two blocks west of the central plaza,* is open Monday to Friday, 8 am-6 pm, Saturday, 9 am-2 pm.

Hospital Mexico Americano, *is on Colomos # 2110,* ☎ *333-641-3141.*

The **IAMAT Center**, *is at Francisco Zarco #2345,* ☎ *333-615-9542.*

Police. *For emergencies,* ☎ *060; for non-emergencies,* ☎ *333-617-6060.* You'll spot numerous police on bicycles around the tourist areas and they are always willing to help or give directions. Many speak a little bit of English.

PUBLICATIONS

The Colony Reporter, *www.guadalajarareporter.com,* is an English-language newspaper that has national and regional news, plus arts and entertainment, restaurant reviews, history, education and sports. They are available at any newsstand for 50¢. You can also subscribe from overseas from between $30 and $45 per year, depending on where you live.

HISTORY

Guadalajara was first located where the villages of Nochistlan and then Zacatecas still stand. After repeated attacks by the Caxcan and Coca Indians, who were living in the area at the time, it was moved to its present site. The move is credited to Beatriz Hernandez, who, along with 60 other Spanish settlers, resettled in the Atemajac Valley. When there were other attacks in the Atemajac Valley, the settlers fought back and won. There is a commemorative monument of Beatriz on one side of the Degollado Theatre on the main plaza in the city.

SIGHTSEEING

Before doing anything in Guadalajara, get on a horse-drawn wagon and take a tour. The wagons are parked along the plazas downtown. Usually, the drivers speak some English and will give you a running commentary about the city for about $10 per hour.

The historical center has a collection of plazas between Hidalgo and Morelos streets. Plaza de los Fundadores is at the east end and Plaza Laureles is at the west end. The plazas form a Latin cross with the cathedral (built in 1616) at the center. The original 14 blocks of arched buildings around the plazas have increased to 30 since the city was first established.

Plaza Tapatia, the center of activity and tourism, can hold up to 15,000 spectators. The

Plaza Tapatia.

plaza is seven blocks long and crosses over Av Independencia at the east end. Degollado Theatre is on this plaza.

The Plaza de la Liberacion is between the cathedral and the Degollado Theatre. This plaza was originally called the Plaza de Las Dos Copas (Plaza of the Two Urns) because of the urn-like fountains in its center. That area also features a statue of Miguel Hidalgo, who helped liberate the Mexican people from oppression under the Spanish.

Plaza de Armas, across from Government House, has a bandstand that was brought from France when Mexico celebrated 100 years of independence. Band music is played there every Thursday and Sunday at dusk.

Plaza de los Laureles is what used to be the courtyard of the cathedral. Now, it has a fountain with the city's coat of arms. Opposite the museum on the north side of the cathedral is the Rotunda of Illustrious Jalsiciences, a mausoleum that holds historical characters from Jalisco's past.

Plaza de los Mariachis starts at the San Juan de Dios Church and is one block long. It forms the top of the cross. Originally it was called the Plaza Pepe Guizar in honor of the composer who wrote the song *Guadalajara*. And, true to its name, you can often hear mariachi music being played here.

The Cathedral, in the center of the plazas, is not the original cathedral built in the city. The original did not have the two towers. In 1818 an earthquake devastated the first building and, when it was rebuilt, the towers were included. Built of gray stone, the church appears austere. However, the fine gothic ceiling, the elaborate arches and the stained-

© Richard Gunion/Dreamstime

glass windows soften the austerity. The cathedral is dedicated to the Virgin of the Assumption. A painting inside by Bartoleme Esteban Murillo shows the Virgin going to heaven and is a good example of colonial art. There is also a 200-year-old organ that is still being played. An image of Nuestra Señora de la Rosa, carved from a single piece of balsam, is also in the church. The carving was given to Mexico as a gift by Carlos V of Spain in 1548.

The Ministry of Tourism is housed in one of the mansions that originally belonged to Juan Saldivar, a settler with means during colonial times. Inside the courtyard are an attractive fountain and a well-preserved colonnade.

Theatre Degollado, a monumental structure with Greek columns and frieze over the portal, was built in 1856. In front of the theater is a fountain and to the side is the monument to the founding mother of Guadalajara, Beatriz Hernandez, holding up the flag of Mexico. Behind the theater is another frieze that is at ground level, which allows for better inspection. It depicts the day of February 14, 1542, when the Spanish won the battle for the Atemajac Valley. It is called El Friso de los Fundadores.

Today, the theater is home to the Jalisco Philharmonic Orchestra and the University of Guadalajara's Folk Ballet. If there is a concert performing while you are here, get a ticket from the tourist office, ☎ 333-614-0123.

> **FACT FILE:** *Plaza de Armas is where Hidalgo made a speech in 1810 to abolish slavery.*

Plaza de Armas features a fountain and the **Palacio de Gobierno** or government house, built in the 18th cen-

Government House.

tury. It now houses the state's legislature. The mural in the central stairway is by the famous painter José Clemente Orozco, who lived from 1883 to 1949. Orozco is considered one of the three great muralists of the last century. (The other two are Siqueiros, whose characters take on a similar appearance to Orozco's, and Diego Rivera, who did the intricate and sardonic murals that are in the Government House in Mexico City.) Orozco was influenced by Rivera and, in turn, influenced painters such as Jackson Pollock, Rupert Garcia and Leonard Baskin.

Public Library, *Av 16 de Septiembre # 849, ☎ 333-619-0480, Monday to Friday, 8 am-8 pm, and Saturday, 9 am-5 pm.* This library holds over 200,000 volumes from as far back as the 1500s. It is the oldest library in Western Mexico and is a pleasure to visit.

Cabañas Cultural Institute, *Hospicio #8, Plaza Tapatia, ☎ 333-617-6734, Tuesday to Saturday, 10:15 am-8:30 pm, Sunday until 2:45 pm.* Constructed in the 18th century, the building has 23 interior patios and a domed chapel. Originally,

The Man of Fire *by Orozco.*

this was an orphanage and named after the man who started it, Bishop Ruiz de Cabañas y Crespo. The dome of the chapel has a mural by Orozco called "The Man of Fire," which is considered one of the most important murals in the world.

Guadalajara Attractions

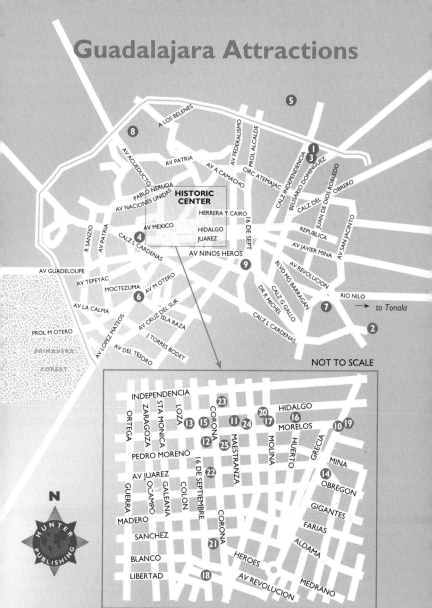

NOT TO SCALE

1. Zoo
2. Bus Station
3. Selva Magica
4. Museum of Art
5. La Barranca Oblatos
6. Los Arcos de Milenio
7. Telaquepaque
8. Zapopan
9. Agua Azul Park, Archeological Museum
10. Plaza Tapatia
11. Plaza de la Liberacion
12. Plaza de Armas
13. Plaza de los Laureles
14. Plaza de los Mariachis
15. Cathedral
16. Tourist Office
17. Theatre Degollado
18. Public Library
19. Cabañas Cultural Institute
20. St. Augustine Church
21. Plaza San Francisco
22. Exconvento del Carmen
23. Regional Museum
24. Museum de Cera, Ripley's Belive It or Not
25. Palacio Gobierno (Govt. House)

SPIRITUAL ADVENTURES

Tarot Card Readings, *Casa de la Sra. Consuelo #248*, ☎ *333-658-6104,* is open for private consultations Monday to Saturday, 9 am-9 pm. The reader has 20 years' experience and will tell you about your love life, give you advice on your job, or confer with the dead. She can even help you with impotency. Such a deal!

San Agustin Church, *on the side of the Degollado Theatre,* was constructed in the late 16th century. It started as a convent, but now houses the music school of Guadalajara.

San Francisco Plaza, *Av Juarez and Av 16 de Septiembre, just a few blocks from the center,* features the San Francisco Church, which has three baroque-style sections. Walking around the outside of this church takes a long time if you want to see all the statues and carvings. Next to San Francisco is the Aranzazu Temple, built in the style of the mission churches with three distinct bells framed into one tower. Inside the church are religious artworks, including three baroque altar pieces, the only ones of their kind in the city.

Exconvento del Carmen (an ex-convent), *Av Juarez*, is a block up from San Francisco Plaza. No longer a convent, the building has been taken over by the arts community and now has plays, literary workshops, movies and visual art exhibitions. There is no entry fee. Stop by the tourist office for a schedule.

The Zoo, *Paseo del Zoologico #600,* ☎ *333-674-4488, Wednesday to Sunday, 10 am-6 pm, $3.* This place is so big (100 acres) that a tram is available to carry you from site to site. There are 360 species of animals here. The main attractions are the aviary, located in a double pyramid-styled building, the herpetarium that has 130 species of reptiles, spiders, scorpions, fish and amphibians. A night zoo houses nocturnal animals.

Selva Magica, *next to the zoo, open daily, 10 am-6 pm, and weekends until 8 pm, $1.* This theme park has about

35 different rides, including a wild roller coaster. Your entrance fee includes a dolphin show.

On the other side of the zoo is the **Planetarium**, ☎ *333-674-4106, that has airplane exhibits along with space and astrological displays. See next page for details.*

■ MUSEUMS

Regional Museum of Guadalajara, *Liceo # 60, on the main plaza, ☎ 333-614-5257, Tuesday to Saturday, 9 am-5:45 pm, $3.* Originally the building was the San José Seminary, built in the late 1600s. It has been used as a seminary, a garrison, a men's college and, since 1918, a museum. The museum is divided into sections depicting different periods. The Paleontology Hall has fossils, including those of a huge mastodon complete with tusks. Another section features modern art.

Paleontological Museum of Federico Solozano, *Av DR Michel #520, ☎ 333-619-7043, Tuesday to Saturday, 10 am-6 pm, Sunday, 11 am-6 pm. The cost is $1 to enter the museum and $2 for entry to the museum and Agua Azul Park next door.* The museum holds a collection of plant and animal fossils in seven different salons. All exhibition halls contain permanent collections, except for one. The main focus around the displays is the importance of preserving these items for science. The exhibits are placed in cases on the floor in some rooms and you walk *above* them to have a good look. Guided tours are offered every day at 10 am, noon and 1 pm on weekdays, and at 11 am, 12:30 and 4:30 pm on weekends. A lot of money has been spent on this museum and it is well worth visiting. There is a café in the building and parking at the back.

Archeological Museum, *Av 16 de Septiembre #889, ☎ 333-619-0104, Tuesday to Friday and Sunday, 10 am-2 pm and 5 pm-7 pm, 50¢.* This museum has objects from the Jalisco, Colima and Nayarit states. Some of the silver and gold items are exceptional in their craftsmanship.

Museum of Arts, *Av Juarez # 975, Tuesday to Saturday, 9 am-6 pm, Sunday, noon-6 pm, no entrance fee.* This building was the original University of Guadalajara. One of the contemporary showpieces is a mural by José Clemente Orozco. The artwork is well displayed and has good lighting.

Museum de Cera (Wax Museum) and **Ripley's Believe It or Not Museum**, *Av Morelos #215, ☎ 333-614-8487, every day, 11 am-8 pm. Adults pay $5 for both museums, $3 for the wax museum only; children pay $2 for both museums and $1 for the wax.* The wax museum has historical figures, actors both national and international, and famous sports figures. The Ripley museum has an eclectic collection of items from around the country. There is a souvenir shop inside.

Planetarium/Museum of Science and Technology, *Periferico North # 401, ☎ 333-674-3978, Tuesday to Sunday, 9 am-7:30 pm, 50¢.* The Severo Diaz Galindo Planetarium is named after Jalisco's first astronomer. There are three areas to the museum; the planetarium, the astronomy hall and the scientific exhibitions. This is a hands-on museum where you can do things like make your hair stand on end.

ADVENTURES ON FOOT

■ HIKING

La Barranca Oblatos canyon is in the Zapopan area of the city, along the Guadalajara/Saltillo Highway. To get here, follow the signs to Tonala-Matatlan and travel along Calle Belisario Dominguez. It ends at the canyon. The area opens at 6 am and closes at 7 pm daily. There is a parking lot (50¢ an hour) at the trailhead.

There are three viewpoints along the canyon. From Huentitan Lookout you can see where the Verde and Santiago rivers merge. Independence Lookout stands over the canyon and gives the best views of its depth. The canyon walls drop 1,900 feet/630 meters to the rivers below. The third viewpoint is the Dr. Atl Lookout, which overlooks Cola de Caballo Falls (Horsetail Falls) that drop about 300 feet/100 meters into the canyon. There are interpretive signs along the trails and a steep, bricked pathway leading into the canyon. Remember that if you go down, you have to come back up again. There are picnic sites along the rivers.

> **FACT FILE:** *El Arcediano suspension bridge, which spans the rivers, was part of the original route into Guadalajara from Mexico City up until 1893.*

La Barranca Oblatos was declared an ecological preserve in 1993 and covers an area of 2,842 acres. An estimated 5,000 visitors run down into the canyon and back each week for exercise. There is a hydroelectric plant at the site and a hotel in the canyon called Casa Colorada. However, I know nothing about the hotel.

GOLF

Atlas Golf Club, *Km. 6.5 on the Chapala/El Salto Highway*, ☎ *333-689-2783*, is an 18-hole, par 72 course with 7,204 yards, designed by Joe Finger. Weekday fees are $25 for 18 holes, weekends you pay $45. Caddies are required and cost $7. Carts are available. For an additional $10 you can use the sauna, steam bath, pool and showers. There is a restaurant on site.

Santa Anita Golf Club, *Km. 65 on the Guadalajara/ Morelia Highway*, ☎ *333-686-0962*, is an 18-hole course designed by Larry Hughes. It costs $21 for nine holes during the week and $29 for 18 holes. On weekends and holidays 18 holes costs $45. Caddies are required and cost $7. The restaurant here is accessible to nonmembers, but you must be "recommended" by one of the five-star hotels in town before you are allowed to play.

Guadalajara Country Club, *Mar Caribe #2615*, ☎ *333-817-2858*, was designed by John Bredemus. There are 18 holes on this par 72, 6,821-yard classic-styled course. Green fees are $65 and caddies cost $10. The course, and its clubhouse, are open to visitors.

ADVENTURES IN THE SUBURBS

Los Arcos del Milenio (Millennium Arches), *Av Mariano Otero and Av Lazaro Cardenas,* is an impressive structure consisting of six arches designed by Julio Chavez Sanchez Sebastian, a famous Mexican sculptor. The arches cover 183,000 square feet/17,000 square meters, took 1,500 tons of metal to make and stand 150 feet/52 meters high.

> **FACT FILE:** *Sebastian also created the Door to Chihuahua in the city of Chihuahua and the Horse's Head in Mexico City.*

TLAQUEPAQUE

Tlaquepaque is the handicraft and art center of Mexico and has been a shopping/trading area since the Tonallan Kingdom ruled this part of the world. Today, the streets are lined with shops selling every art or craft ever made in Mexico. Some are of very high quality. But shopping isn't all you can do here. Visit **The Pottery Museum**, *Independencia #237, ☎ 333-635-5404, Tuesday to Saturday, 10 am-4 pm, and Sunday until 1 pm, free.* Housed in a colonial mansion, the museum has been exhibiting art since 1954. Of special interest are the miniatures and elaborately designed pre-Hispanic pieces. The kitchen is also worth visiting. It has one wall decorated with traditional coffee cups.

> **PETATILLO**
>
> The Petatillo style of painting on ceramic pieces is a crosshatch design that looks like long strands of metal woven together. This design is difficult to achieve and has been used by artists for several generations.

The **Pantaleon Panduro Museum**, *Sanchez # 91, ☎ 333-635-1089, Tuesday to Sunday, 10 am-6 pm, free*, displays the best pieces of pottery produced in the country for that year. There are contemporary and antique designs and some miniatures.

The central plaza will lead you to **El Parian**, a building with a food court where you can get just about anything to eat. From the plaza, continue on to the **Refugio**, *Donato Guerra # 160,* a cultural center that was once an asylum for women. It has been renovated and turned into a collection of chapels and singing rooms.

Walking between Tlaquepaque and Tonala you will pass some old mansions built before the 1900s.

To get to Tlaquepaque from either the bus station or the airport, take a taxi or city bus marked *Tlaquepaque.*

TONALA

Tonala, now an extension of Tlaquepaque, is the pottery center of the country. The word *Tonala* comes from the local Indian language and means the Place of the Sun. When the Spanish arrived, the village was governed by Atzahuapili, a queen who was known to keep numerous jewelers who designed elaborate pieces for her. Today, the area still has fine jewelry shops, but it has switched its focus mainly to ceramics.

There are about 400 shops in the area supporting artists who do both high- and low-temperature pottery. They also work with iron, stone, brass, copper, marble, papier mâché, textiles and glass. Some of the more interesting items are miniatures. Market days are Thursday and Sunday, when temporary stalls display food, herbal medicines and crafts, and magicians and street buskers offer entertainment.

Pottery display.

> **AUTHOR NOTE:** *You may find shopping during non-market days easier, as there are fewer people.*

Visit the **Museum Nacional de Ceramica**, *Constitución #104,* ☎ *333-683-0494, Tuesday to Friday, 10 am-5 pm, and weekends, 10 am-2 pm.* There is no charge to enter but you must pay $8.50 for the use of a camera. The museum, housed in a colonial mansion, displays ceramics and pottery from around the state. There are hundreds of shops from which to purchase items made in Tlaquepaque and Tonala. For an overview, visit www. mexweb.com/tonala2.htm.

■ ZAPOPAN

Zapopan is five miles/eight km northwest of the city center. To get here, follow Av Calzada Avila Camacho to Zapopan suburb, recognized by an ancient and decorative arch at its entrance. The walkway inside the arch, Paseo Teopiltzintli, is lined with bars, restaurants, gardens, fountains and shops. Continue along the *paseo* to Plaza de las Americas and the **Virgen de Zapopan Basilica**, built in 1730 and now the largest pilgrimage site in Mexico. Every spring at the beginning of rainy season (March), the village becomes a hub for the pilgrims. At that time, the Virgin of Zapopan, a tiny image carved from corn-husk paste, is taken out of the Basilica to visit 130 parishes in the city. She is supposed to offer protection from rains and floods. On October 12th, when her tour is over, she is taken back to rest for the winter. About a million people welcome her back. After she is safely tucked away, the people enjoy a festival in the courtyard. The devotions to the virgin started when the original church collapsed in 1606, destroying everything but her. Besides her protection to the parishes, she also protects Guadalajara from lighting, plagues and storms.

Next to the Basicilica is the **Huichol Art Museum**, ☎ *333-636-4430, Monday to Saturday, 9:30 am-1:30 pm and 3:30-6 pm, Sunday, 10 am-2 pm.* A "must stop" if in the area. The art is done on shirts, knapsacks, pants, skirts, rings, necklaces and masks. Like petit point, the intricacy of the beadwork is amazing. Also nearby is the **Albarran Hunting Museum**, *Paseo de los Parques #3540*. It costs $2 to enter. The house looks like it was constructed in Africa and is stuffed with 270 animals that were killed by Benito Albarran, the original owner of the house. He traveled to five continents to get the animals.

Rodeos and Bullfights, *Plaza de Toros Nuevo Progresso, Av R. Michel # 577,* ☎ *619-0315,* has bullfights on Sundays between October and March. They start about 4:30 pm and cost $8-$15 to enter, depending on the seat (those in the sun are cheaper). They also have a two-hour rodeo show that starts every Sunday at noon. Across the street is the **Jalisco Stadium**, where football (soccer) games are played. See the tourist office in the center of town for game schedules.

ADVENTURES IN NATURE

Parque Agua Azul, *Calz. Independencia Sur between Gonzalez Gallo and Las Palmas (you can also enter from Av. Dr Michel), $2 to enter the park and museum; $1 to enter the park only.* This is the most popular park in town. Located next to the Archaeological Museum in the southern section of the city, it has two areas connected by a bridge. A lush green section has a tree-lined walkway, called Avenue of the Musicians, with gardens on each side. Along here are benches and tables, as well as food vendors. But the most interesting things are on the other side of the bridge. They are the butterfly house, the orchid house, the solarium and the aviary. Guided tours are available hourly at the butterfly house. There is also the Concha Acustica, an outdoor stage where

Butterfly House.

cultural shows are held. Ask at the tourist office on the main square in town about events.

Primavera Forest, *Km 20 on Highway 15,* is on the way to Tepic/Puerto Vallarta, before the tollbooth. The park has 154 square miles/400 square km of forest with picnic tables and walking/cycling paths. Birding is good here. There is a hot spring just over the hill from the park (you will see signs). The spring is on privately owned land and the owners charge to enter. To get here, pass the country clubs of Rancho Contento and Pinar de la Venta on Highway 15 (the road to Tepic/Puerto Vallarta). This is where the toll road begins. Watch for signs indicating the *Canon de las Flores* and *Ejido La Primavera.* This is where you turn and follow the signs to the site.

ADVENTURES OF THE BRAIN

Español Para Todos, *Torres Quintero # 39,* ☎ *333-364-0897, www.espanolparatodos.com.mx,* offers all levels of language school with either a private tutor or group lessons. There are classes for beginners, business needs, advanced grammar or Latin American literature. The classes are for two hours a day, five days a week, and cost $150 per month. Private lessons cost $8 an hour. Studying literature, culture and the arts is $75 a month.

OUTFITTERS/TOUR OPERATORS

During my visit, few tourist agencies could make arrangements for hiking, biking, rafting or birding excursions. Most seem to sell tickets to other places and book expensive hotels. You are mostly on your own to explore.

Andale Mexico, ☎ *442-212-2899, www.andalemexico. com/tour_tqexp.htm,* an Internet travel agency in Queretaro, offers a trip on the Tequila Express that runs to Tequila and Amatitan. It starts in Guadalajara and covers the tequila tour plus two nights in a hotel for $300.

DAY TRIPS

The village of **Tequila**, at the foot of Tequila Volcano, can be reached by taking a bus from the old bus station or by taking a tour on the Tequila Express (see next page). The village of Tequila is classified as the "denomination of origin," meaning it is recognized internationally as the place that originally discovered tequila.

The volcanic soil deposited during eruptions makes the ground here (along with the ground in Amatitan, just down the road) perfect for growing the blue agave plant that is used in making tequila.

AGILE AGAVE

The mescal, or agave azul, is a cactus-like plant that is used to produce tequila, vinegar and sugar. Its leaves are also used for roofing and the stalks are used as construction beams. Threads pulled from the leaves are used for sewing and the spines can be used as nails. Once the plant has been cooked, it can be pressed into bricks.

If touring on your own, take a bus (or drive on the highway toward PV) from the old bus station and get off at **Arenal**, 45 km/30 mi from Guadalajara. Along the way you will see agave in the fields. In Arenal, go to the **Hacienda de la Providencia** (ask directions or follow the signs). The hacienda has been producing tequila for more than 100 years. Tours of the still and the colonial hacienda, decorated in period furniture, are available. From Arenal, take a local bus to **Amatitan** just six miles/ nine km farther, where you will find the **Hacienda de San José del Refugio** that has been producing tequila since 1870. This is a mule-driven mill. After seeing the still, you will be taken into the cellars where the fermentation vats are sunk into the floor. This is the most unusual of the three distilleries along this route and really worth the stop. A factory in town, next to the Pemex station, produces handmade oak casks and barrels for the tequila industry. You can purchase a decorative cask

that has side arms on it where tequila glasses can sit. After visiting Amatitan, catch another bus to Tequila, where you can again visit a tequila factory, (there are dozens from which to choose), have another taste of the sacred brew and hope that you can make it back to your hotel in Guadalajara. Tequila has the **Tequila Sauza Museum** on the town square. Inside is a mural that is reminiscent of Hogarth's Gin Mill. This one depicts the effects of tequila, rather than gin, on the general population. Just beyond the city you will see **Tequila Volcano** (9,500 feet/3,000 meters above sea level).

TEQUILA TWO-STEP

It takes eight to 10 years for the plant to grow to maturity. Once the heads, called cones, are ripe, they are picked and heated in ovens for 24 hours, then cooled for another 24 hours. The next step requires the cones to be ground, so the juice can be extracted. The juice is left in tanks for 72 to 96 hours. It is then distilled and left to age, which can take anywhere from a few months to several years.

To travel from one community to the next, take local third-class buses (they run every half-hour) from each village center about. If you find the tequila has gotten ahold of you, there is a private sanitarium in Tlaquepaque where you can get a very comfortable cure.

The **Tequila Express**, ☎ *333-880-9099, runs every Saturday (register by 10 am; the train leaves by 10:30 am), $55 for a return trip to Tequila.* It leaves from the Ferrocaril Mexicano Station, Camara National de Comercio for this full-day adventure. As you wait at the train station with your ticket in hand, a mariachi band will play for you. On the train, you can start your consumption of tequila or local beer. The train has reclining seats, tray tables and air conditioning. After a short time traveling, you will be served some vegetables and fruit. Once in the village of Tequila, you will be taken to the museum, located in a colonial house that once belonged to a tequila baron. It features harvesting implements, wooden carts and a collection of bottles. From there you go to the factory and actually see the production firsthand. The final stage of the tour includes a true Mexican fiesta, where you can eat traditional Mexican food served as a buffet. Back on the train (about 6 pm) the party continues with more mariachi and dancing in the aisles. By the time you're in Guadalajara, you will be ready for bed.

SHOPPING

Everyone comes to Guadalajara to shop for authentic high-quality art. The places to shop are mainly in the art centers of **Tlaquepaque** (see page 202) and **Tonala** (page 203). I have recommended a few other places in the city, but I also suggest you mainly walk the streets and see what appeals to you.

The enormous **Libertad Market** in the central square, is also called the San Juan de Dios Market. This spot has always been a market, even before the Spanish settled in the city. It sells mainly produce and items for use in the home, but tourists will also be able to find numerous handicrafts.

Omar Centeno, *Av Vallarta # 1075*, ☎ *333-827-1497*, sells high-quality fine art. Some of the bronze workings are magnificent (and expensive).

Handicraft House, *Calzada Gonzalez Gallo #20*, ☎ *333-619-1369, Monday to Friday, 10 am-4 pm, Saturday until 5 pm, Sunday until 3 pm*. Handicraft House features art from around the state, including over 2,000 ceramic pieces designed by Roberto Montenegro. There is also an exquisite collection of blown glass and metal handicrafts.

Artesanias Arzola, *Juarez #286*, ☎ *333-683-3761, or Fco. Madero #197*, ☎ *333-683-0134*, has unique articles such as frames, candlestick holders and birdcages (used to hold incense). They are made from gold, silver or copper.

Art V, *Av Tonala #273-A*, ☎ *333-683-5570*. If you are searching for hand-painted glass, this is one of the better shops. They bake their painted glass at 1500°F/800°C to ensure longevity. Numerous items sold here include party glasses, decorative glass chests and glass masks.

PLACES TO STAY

Hotels are spread all over the city. There is one at the new bus station and many along the highway into town, but they are a long way from the center. If you have a car, they may be an option. Go to one that has off-street parking and use public transportation from there. The one hotel by the bus

HOTEL PRICE SCALE	
Room price, in US $	
$	up to $20
$$	$21-$50
$$$	$51-100
$$$$	$101-$150
$$$$$	$151-200

station is rather expensive, but if you are catching a bus early the following morning, it works out costing about the same as staying in town and catching a taxi both ways.

Hotels around the old bus station in town are numerous and cheap. The Royal is an example of what you will get.

Hotel Royal, *Los Angeles #115 at Reforma,* ☎ *333-619-8473, $,* is fairly clean. The rooms have color TVs, fans and hot water all day. If you take a room with two beds good for four people, the cost is just $20. This is a family-run establishment.

Guadalajara Hostel, *Maestranza #147,* ☎ *333-562-7520, www.hostelguadalajara.com, $,* is in the center just off the plaza and located in a building built in the 1800s. The hostel has 30 beds and is secure. There is hot water in the bathrooms, full kitchen facilities, lockers (bring your own lock), Internet access, a games room and laundry service. However, if sharing a room, it may be cheaper for you to stay at other hotels such as the Sevilla.

Hotel Seville, *Calle Prisciliano Sanchez #413,* ☎ *333-614-9172, $$,* is a three-star hotel that offers a double for just $22. Rooms are clean, although a few are not overly big. There are fans, TV, lots of hot water, fluffy towels and even a shower curtain in the tiled bathroom. The bedrooms are tiled and carpeted and each room has a closet and desk. The hotel personnel speak some English. There is parking available and a restaurant.

Hotel San Francisco Plaza, *Degollado #267*, ☎ *333-613-3256, $$,* is located in the center near the Degollado Theatre. This colonial house has 76 renovated rooms that are comfortable, but not plush. They are set around three inner courtyards. The biggest draw for this price range is the central location.

Posada San Rafael, *Lopez Cotilla # 619*, ☎ *333-614-9146, $$*, is a restored historical hacienda in the center of town. The 12 big rooms are comfortable and set around a central courtyard. The front door is always locked and kitchen facilities are available for those staying longer than a few days. There is air conditioning and the bathrooms are tiled and have hot water. I love this place. The staff is friendly and there is Internet access for a small fee.

Hotel Frances, *Maestranza # 35*, ☎ *333-613-1190, www. hotelfrances.com, $$$,* is an elegant hotel with a historic past. The building, 375 years old, has always been a hotel. The entrance has a marble fountain and the inner courtyard is surrounded by arches held up by classical columns. The center of the courtyard has an enormous gilt chandelier and a wide stairway leading to the upper levels, where the rooms are located. When the building was remodeled in 1981, it was declared a national monument by the Governor of the state. Back in 1610 when the hotel was built it was called the Mezon de San José and provided short-term shelter for traders traveling from the northwest of Mexico to Mexico City. During renovations many of the early items were preserved. For example, what looks like garbage bins are actually troughs used to feed horses. In more recent years, the hotel was chosen as the site to film scenes for the movie *The Evil that Men Do*, starring Charles Bronson. The movie also has some of the owners in it. No two rooms in the hotel are alike, but the choice ones have a balcony facing the government building across the street. The on-site restaurant has a splendid lunch buffet for $5 per person.

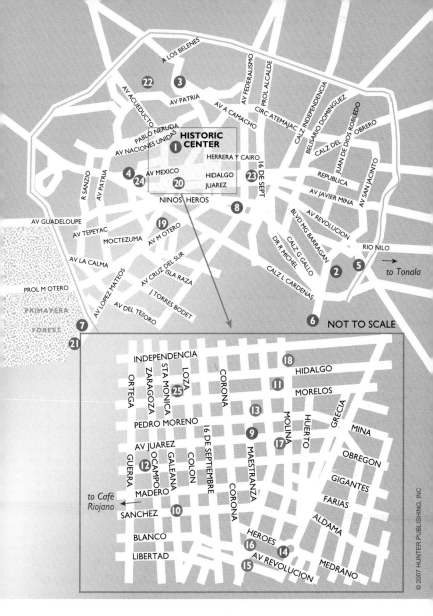

Places to Stay & Eat

1. Hotel Royal
2. Casa del Rotoño
3. Hotel Country Plaza
4. Hotel Plaza los Arcos
5. Villa del Sueño
6. Hotel Casa Grande
7. Hotel Crown Plaza
8. Holiday Inn
9. Guadalajara Hostel
10. Hotel Sevilla
11. Hotel San Francisco Plaza
12. Posada San Rafael
13. Hotel Francis
14. Hotel Colon
15. Hotel Galecia
16. Hotel Aranzazu
17. Hotel Genova
18. Hotel Mendoza
19. Rincon del Sol Restaurant
20. Hare Krishna Restaurant
21. El Carnal Restaurant
22. Boni's Restaurant
23. Hacienda de Tequila Restaurant
24. La Charla Restaurant
25. Antigua Restaurant

Hotel Colon, *Av Revolucion #12*, ☎ *333-613-3390, $$$*, is a three-star hotel. The clean rooms have a TV, phone, tiled bathroom and carpet in the bedroom. There is a restaurant and front desk service 24 hours a day.

Hotel Nueva Galicia, *Av Corona #610*, ☎ *333-614-8780, $$$*, is a sister hotel to the Colon and is convenient for those wanting to be in the commercial area of the city. The rooms are clean and the English-speaking staff is friendly.

Hotel del Parque, *Av Juarez #845*, ☎ *333-825-2800, $$$*, is close to Plaza Revolucion. The rooms are simple and clean and the staff speaks some English. The big draw to this hotel is its jazz bar, one of the most popular in town.

Casa del Retoño B&B, *Matamoros #182*, ☎ *333-639-6510, $$$*, is in Tlaquepaque. This is an adobe-brick house built in traditional Mexican style. There are eight colorful rooms with private bathroom and tiled floors. The garden is decorated with potted plants and old trees where birds are often seen. Complimentary breakfast consists of juice, coffee, tea, milk, cereal, toast, yogurt and fruit. This is a lovely place.

Hotel Country Plaza, *Av Americas #1170*, ☎ *800-359-7234, $$$*, is close to the country club. It has 119 rooms, some wheelchair-accessible. The rooms are large, some with king-sized beds and sitting areas. They have carpeting, private bathroom, purified water and cable TV. There is a pool, tennis courts, a business center, laundry service, free parking and a casino.

Hotel Aranzazu, *Av Revolucion #110*, ☎ *333-613-3232, $$$*, is a Best Western Hotel. There are 468 rooms on 10 floors. Each has cable TV, a mini-bar, alarm clock, private bathroom, VCR and Internet connection. You have a choice of either two twin beds or one king-sized bed. The hotel has a restaurant, bar, parking, babysitting service, laundry, valet, a spa, pool and tennis courts. The buffet breakfast is expensive. Watch your bill in the restaurant.

Hotel Genova, *Av Juarez # 123*, ☎ *333-613-7500, $$$*, is another Best Western hotel, but much smaller than the Aranzazu. The 185 rooms on seven floors have either two doubles or one king-sized bed, mini-bar, cable TV, coffee maker and Internet connection. There is off-street parking, a restaurant, a beauty parlor, laundry service and a spa. Breakfast is included in the price, as is a welcoming tequila drink on arrival. They also provide a morning newspaper.

Hotel Plaza Los Arcos, *Av Vallarta #2477,* ☎ *333-615-1845, www.magnohotel.com.mx, $$$,* has large but spartan rooms, some with kitchenettes. Rooms are carpeted, and have a private bathroom with purified water, cable TV and a sitting area. Continental breakfast is included. There is private parking available. The hotel is close to the newest shopping mall in Guadalajara and to restaurants, bars, galleries and the Expo center. This hotel is associated with the Magno Hotel Chain.

Villa del Ensueño, *Florida #305,* ☎ *333-635-8792, $$$/ $$$$,* is located in Tlaquepaque. It is a first-class hotel/ B&B with 18 large modern rooms/suites surrounding a central courtyard that has a heated pool, potted plants and deck furniture. There is a second pool indoors. The rooms are furnished with solid wood furniture and have open beam ceilings, fans, good lighting and tiled floors. The entire hotel is hospital clean. Internet service and off-street parking are available.

De Mendoza Hotel, *Av Carranza #16,* ☎ *333-614-2621, $$$$,* is a colonial building in the heart of the historical area. Each large room has a sitting area, air conditioning, cable TV, carpet, open beam ceiling, private bathroom, mini-bar and heavy wood furnishings. There is a pool, restaurant, bar, travel agent and off-street parking. The staff speaks English.

Hotel Casa Grande, *International Airport,* ☎ *333-678-9001 or 888-306-2487, www.casagrande.com.mx, $$$$,* has large carpeted rooms with private bathrooms, night tables with reading lights and sitting areas. There is a pool, a fitness center, a restaurant (7 am-1 am), a bar (5 pm-1 pm) and a business center.

Hotel Crown Plaza, *Av Lopez Mateos Sur #2500,* ☎ *333-634-1034, $$$$/$$$$$,* has almost 300 rooms on eight floors. All have private bathroom, air conditioning, com-

North from Puerto Vallarta

fortable beds and a sitting area. The well-tended grounds have a pool, a children's play area and two tennis courts. There is a gym, a beauty salon, massage service, a bar, a restaurant and babysitting service. The hotel also has free parking, an airport shuttle and even a kennel for Rover. The only drawback is the distance from the center of town. It is too far to walk. I sent my husband, John, out to pace the distance, but after two days of walking he gave up and returned to me by cab.

Holiday Inn, *Av Niños Heroes #3-89,* ☎ *333-622-2020 or 800-364-7700, www.selectgdl.com.mx, $$$$$,* is like any Holiday Inn found around the world. The rooms have a private bathroom, air conditioning (or heat, if need be), a table and a chair. There is a rooftop pool and a restaurant on site. There are special prices during off-season, but even these are international prices rather than Mexican ones. The service is good and the staff is helpful. Most speak some English.

PLACES TO EAT

The people of Jalisco are especially proud of their food. If you see some of the items listed below on the menu be certain to try them.

JALSICO SPECIALTIES

- **Tortas ahogadas** is a meat-stuffed roll covered in a hot chili sauce.
- **Birria** is a spicy meat stew.
- **Menundo** is a dish made with tripe.
- **Pozole** is a corn-based soup.
- **Charales** are tiny fried fish.
- **Jejuino** is the traditional sour-sweet, non-alcoholic drink.

Antigua Restaurant, *Morelos #371,* ☎ *333-614-0648,* is open 8 am-10 pm daily, and on Friday and Saturday it stays open until midnight. This building was constructed in 1802 by a member of the Calzado family and is still owned by them. In 1802 the area that is now used as a restaurant was the Library of Santisima Trinidad (Holy Trinity). The family started a pastry shop in the rooms next to the library. It became popular and, eventually, expanded into a restaurant. Pastry is still their specialty. Antigua offers an excellent breakfast buffet for $5.80. The scrambled eggs have a unique spice added for flavor. Their evening specialty is *arrachera tapatia*, a spicy beef dish that is filling. Also good is the chicken Cordon Bleu (azul). The bar has live music on weekends.

Rincon del Sol, *Av 16 de Septiembre #61,* ☎ *333-683-1989*, specializes in Mexican food. The chilies in walnut sauce or mutton with seafood are the best dishes. A moderate-sized serving costs about $12. The food is always nicely presented.

Hare Krishna, *Pedro Moreno #1791,* ☎ *333-616-0775*, is a vegetarian restaurant that serves Indian cuisine. Their food is delicious, but I often have a hard time finding the restaurant open. Phone before you go.

Productos El Jardin, *Av La Paz # 1558,* ☎ *333-825-6885*, is a vegetarian restaurant that has an à-la-carte menu and a buffet. The cost for the buffet is $8. Drinks are extra.

El Carnal, *Av Lopez Mateos Sur # 6160, no phone,* is open every day from 10 am-7 pm. The restaurant specializes in seafood and their best meals are made with huge shrimp or lobster. The special Jalisco dish is *charales* (see above) and they also have the best ceviche in town. Unintrusive live music plays and there's an activity area for children. The off-street parking is a draw for those driving.

Boni's, *Av de las Rosas #543,* ☎ *333-647-2551*, in Zapopan, is a new-wave place that offers many vegetarian dishes. The cost is a tad expensive – around $9 for a large salad.

Hacienda de Tequila, *Av Hidalgo #1749,* ☎ *333-630-5090*, is a block from Av Las Americas. If you haven't had enough steak and tequila, then maybe you need to come here. They use Angus beef and their tequila is never watered down as it is in many bars in Mexico, especially the establishments that charge lower prices. The atmosphere is comfortable and quiet. A perfectly cooked steak costs $12.

Café Riojano, *Av 8 de Julio #164, between Cotilla and Madero,* ☎ *333-820-3323, bullyfo@yahoo.com.mx,* is a tiny place that offers delicious coffee and cake. This is a good midday hangout. An espresso is $1 and a latté is $1.50. If you want something sweet, try a chocolate soda.

Restaurant Chez Pierre, *Av España #2095,* ☎ *333-615-2212*, is open Monday to Saturday, from 1 pm-1 am. The restaurant, which has been in business for 32 years, offers first-class French cuisine cooked by famous chef Pierre Pelech. The best meal is the oysters and roast duck ($14). But no matter what you try, it will be good. The French like to take hours to enjoy a meal – plan to do the same when you come here. If in Guadalajara during Christmas, the meal served after midnight Mass is always exceptional. For this you must book in advance.

Unico Restaurant Folklorico, *Av Lopez Mateos Sur #4521,* ☎ *333-632-9222,* is open Tuesday to Saturday from 4 pm-1 am for meals and during holidays, until 3 am for music and dancing. This is a good spot for first-class Mexican food and entertainment. The Folklorica shows are at 4 and 9:30 pm, Tuesday to Saturday. There is valet parking until 1 am.

Genghis Khan, *Av Mariano Otero #1499,* ☎ *333-671-0130*, opens daily for supper at 5 pm. It is a large Mongolian-style restaurant with brass urns and shields that lend an exotic atmosphere (although they have given in to their conquerors and now serve Chinese food). Prices are somewhat high. A meal of sweet and sour meat costs $9 per serving.

Il Magazzino Café and Bar, *Av Manuel Acuña #2938,* ☎ *333-641-9775,* is an Italian restaurant that serves pastas, pizzas, fish and barbequed steaks. One of these dishes, with a bottle of imported wine, will run $25.

La Charla, *Av Vallarta # 1095,* ☎ *333-825-0393*, is open daily for breakfast. A full plate of *huevos rancheros* and toast costs less than $7. This is a very clean place set in a trendy part of town.

NIGHTLIFE

Don't stay out late in Guadalajara, as the city transforms itself from an interesting historical center in the day to a rowdy, brawling zone at night. Even in the quiet areas, beer bottles seem to fly out of windows and drunks take pleasure in sleeping along your walkway. If you want some entertainment, go to the bar in your hotel or plan on taking a taxi everywhere.

Alcatraz Prison Bar, *Marcos Castellanos # 114-Z*, ☎ *333-826-5886*, is a lively drinking joint/eatery that attracts locals wanting to drown their sorrows with lots of booze and loud music. However, I found it to be fun.

Peña Cuicacalli, *Av Niños Heroes # 1988*, starts their live entertainment at 8 pm; a second show starts at 9 pm. They bring in artists from around the country for the shows. If you want to have a meal here, reservations are highly recommended.

Laguna Chapala

Chapala Lake, the largest natural lake in Mexico, is about 50 miles/75 km long and 13 miles/20 km wide. Although large in area, the lake averages only 10 feet/three meters deep and is just 30 feet/10 meters at its deepest. The area is famous for its warm climate and has attracted over 6,000 Canadians and Americans as permanent residents, many of whom are artists. The lake is 30 miles/45 km from Guadalajara, about one hour by bus.

Currently, the lake's water level is low, making the dock and "lakeside" restaurants about a quarter-mile from the shore. The distance is so far that, if you hire a boat to take you around the lake, there is a bus to take you from the end of the pier to the shore of the lake.

Fluctuating water levels are not uncommon, although floods have been more common than droughts. The lake flooded for a few years in the 1940s and receded in the

North from Puerto Vallarta

1950s. It flooded again in the 1980s and is receding now. Since the building of the Maltarana Dyke in the 1950s, fluctuations have become more severe.

LEGISLATIVE LOOPHOLE

A mistake in legislation allowed foreigners to purchase land that was on the waterfront, so many North Americans living at the lake purchased the land they had previously leased. The law was in effect for only three months. Once the government realized what was happening, they changed the law so foreigners could no longer do this. They also cut off water supply to the lake, in the hope that the foreign landowners would sell the property back to Mexicans. A side effect of this move was that it caused the shoreline to recede a long way from business establishments.

> LOCAL LINGO: *The word* Chapala *means "Place Soaked in Water," according to some, while others believe it means "Grasshoppers in Water."*

GETTING HERE & AROUND

The **bus** to Chapala leaves from the old bus station in Guadalajara. You must pay 5¢ (50 centavos) to enter the bus station (once inside, toilets are free). Buses run once every half-hour between 5:30 am and 9:30 pm. The fare is $3.50 per person, each way.

Buses to other destinations around the lake can be boarded in Chapala, either at the station where the Guadalajara bus arrives, or a little farther up the street.

Lakeside Linea Profesional Rent-A-Car, ☎ *333-766-2555, Monday to Friday, 9 am-4 pm, and Saturday till 1 pm.* A Chevy with five-speed standard transmission costs $48 a day and includes insurance, tax and 155 miles/250 km of driving. For a week, the cost is $280, including unlimited mileage. The same model automatic costs $60 a day. A Nissan Sentra automatic with air conditioning costs $75 a day with 155 miles/250 km each day of free mileage, $450 a week with unlimited mileage. Insurance deductible is 10% of the value of the car in the event of theft and 5% in the event of collision. You are covered for two drivers at no extra charge, as long as each driver has a valid driver's license.

HISTORY

Records show that the **Nahuatl Indians** lived in the area as early as the 12th century. Fishing in the lake was good and the climate comfortable. When **Franciscan Friar Antonio Tello** arrived in 1524, he found a large community. He started evangelizing and constructed religious buildings at Chapala and around the lake. Life remained rather isolated except for the religious activity until the 1900s, when elaborate homes started to spring up. Some of the hotels from that time are still operating today. Once the railroad was completed in the 1930s, more people came to settle. The railway made transportation to and from Guadalajara much more comfortable than the horse and buggy method used before. The trip was also nine hours shorter.

SERVICES

The **post office**, *Hidalgo #242B on the road to Ajijic, Monday to Friday, 8:30 am-3 pm, Saturday until 1 pm.*

Municipal Police, *Niños Heroes & Zaragoza,* ☎ *333-765-4444.*

Health Center, *F.R. de Velasco # 406,* ☎ *333-765-2623.*

PUBLICATIONS

El Ojo del Lago is a local newspaper publication in English, free for the visitor and packed with useful information from historical stories to cultural events. The *Lake Chapala Guide*, by Teresa Kendrick, has detailed information about the lake and its ecological history. It also has suggested tourist attractions, including details on how to reach them.

FESTIVALS

October 4th is the **Festival of San Francisco de Asis**, Chapala's patron saint. Celebrations include a special church service followed by street dancing and parades.

SIGHTSEEING

■ HISTORICAL WALKING TOUR

Chapala has some interesting historic houses. Prior to the 1900s, the only building around the lake taller than one story was the church. Then Luis Barragon, a Mexican architect, built his family home, an ostentatious mansion on Av Frederico Madero between Morelos and Niños Heros. It became the highest building in town. **Hotel Arzapalo** faces the lake at the end of Av Frederico Madero. It was built in 1898. **Hotel Nido**, along Calle Madero, is now the municipal office. It was built in the early 1900s and is located just north of Hotel Arzapalo and across from the Beer Garden, the longest-operating restaurant in Chapala. Inside the Nido are numerous photos of Chapala during the lake's high-water days. **Hotel Niza**, just a bit farther along Calle Madero, was built in 1908. **Villa Monte Carlo**, on Hidalgo just off Madero, was built in 1895 by Septimus Crow. He liked the area because he could treat his arthritis in the nearby hot springs.

During the late 1800s, a visit by the president made the area popular with the rich, and villas Ferrara, Niza and Josefina were built in a style similar to the Monte Carlo. These houses are the big mansions along the Madero. The church with the double steeples is the **Church of San Francisco,** built in 1528 and reconstructed in 1580. The Queen Anne mansion that houses the Cazadores Restaurant, located on the street facing the lake, is called

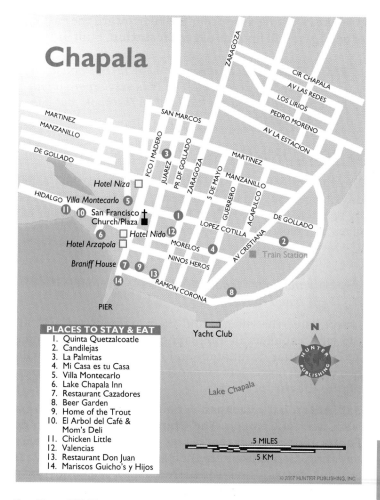

Chapala

ZARAGOZA
CIR CHAPALA
AV LAS REDES
LOS LIRIOS
PEDRO MORENO
SAN MARCOS
MARTINEZ
MANZANILLO
DE GOLLADO
AV LA ESTACION
FCO I MADERO
JUAREZ
PR DF GOLLADO
ZARAGOZA
5 DE MAYO
MARTINEZ
MANZANILLO
Hotel Niza ☐
GUERRERO
ACAPULCO
DE GOLLADO
HIDALGO Villa Montecarlo ❺
San Francisco ✝
❶❶ ❿ Church/Plaza ■
LOPEZ COTILLA
❶
❷
Train Station
Hotel Nido ❶❷
❻ ☐
Hotel Arzapola ☐
MORELOS ❹
AV CRISTIANA
Braniff House ❼ ❾
NINOS HEROS
❶❸
❽
❶❹
RAMON CORONA

PIER

Yacht Club

PLACES TO STAY & EAT
1. Quinta Quetzalcoatle
2. Candilejas
3. La Palmitas
4. Mi Casa es tu Casa
5. Villa Montecarlo
6. Lake Chapala Inn
7. Restaurant Cazadores
8. Beer Garden
9. Home of the Trout
10. El Arbol del Café &
    Mom's Deli
11. Chicken Little
12. Valencias
13. Restaurant Don Juan
14. Mariscos Guicho's y Hijos

Lake Chapala

N

.5 MILES
.5 KM

© 2007 HUNTER PUBLISHING, INC

the **Braniff House**. It was built in 1906 by Luis Verdia and purchased by Alberto Braniff in 1906.

> **FACT FILE:** *Although these Braniff's did not own the American Braniff Airlines, Alberto is credited with being the first to fly a plane in Latin America. He did this on January 8, 1910.*

Farther along the street that follows the lake is the **Chapala Yacht Club**, constructed in 1910 by Chistian Shjetnan, a man instrumental in getting the rail line to the lake. Walking away from the lake toward the east end of town, you will find the old **train station**, built in 1930.

> **FACT FILE:** *DH Lawrence* lived in the house at Zaragoza #307 and wrote The Plumed Serpent while here. He calls the lake "Sayula" in the book, but it is clearly Chapala.

■ EXPLORING LAKE VILLAGES

Touring the villages around the lake could take a few days, depending on your interests. This tour can be done by boat, car, bus or on foot. However, travel by bus or car gives you more time to explore.

> **AUTHOR NOTE:** *Boats cost far less when rented for the day, rather than by the hour. Negotiate with the operators located at the pier.*

I have listed the villages and their main attractions. Although Chapala is an interesting town, Ajijic has become a very popular destination and has all the tourist facilities you will need. Some make it a base camp for exploration to the rest of the area.

San Antonio Tlayacapan is an easy three-mile/five-km walk west of Chapala. The **Church of San Antonio de Padua** and the tower that is now part of the school are interesting. San Antonio is the patron saint of the village and his day is June 13th. The village celebrates for a week before with mass, fireworks, food and dancing. On the 13th, people from around the lake come to spread flowers around the streets and church and to help celebrate with an exceptional fireworks display. Overnight options in San Antonio Tlayacaoan are **Casa Tlayacapan**, *Colon # 100*, ☎ *333-767-0182*, or the **trailer park**, *Allen Lloyd # 149*, ☎ *333-766-0040*, which has a pool, clubhouse, satellite TV and flower gardens. There are numerous restaurants, including an Italian and a fried chicken place.

The traditional village of **Ajijic** is five miles/seven km from Chapala. It has cobblestone streets and adobe brick

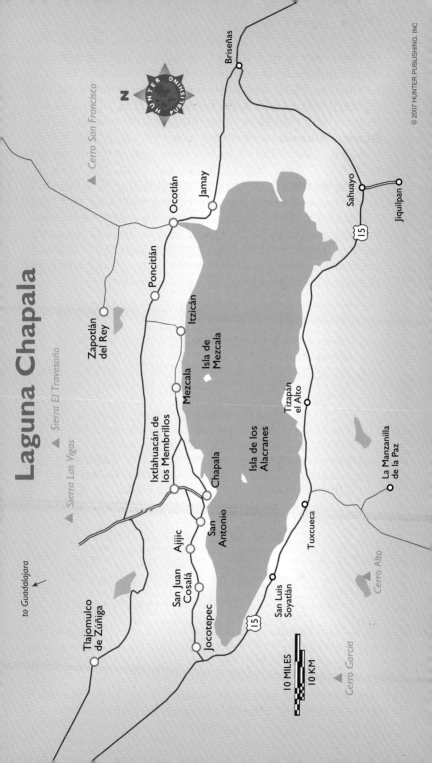

houses, and is now attracting tourists more frequently than Chapala. It is one of the oldest villages in Mexico, founded in 1531. The town has become popular for foreign artists to make their homes. If art is what you are looking for, this is a must stop. In the village is the **Rosario Chapel**, a beautiful stone building with a central bell tower. The plaza has been restored into an attraction. During the rainy season, you can walk to **Tepalo Waterfall**, reached by a trail that goes up the hill at the back of town. It's a fairly long walk that will take about two to three hours. Be aware that during dry season (November to March) there may be little or no water falling. There are numerous places to stay (over 20) and even more places to eat (over 50). Many of the B&Bs in this area are exceptional by world standards.

ARTSY AJIJIC

The annual **film festival** has been held in Ajijic every October/November since 1999. It has received international acclaim. Check at the tourist offices in Guadalajara, Chapala and Ajijc for details.

The **Ajijic Arts Society** has been instrumental in promoting local art. Among their members is Georg Rauch, an Austrian who developed his style in Mexico. **The Galeria Americas, Casa de la Cultura, Galeria Daniel Palma** and **Galeria de Paolo** are all first-class galleries that carry the works of Chapala artists.

The **Music Appreciation Society** promotes and supports concerts, dance performances and chamber music events. They are affiliated with the Degollado Theatre in Guadalajara.

San Juan Cosala is another mile/1.5 km past Ajijic. The big draw here are the hot springs that have temperatures of around 95°F/35°C. They are located at Km 13.5 along the Chapala/Joco Road at the Motel San Juan Cosala. The waters are said to help detoxify the body, although some believe the water is also good for arthritis. I think it is just good to soak in. The town has about 10 little places to stay; food is best around the Piedra Barrenada section of town.

Jocotepec (Place of the Citrus Fruits) is at the most western point of the lake. Although inhabited by locals for centuries, it didn't become a town until 1832. **Señor del Monte Church**, in the center, is worth stopping at. The festival honoring Señor del Monte (with pineapple?) is held on the third Sunday in January. Like the rest of the villages on the lake, Jocotepec has numerous places in which to stay and/or eat.

Poncitlan, 15 miles/25 km east of Chapala along the rail line (no trains running), is laid back and quiet. It has an old church made of stone with a triple bell arch on top. The old wooden door is rugged, thick and arched with stone. Just on the outskirts of the town are the ruins of the **San Jacinto Hacienda**. Also of interest is the **Convent of San Pedro and San Pablo**, built in 1553. On the altar of the convent's church is a sculpture of the Nuestra Señora del Rosario. It was given to the town by King Carlos V of Spain. There are a couple of hotels and B&Bs in town, as well as numerous restaurants. The most popular of these is El Patio on Emilio Carranza #45.

Ocotlan (Place of the Pines) is on the rail line at the eastern end of the lake and at the only natural outlet of the lake. The town was founded in 1530 and the imposing **Misericordia Church** was built in the 1800s. It features twin bell towers and outside niches that hold religious statues. Inside are records of the earthquake that destroyed the town. Another attraction is the **Anthropological Museum**, which contains rock paintings found in the nearby hills and along the northern lakeshore, along with ceramics created after the Spanish arrived. There are more than a dozen hotels in the village.

Jamay is at the eastern end of the lake and has been inhabited for centuries. The main attraction is the monument in the plaza honoring Pope Pius the IX. It stands about 100 ft/30 meters high and is carved from stone. Walking to the **Guadalupe Chapel** on the hill will give you an excellent view of the village and lake. There are three or four places to stay in town. Most people come here for the food; over a dozen good restaurants serve local lake dishes.

La Barca, founded in 1553, is not on the lake but rather on the Chapala Marsh where the Lerma River enters the lake. Birding is good here. It is **La Morena Hacienda**, now restored and made into a museum, that is the draw. The murals on the inside of the hacienda cover about 5,300 square feet/500 square meters of wall space. The paintings are of life around the lake in the 1800s and were done by Gerardo Suarez. He was inspired by the work of Casimiro Castro, whose lithographs published in 1855 were exceptional. You will notice from the mural that there were beggars in Mexico even then. There are about a half-dozen places to stay in town and twice as many restaurants.

ADVENTURES ON FOOT

Stations of the Cross, just out of Ajijic, can be reached by walking. From the center of Ajijic, follow Galeana Street just east of the Ajijic Clinic. Go uphill. Within 15 minutes you will get your first view of the lake. During rainy season, the vegetation is lush and the flowers are numerous. In fact, the trail becomes hard to follow because the vegetation is so dense. However, in dry season the route is hot and dusty. Once past the crosses depicting the life of Christ during his last week on earth, you will come to a small chapel that overlooks the lake. Wear boots on this hike as the terrain is uneven and often has loose rocks. You will also need water, a hat and sun protection. It is about an hour up and half an hour down.

> **BIRD WATCH:** *There are some birds in the Stations of the Cross area; eagles are common.*

ADVENTURES ON WATER

You can rent a boat at the pier to take you out to the islands. Boats cost far less when rented for the day, rather than by the hour. Negotiate with the operators located at the pier.

Isla de los Alacranes (Scorpion Island) is in the middle of the lake. Thankfully, the island is named for its shape, not for the insects. However, due to the appalling condition of the lake, the wildlife on this island has decreased.

DAMMED IF YOU DO

Eleven dams have been built up the Lerma River, a major contributor to the lake. Between the 1970s and 2002, the volume of the lake was reduced by 83%. Because of the diversion of water, a waterfall that once plunged 150 feet/50 meters into the lake has also disappeared. The level of toxic chemicals is up so high that fish are mutating. Phosphorus is 80 times higher than permitted by international standards. This statistical information was taken from www.livinglakes.org/chapala/#biology. If you are interested in the health of this lake, go to the website or contact Sociedad Amogos de Chapala, www.amigos-delago.org, ☎ 376-765-5755 in Chapala.

Mezcala Island is interesting because it has the ruins of a prison. These include stone paths, crumbling walls and photogenic doors and windows. This was once a fort during the 1812-1816 Revolution, when locals took their stance against the Spanish. They fought heroically, trying to win independence for Mexico and finally succumbed to hunger and thirst rather than military defeat.

Transport to Lake.

An account of the fight has been published in the ***Heroic Defense of Mezcala Island***, by Alberto Santoscoy, and is available as an e-book at www.epmassoc.com/catalog/175.php?sp=3. If this link is broken, type the book title in your search engine to find another link.

Bull's Cave on Mezcala has petroglyphs and rock paintings. You can take a boat to this island either from the village of Mezcala or from the pier in Chapala. The island is about 15 miles/25 km from Chapala.

OUTFITTERS/TOUR OPERATORS

Boats to go around the lake can be hired at Chapala ($33 for half an hour for up to eight people; $38 for an hour). Boats to Isla de los Alacrines cost $22 for half an hour and $27 for an hour. Rates go down when hired for longer periods of time.

Horses can also be hired at the pier in Chapala for trips around the dry lakebed. The cost is $10 an hour.

Charter Club Tours, *Plaza Montaña Center, Main Highway and Colon St,* ☎ *376-766-1777, charterclubtours@ hotmail.com,* offers bus tours with bilingual guides. On Wednesday they have a tour around the lake; on Saturday they do a tour of Guadalajara city. Custom tours are available. Prices vary but, as an example, you can do a shopping trip to Guadalajara for just $7 (not counting your purchases). They also know when and where the monarch butterflies appear; ask them about it.

SHOPPING

Artisans near the docks and lake sell souvenirs. However, if you want something special in the way of embroidery or ceramics, try **Galeria de Artesanos de Chapala**, *Av Madero #220,* ☎ *376-765-5487,* which carries a collection of work from local artists.

Isabel's Bazaar, *Hidalgo #76,* has exquisite paintings by Isabel. Also for sale are other items, like Mexican jewelry, but I think Isabel's paintings – many of which are less than $100 – are the best.

PLACES TO STAY

Each village around the lake has a bed and breakfast and a moderate hotel. The ones listed below are just a sampling. Be adventuresome and look for new ones – let me know when you find an exceptional establishment. The hotels in Chapala and Ajijic are numerous – and Ajijic has more places in the moderate price range.

HOTEL PRICE SCALE	
Room price, in US $	
$	up to $20
$$	$21-$50
$$$	$51-100
$$$$	$101-$150
$$$$$	$151-200

Candilejas, *Lopez Cotilla # 363, Chapala,* ☎ *376-765-2279, $,* has 15 basic rooms with private bathroom and fans. This is a very well-kept place, run by an amiable man whose care of the gardens seems to attract guests. Just a block from the bus station, this is an excellent choice in this price range.

Mi Casa es Tu Casa, *Guerrero # 190-A, Chapala,* ☎ *376-765- 5059, $$,* has large, clean rooms with private bathroom and cable TV. There is a laundry service and breakfast is included in the price. Vegetarian cooking is available upon request.

Los Dos B&B, *Calle Rico 191, Jocotepec,* ☎ *376-763-0657, $$$,* has a pool, an artist's studio, extensive gardens and a shuttle bus just outside the house that will take you to and from town. The rooms are large and have private bathrooms. Breakfast, included in the price, is served on the patio.

Nueva Posada, *Donato Guerra #9, Ajijic,* ☎ *376-766-1344, $$$,* is a luxuriously restored hacienda. It has huge arched windows, high ceilings, ornate chandeliers and antique furniture. The stone staircase leading to some rooms is an amazing work of masonry. There are lush

North from Puerto Vallarta

potted plants in every hall and a stone walkway leads to the pool that is hidden by flowering vegetation. The restaurant has a huge rubber tree in its center. The 17 rooms, located on three floors, are decorated with watercolors by local artists. This is an exceptional place.

Hotel Real de Chapala, *Paseo del Prado #20, Ajijic,* ☎ *376-766-0014, $$$,* has 79 rooms with air conditioning and private bathrooms. The hotel also has a restaurant, a bar, a pool, two tennis courts and a volleyball area. Everyone I spoke with recommended eating at the rooftop patio and restaurant because the food, service, prices and views can't be beaten. The rooms have air conditioning, night tables and a sitting area.

Quinta Quetzalcoatle B&B, *Zaragoza #307, Chapala,* ☎ *376-765-3653, $$$,* has nine rooms, some of which are wheelchair-accessible. Each room has a shower and bathtub, a sitting area and reading lights. They are also tastefully finished. There is a hot tub and pool on site.

> **FACT FILE:** *Quinta Quetzalcoatle B&B is where DH Lawrence wrote his famous novel, The Plumed Serpent. All you wannabe novelists may get some inspiration by staying here.*

Villa Monte Carlo, *Hidalgo #296, Chapala,* ☎ *376-765-2024, $$$,* is the old house built by S. Crow (see *Walking Tour,* page 222) and has 48 renovated rooms with air conditioning and private bathrooms. If history is your thing, you may want to try this place.

Lake Chapala Inn, *Paseo Ramon Corona #23, Chapala,* ☎ *376-765-3070 or 800-501-9446, $$$,* has rooms with private bathrooms, king-sized beds, TVs, telephones,

© Lake Chapala Inn

hair dryers and bedside reading lamps. There is a flowered terrace overlooking the lake and a tiny pool in the garden. There is also laundry service, a library and a music room.

PLACES TO EAT

Acapulquito Zone, *Ramon Corona,* ☎ *376-765-4595,* is located along the lakeshore, where numerous restaurants and bars are found. At Acapulquito's you will get delicious seafood for around $10 per meal. This is a favorite of ex-pats.

LAKE CHAPALA FISH DISHES

- **Carp roe** is whitefish.
- **Birria** is catfish.
- **Charales** – Charal is a small fish caught in the lake that has been used to make a traditional dish for hundreds of years.
- **Caldo michi** is fish soup.

Restaurant Cazadores, *Braniff House, Ramon Corona #18,* ☎ *376-765-2162,* is across from the lake. Save this elegant restaurant for a special lunch or dinner. The waiters are in black ties and vests, the food is good and the meal will take a few hours to consume.

The Beer Garden, *Ramon Corona,* ☎ *376-765-3817,* opened in 1929 and has been a popular restaurant ever since. There is a rooftop patio where you can enjoy the sunset while sipping a margarita or a glass of wine before the disco starts. It is located at the far end of town, along what used to be the shore and across from the Nido.

Home of the Trout, *Paseo Corona # 22,* ☎ *376-765-4606,* is closed Monday. On Wednesday when they feature live music, reservations are necessary. The special on that day is chicken Cordon Bleu, which includes a margarita or white wine, nachos appetizer and dessert – all for $10. Fridays they offer a steak and seafood combination for $12, including all the extras that you gct on Wednesdays. They also serve things like stuffed squid or frog legs.

Mariscos Guicho's y Hijos, ☎ *376-765-3232, at the Chapala pier,* serves the best seafood in town. They also have some gourmet dishes like frog legs, caviar tacos and seafood soup.

El Arbol del Café (Coffee Tree), *Calle Hidalgo #236,* ☎ *376-765-3908*, is the place to find a good cheesecake to go with your afternoon coffee. It is fun to hang out here.

La Casa del Waffle, *Chapala-Jocotepec #75, next to Thrifty Ice cream (which serves Starbucks coffee), no phone*, is open 10 am-midnight every day except Tuesday. Come here for a late breakfast and, while sipping on a coffee, decide which of the 12 flavors of big Belgian waffles you'd like. Options include things like mango and strawberry. The kids' favorite (and mine) is the Winnie the Pooh waffle, with honey. All meals are about $7.

Ajijic Grill, *Morelos #5,* ☎ *376-766-2458*, in Ajijic, offers a good Japanese dinner. They have a sushi bar – like a salad bar, only with sushi. They also have lunch specials that include dishes such as tempura, tonkatsu, yakitori and kushi age. Other non-Japanese dishes are quail and lobster.

Mom's Deli, *Hidalgo #79-I, Plaza Maskaras,* ☎ *376-765-5719,* has a different lunch special every day starting at 11:30 am. As an example, they have French dip sandwich or roast pork on Mondays and meatloaf on Wednesdays. The cost is $6 per serving and the meals are offered until the food is gone, so get here early.

Valencianas, *Morelos #209,* ☎ *376-765-4182,* has the best pizza in town. This is a rare find, as fish is the most common meal in the area.

Chicken Little, *Av Hidalgo # 101-B,* ☎ *376-765-4399*, is the most popular chicken-aria in town. There is a small seating area at the restaurant, but most patrons take the food with them and snack on the beach or at the docks.

NIGHTLIFE

Because the lake has attracted many artists, the area is alive with workshops, theater performances, readings and art shows. Pick up local publications for information on these events.

South from Puerto Vallarta

The Costalegre:
Puerto Vallarta to Barra de Navidad

The Costalegre stretches 80 miles/150 km south from the Bay of Banderas to Barra de Navidad. This section of coast was decreed by the president in the 1990s to be an ecological tourist corridor. He did not want it to be developed into another sprawl of luxury hotels. The corridor is bordered by Puerto Vallarta in the north, Colima in the east and Manzanillo in the south. Although there are a few huge estates and hotels along this stretch, most of the area remains remote, dotted only with isolated fishing villages. If you are totally self-sufficient, you can camp in some of these villages and beaches. However, I do not recommend this because the robberies in this part of the country have often been violent.

© Jacus/Dreamstime

Besides sunning, surfing and wildlife viewing, windsurfing is good along this stretch of coastline. If you are independent and have your own car, you could spend a year exploring all the coves, bays and villages and never see them all.

> **WARNING:** Because of the curves and narrowness of the road, do not drive along here at night. Large transport trucks use this highway and often drive in the middle of the road, squeezing any little guy onto the non-existent shoulder and down the bank.

To get here, take local buses from town to town (carry a map – the one I used was Mexico Pacific Coast by International Travel Maps, Vancouver), or drive.

Hotelito Desconocido, ☎ *322-223-0293 or 800-851-1143 from the US, http://hotelito.com,* is 60 miles/90 km south of Puerto Vallarta and three miles/4.5 km toward the coast from La Crus de Loreto along Highway 220. The hotel is one of Mexico's most ecologically friendly resorts. It offers an all-inclusive package that costs anywhere from $500 to $650 a day, depending on the season and/or a special sale. The packages include pick-up from Puerto Vallarta airport, four nights and five days for two people, breakfasts and dinners, tea and fruits all day, introductory use of the spa plus one massage and one body mud treatment, one mermaid bath and one facial, one horse trip, free use of kayaks and a trip to see the turtles. This is a luxury vacation geared toward the ecologically sensitive.

VIEW TURTLES HATCHING

Every August to February, Olive Ridley turtles lay their eggs on the beach here and, six weeks later, the eggs hatch. Because most sea turtles have three different egg-laying sessions two to six weeks apart, viewing these events is possible for almost six months. There is a biologist available at the hotel to answer questions and to help you find the turtles during their laying/hatching times.

The bungalows, called *palafitos*, are located over the estuary. They are constructed with natural products; the support beams are wooden poles, the walls are bamboo and the roof is thatch. Wood floors complement the thatched roof. The furniture is mostly rattan and the walls are decorated with antiques and local art. There is solar power for electrical use and candles are used for light at night. Each room has a ceiling fan, a mosquito net over the bed, a safe deposit box, a private bathroom and a bamboo shower stall. Bathrobes, soap, shampoo and body lotion is supplied. Breakfast

© Hotelito Desconodido

and supper are served buffet style in the palapa hut overlooking the lagoon and lunch is served at the smaller beach club. Activities include wildlife-viewing, horseback riding, mountain biking, hiking, windsurfing, rowing, canoeing, volleyball and billiards. All of the equipment is supplied by the hotel.

> **BIRD WATCH:** *Birders can cross to the estuary where the bird life is rich. There is also a viewing platform for birders.*

The health spa has a steam bath, Jacuzzi, showers and massage chambers. They also offer specialized treatments such as aromatherapy, Swedish massage, Shiatsu massage, reflexology and a mud bath treatment that is said to stimulate metabolic functions and rejuvenate the skin. There is also the mermaid's bath or stone therapy (rocks are used to remove the stress from your body).

Tomatlan

This little village of 10,000 people is a good place to stop and shop if you are heading back to the beach roads. There are numerous places to eat and a few places to stay. If you are interested in wide-mouth bass fishing, then a trip to the dam is suggested.

ADVENTURES ON WATER

Cajon de Peñas Dam is the largest in the state and has a capacity to hold 186 billion gallons of water. This dam supplies water to Tomatlan and generates power for the area. Fishing for tilapia, bass, prawns and *bagre*, a catfish belonging to the *Doradidae* family (the species originated in Peru), is popular. Some people collect the tegolobo mollusk that lives here, which is known for its flavor. A family living near the dam and just off the road will rent you a boat for about $15 an hour. They will also prepare a meal for you. If you are self-sufficient, you can camp near the water. To get to the dam from Tomatlan, return to Highway 200 and go north (turn right at the highway) and follow it to the Km 130 sign. Turn onto an unpaved road toward Viejo Santiago and follow it for 11 miles/18 km to the dam. There are signs indicating both the dam and the village of Viejo Santiago.

Playa Chalacatepec is half an hour from Tomatlan by car and six miles/nine km from the highway. Playa

Chalacatepec encompasses three beaches in all. The north beach has gentle waves, making it good for swimming. It has a long expanse of sand protected by a rocky point at the center, where you can fish,

© Papelius

watch for birds and find little coves in which to sit. The southern span of beach has strong surf. The entire beach is an exceptional stretch of land that is seething with birdlife. The remains of a pirate ship that sits on the sand here has become part of a legend that says there is gold at the bottom of the ocean, not far from the ship. From Tomatlan, return to Highway 200, turn south (left) and follow it for about 17 miles/28 km until you see a sign indicating Playa Chalacatepec. Turn toward the ocean.

ADVENTURES IN CULTURE

The white **mission church** on the plaza was constructed between 1769 and 1774 and the bell in the tower is dated from 1730. Inside, two statues date back about 150 years and are considered exceptional pieces of art.

La Peñita Pintada (rock paintings) is along one of the small tributaries of the Tomatlan River. To get there, ask a taxi driver to take you to "La Pintada." The fare should be less than $5 for the one-way trip. He will take you to a spot on the Tomatlan River and you must walk from there. As you walk up the river, watch for a rocky outcrop and the painted wall that is filled with ancient hieroglyphics. The paintings are on the ceiling of the outcrop, 30-45 feet/10-15 meters above ground. The rock itself was hand-sculpted so that the paintings are protected from sun and rain. Some believe these paintings are very old, around 10,000 years, and like those found in Spain.

PLACE TO STAY & EAT

Hotel San Miguel, *Galeana #52*, ☎ *322-298-5522, $$*, has large, clean rooms with large windows, cable TV, air conditioning, tiled floors and sitting areas. The hotel has a pool, a restaurant, a bar and Internet connections.

Quemaro

Quemaro is home to little more than Las Alamandas, a luxury hotel that has been featured in prestigious magazines like *Town & Country* and *Travel + Leisure*. The resort is a little way outside of the village.

PLACE TO STAY

Las Alamandas, *San Patricio Melaque #201,* ☎ *322-285-5500 or 888-882-9616 from the US, www.alamandas.com*, is an exclusive retreat on the beach. The 11 villas, which cost between $390 and $790 each night, are surrounded by 1,500 hectares of jungle. Each is designed in a unique Mexican style and decorated with artistic ceramic tiles. The villas have wooden shutters, private balconies, private kitchen areas and oversized tubs in the bathroom. The furniture is high-quality rattan with fuchsia covers and the walls are decorated with tasteful artwork. Benches are hidden in the gardens and flowered walkways lead between the villas. The service is outstanding. If you want a romantic drink while enjoying the sunset, the staff will take you to a point overlooking the ocean, open a bottle of champagne and ask when to pick you up. Then they will disappear until your pickup time. For leisure activities there is a health spa, horses for riding and tennis courts. You can also go cycling or take a river excursion and look for wildlife. Meals, not included in the price of the room, can run about $200 a day extra. However, you get to order

© Las Alamandas Resort

from a gourmet selection that is exceptional.

Airport pick-up is included in the price. Those with their own plane can use the 3,300-ft landing strip. However, don't arrive at the gate without reservations, because the guards will not permit you to enter.

Chamela Bay

On the road to Barra de Navidad along Highway 200, at Km 72 El Super, is a road that leads to Chamela Bay and a delightful little fishing village (the turn off is signed Km 72/El Super). The bay holds four beaches referred to as Playas Perula, Fortuna, Chamela and Rosadas. The bay is dotted with small islands, some vegetated, some just large rocks with a name. There is little at the turnoff except a few stores, but the bay has some low-key places to stay, including a couple of RV parks. There are lots of places to eat.

ADVENTURES ON WATER

The best **snorkeling** is from Playa Perula, a wide expanse of gentle water and soft sand. Boats along the bay will take you around the islands to good snorkeling spots for $15 an hour. If you want to go for longer, a deal can be worked out. There are many palapa huts offering fish dinners for sale along this stretch.

Snorkelers observing undersea life.

Playa Fortuna is where the waves get a bit stronger, so body surfing and windsurfing can be good. There are also a few hotels and restaurants along this beach.

ADVENTURES IN NATURE

Cumbres de Cuixmala Reserve is a nature preserve bound on the north by the San Nicolas River, on the south by the Cuixmala River, and on the west by the ocean. The reserve goes about six miles/10 km inland. It has both deciduous and semi-deciduous forests that house a myriad of birds and animals. There are over 1,120 vascular plant species, some of which are considered threatened.

A LESSON IN BIOLOGY

A vascular plant is one that has xylem and phloem cells to conduct water, nutrients and photosynthetic products in flowering plants, ferns and fern allies. Xylem cells transport water and nutrients to the leaves and the phloem cells transport photosynthetic products to the roots.

About 270 bird species use the reserve, 40% of which are migratory. Threatened bird residents include the yellow-headed parrot and the wood nymph. The reserve is also a healthy area for crocodiles.

CROC ALERT

One incident between a crocodile and human has occurred here. A fisherman was diving with a spear and he carried a sack of fish over his shoulder. He was bitten in the foot by a croc. It is believed that the croc was not after the man, but the fish.

Birding on the numerous small islands around the bay is good. **Isla Pajarera** is home to brown boobies and is also a good diving spot.

> **AUTHOR NOTE:** *The closest place offering dive gear rentals is Melaque, 45 miles/72 km south of Chamila.*

Isla Cocinas has a small birding beach. Watersports, especially windsurfing, are popular. **San Andres, Novilla, Esfinge, San Pedro, San Agustin** and **La Negrita** islands all provide wildlife-viewing opportunities. You can kayak around these islands (see *Immersion Adventures*, page 255, for information).

Chamela Bay.

PLACES TO STAY

A one-lane village follows the shore of the ocean. Because finding places does not require directions, the hotels/motels don't offer addresses.

HOTEL PRICE SCALE
Room price, in US $
$ . . . . up to $20
$$ . . . . $21-$50
$$$ $51-100
$$$$ . . . . $101-$150
$$$$$ $151-200

Don Pillos RV and Tenting, *$*, *no phone*, is at the south end of the bay at El Negrito. The $20 daily rate includes use of washrooms and showers. There are a few shaded areas to park an RV, but most are in the sun. The gate is locked at night.

Bungalows Mayar Chamela, ☎ *315-333-9711*, *$*, in Chamela, has 18 rooms with kitchens, private bathrooms and fans. The site is clean and has a pool. This is a two-star property.

Hotel Vagabundo, *Independencia and Ballena*, ☎ *315-333-9736*, *http://www.costalegre.ca/perula_Places_To _Stay.htm*, *$$*, in Perula, has simple rooms with private bathrooms, fans and tiled floors. A couple of bungalows also have kitchen areas for cooking. For added comfort, there is a swimming pool.

Playa Dorada, ☎ *315-333-9710, $$,* in Perula, has bungalows with two double beds, ceiling fans, bathrooms with hot water, full kitchens and small living rooms. The rooms in the main, three-story building have one double and one single bed, fans, private bathrooms and small sitting areas. There is a pool and the grounds are well shaded.

Centro Vacacional Chamela, ☎ *315-285-5224, $$,* is a clean place with 22 rooms right on the beach. They do not take reservations. There is a pool and well-maintained gardens. This is the best moderately priced place near Chamela (turn off at mile marker 66.5 on Highway 200).

Paraiso Costalegre Resort, ☎ *315-333-9778, $$$,* is at the old Villa Polynesia site. It has 11 cabins, two larger houses and 16 RV spots, as well as tenting. To guarantee shade, RVs park on a pad under a palapa roof ($12 per night). Shade trees dot the property. The rooms are inviting and have a private bathroom and comfortable beds. There is a large sign on Highway 200 pointing the way to the resort.

Villa Vista Hermosa, ☎ *877-845-5278 in the US, www. villavistahermosa.com, $$$$$,* sits on five acres on a hill overlooking the bay. The flowered grounds are well tended; potted plants surround the fountains and pool. If you prefer the beach to a pool, use the private cove just below the resort. Each villa is exquisite, featuring large beds in big rooms, tiled floors, brick walls, Mexican furnishings and air conditioning. There are numerous patios and hideaways where guests can sit. All meals are included in the price and you are even invited to sneak into the kitchen for a midnight snack. Wine is served with dinner. Gourmet meals are made using fresh fish, chicken or shrimp.

© Vista Villa Hermosa

Pick-up at the airport in Manzanillo or Puerto Vallarta can be arranged.

PLACES TO EAT

Restaurant Tejeban, ☎ *315-333-9705,* is at El Super, on the south side of the Chamela River. **La Viuda Restaurant** is on the north side of the river at Km 64. On the other side of the bridge is **Don Lupe's Mariscos**. **Restaurant Tejeban** is a truck stop where chicken and hamburgers are the mainstay of the day, while Don Lupe's Mariscos sells seafood. I have no information about La Viuda except that it has been around for quite some time.

Beachfront palapa restaurants between Playa Fortuna in the north and Playa El Negrito in the south serve mostly seafood. You can expect to pay between $5 and $10 for large meals and much less for snacks. Beer runs $1.50-$2 for a large bottle.

Costa Careyes

This small bay has gentle waves and is good for swimming. At the village of Careyes, the shore becomes rocky with tiny stretches of white sand. Birding is good here.

ADVENTURES IN NATURE

In 2002, the Mexican National Commission for Protected Areas set aside 17 marine turtle refuges as protected areas. One of these places is **Teopa Beach**, at the north end of the bay, where the workers have collected, protected and hatched over half a million eggs so far. The Mexican division of the World Wildlife Federation has joined forces with the National Commission to give these areas the highest form of wildlife protection in the Mexican system. For more information visit the World Wildlife Federation website, www.wwf.org.

ADVENTURE ON HORSEBACK

Costa Careyes Polo Club, *no phone,* was established in 1989. It is three miles south of the Costa Careyes Resort. The greens are open mid-November to mid-April and the fees are $70 per game during the day, but $50 for early morning sessions. The club has two fields and games are played most weekends. Beginners and pros are both welcome to play and/or take lessons. There are about 40 horses available for rent to play the game.

Cuitzmala

Cuitzmala is 25 miles/44 km south of Careyes along Highway 200 and is the location of the **Goldsmith family mansion**. The Goldsmiths are descendants of the rich Bolivian A. Patiño, the first Indian since the days of the Inca to become rich. He made his money from mining. With things looking a bit shaky in Bolivia, Patiño moved his family to France and got into banking. Family fortunes grew. The mansion at Cuitzmala is just one of many owned by this family. The Alamandas Resort, just out of Puerto Vallarta, is also owned by them. Access to the beach near the Goldsmith mansion is restricted because part of the beach has been set aside as a turtle preserve.

PLACES TO STAY

Casitas de La Flores, *Km 53.5 on the Barra de Navidad road,* ☎ *315-6510-240, www.mexicoboutiquehotels.com/thecareyes/index.html,* $$$$$+, has brightly colored Mexican pueblos that can be purchased or rented. They come with one, two or three bedrooms and fully equipped kitchens, air conditioning, cable TV and telephones. The tiled bathrooms are spacious, the balconies have views and there are plunge pools to soak in. The courtyards are decorated with exotic plants. This is a luxury five-star establishment, where the rent starts at $900 a day during low season. High-end pueblos with five bedrooms and seven bathrooms cost $2,000 a day.

El Careyes Beach Resort, *Km 53.5 on the Barra de Navidad road,* ☎ *315-351-0000 or 877-278-8018 from US and 866-818-8342 from Canada,* charges $225 to $550 per night for a pueblo-styled room that has air conditioning, cable TV, a private balcony and either a garden or an ocean view. Some rooms have private plunge pools, while others have an indoor Jacuzzi. On the property is a meandering pool, shaded in places by palm trees. There is also a full-service spa, a restaurant, a bar, tennis courts and a workout and weight room. Equipment is provided for

© Producciones ViVa

watersports, including boogie boarding or kayaking. Horses and bicycles are also available for guests to use. You can even play a game of polo. El Careyes is another exotic place and the only one tucked into this little bay.

TURTLE TENDING

The beach near the Careyes resort is where the Carey turtles, now endangered, come to lay their eggs. The conservation practices around this event are strict and only respectful visitors are permitted entrance to the beach to watch the laying or hatching of the eggs. The Careyes Beach Resort will escort those interested in seeing the turtles (see above). However, any beach where a Carey hawksbill turtle decides to come ashore is now under strict protection according to the Mexican National Commission for Protected Areas and this beach is part of a preserve.

PLACES TO EAT

Playa Rosa is a waterfront restaurant that serves good quesadillas and lobster (in season). Meals cost between $6 and $12. No waterskiing, Jet Skiing or spear fishing is permitted in the area around the restaurant. Open noon until 10:30 pm.

Tenacatita

This village is five miles/eight km off the main highway toward the ocean. Turn toward the ocean at the Km 30 sign. Going in the opposite direction leads to Agua Caliente. The village of **Rebalcito** (with hotel) is two miles/three km before the beach. Some travelers stay here and walk down to the water.

Tenacatita is a tiny village that has a few palapa huts along the beach selling seafood and beer. The beach is two miles/three km long and is good for snorkeling and swimming. It is also popular for catching lobster, octopus, crabs and snails.

> **LOCAL LINGO:** *The name* Tenacatita *means "colored rocks" in Nahuatl. The town was named after the reddish rocks at the south end of the bay. It is believed that locals used to cut pieces of stone from the rock to build into their homes.*

Because indigenous people have lived here for centuries, it is possible to find pieces of pottery and figurines in the hills near the bay, especially after a heavy rain when the water washes away the earth.

ADVENTURES ON WATER

At the mangrove swamp near the lagoon behind the isthmus and Playa la Boca, *pangas* can be hired to take you upriver in search of wildlife. See *Tour Operators*, below.

> **AUTHOR NOTE:** *Playa la Boca has knee-deep black sand and lots of sand fleas, especially at night.*

The bay is one of the best in the country for **snorkeling** because of the calm water. The sport is especially popular at a spot called **The Aquarium**, located to the right of the village and over the hill. This route will also get you to **Playa Mora**, which has a colony of black coral. Black coral is now protected and only a small amount is harvested each year. It is recommended that you not purchase black coral jewelry so that even less will be harvested. Damselfish are often seen in this area.

> **FACT FILE:** *It takes black coral a hundred years to grow half an inch.*

Playa de Oro is known for the American steamship (named *The Golden Gate*) that sank on July 27, 1862, killing 250 people and losing $1.5 million in gold. The vessel caught fire and sank just offshore. Only 80 people survived. Two years after the accident, a few cases of gold were recovered. In the 1960s, the ship was found and salvaged. It was just 50 yards from the shore. It is believed that a lot of the gold is still out there and, occasionally, someone finds a piece washed up on shore. Look for some. This is a popular spot for snorkeling and diving. Diving gear and guides can be hired in Malaque.

ADVENTURES IN NATURE

A walk along this shore will bring you to a huge rock at the water's edge that looks a bit like a mini Macchu Piccu. There you will find a small cave inhabited by **bats**.

> **WARNING:** Be careful when in the water near the cave, as the waves are very strong.

OUTFITTERS/TOUR OPERATORS

The **Palapa la Sirenita restaurant** has boats for trips into the mangroves that cost $25. The excursion will take a few hours.

PLACES TO STAY

Remember, no area code is needed when making a local call.

HOTEL PRICE SCALE	
Room price, in US $	
$	up to $20
$$	$21-$50
$$$	$51-100
$$$$	$101-$150
$$$$$	$151-200

Playa Tenacatita Trailer Park, *Av Tenacatita, across from Hotel Paraiso,* ☎ *333-115-5406 (cell),* has 15 RV spaces with water, sewer and electricity. They cost $15 a night, with discounts for longer stays. The gate is kept locked at night.

Hotel Paraiso de Tenacatita, *Av Tenacatita # 32,* ☎ *315-353-9623, www.costalegre.ca,* $, has 13 rather small and plain rooms that have either a fan or air conditioning. They are located around an inner courtyard. Look for the bright orange exterior.

Hotel Costa Alegre, *El Rebalsito,* ☎ *315-351-5121,* $, has simple rooms with air conditioning and fans. There is a restaurant on site.

Blue Bay Village, *Km 20.7 on Highway 200,* ☎ *315-351-5020 or 800-258-3229,* is a five-star all-inclusive resort. It has over 200 rooms and suites; rooms go for $110 during low season and suites run $490 during high season. There are two restaurants (one buffet, one à la carte), four bars, a disco, a snack bar, pool, sauna, tennis courts, a gym and an open-air theater that has nightly shows. The hotel also offers horseback riding, boats and watersports equipment for rent.

> **FACT FILE:** *Blue Bay Village is called Los Angeles Locos by the local population. The original owners were so rich that, to the locals, they seemed to be wasting money coming to this isolated spot, hence the name.*

Las Villitas Club Deportivo, *Av Tenacatita # 376,* ☎ *315-355-5354, $$$,* has large and small bungalows with kitchens. Each bungalow has a full stove, fridge, stools, TV, tiled floors, white walls and fans. The larger bunga-lows have sitting ar-eas separated from the bedrooms by a curtained window. The place is funky and painted in every bright color imagin-able. However, every-thing is very clean. Guests can rent mountain bikes.

Punta Serena, *Km 20 on Highway 200, beside Blue Bay Village,* ☎ *315-351-5100 or 800-551-2558, www.puntaserena.com, $$$$,* is an adults-only holistic spa re-sort with 26 rooms. According to *Spa Magazine,* Punta Serena offers "a heaven of tranquility and true personal pampering... where you can free your mind, spirit and soul with a (clothing optional) stroll along the beach." I agree that the hotel is first class. It offers treatment pro-grams that include facials, body wraps, exfoliation treat-ments, massages, Mexican sweat lodges, manicures and pedicures. There are two hot tubs, a spa with sauna, a steam room, an indoor Jacuzzi and a fully equipped gym.

PLACES TO EAT

There are numerous eateries along the beach, and more restaurants at Rebalcito. **Restaurant Yoly** is recommended for good Mexican food if you want to walk the two miles/three km up to the highway and on to the village of Rebalcito. There are no taxis available. I have no phone listing for this restaurant. However, prices are under $10 for a seafood dinner.

In Tenacatita, **Chito** and **Fiesta Mexicana** *(no phones)* are close to one another. Both offer Mexican food for reasonable prices.

Restaurant Palapa la Sirenita, ☎ *315-351-5208,* has dinner specials on Tuesday (*tomales*) and Friday (*birra de chivo*, or goat meat) for $8 a meal. The cozy place with just 10 tables has been in business for almost 20 years.

Cihuatlan

This town of 20,000 people is 22 miles/33 km from Barra de Navidad. Besides visiting the plaza, golfing at Tamarindo and walking the Marabasco River, there isn't much else to do here.

ADVENTURES ON FOOT

■ HIKING

At the side of the **Marabasco River** about four miles/six km from town is a painted rock with circular engravings on it. The rock sits in the middle of a field. Walk up the river (the same side as the town) to reach it. You can also ask a taxi to take you here, but the river is good for swimming, so I prefer to walk.

■ GOLF

El Tamarindo resort has an 18-hole, par 72, 6,682-yard course that features some of the most dramatic golfing scenery in Mexico. After the ninth hole, players can stop for a drink at the snack bar before going down the shallow green to a stretch of rocky coastline. There, they play three holes along the shore and end at a par five on the last hole. Signs warn you not to go into the bush looking for golf balls as snakes and other dangerous creatures inhabit the brush. The cost to play is $150 for green fees and cart and $25 for the mandatory caddy. A tip is extra and expected.

ADVENTURES IN NATURE

Playa Peña Blanca, at the north end of the beach that is south of the village, is under protection when turtle eggs hatch. You will need special permission to pass this way during that time. For more information about the protection, visit www.wwf.org.

The white rock just off shore that is covered in bird-dung gives the place its name. The bird most commonly seen here is the blue-footed booby. This is also a popular dive site because of the canyons and the artificial reef that was created in 1996.

La Vaca Mountain is a scenic spot along the beach, but it is inundated with ATVs every day from 9 am to 3 pm. For a thrill in speed, you can join a tour that starts at Peña Blanca and goes for three hours along the beach, through a river, around the mountain and back again. The faster you go, the better. The machine (Honda TRX-250), a scarf, helmet and goggles are included in the cost of the tour.

OUTFITTERS/TOUR OPERATORS

Off Road & Trails Adventures, *Rancho Peña Blanca,* ☎ *315-333-1707*, offers a tour to La Vaca by high speed ATV. Call for prices.

Playa Manzanilla

This is not to be confused with the larger center of Manzanilla, a little farther south. To get here, turn at

Km 13 off Highway 200 and follow the dirt road down a mile. Those without a car can walk from the highway. The beach has gentle waves and palapa food places (there are also lots of restaurants in the village). There are numerous guesthouses for rent if you want to stay awhile, plus a few smaller, basic hotels for shorter stays. Internet access is available. This is turning into another desired destination.

ADVENTURES ON FOOT

Take the **waterfall hike** starting at the footbridge on the road going to Campo. Turn left at the river and follow the trail past an odd tower with a thatch roof. Continue along the road/trail that runs beside the river to a goat farm with a gate across the road. Pass through, but be certain to close the gate. Once back on the river follow a small trail on the left or walk on the riverbed if there isn't too much water. The walking gets a bit rugged farther in, and eventually you will come to a pool with high rocks around it. The waterfall is at the far end. It is never dry, although in summer it is just a trickle.

ADVENTURES ON WATER

For a tour of the bay see Pancho, Alex or Monty at **Restaurant Fiesta Mexicana** in Tenacatita, ☎ *315-338-6316*. They can take you out to view dolphins, turtles and whales (in season). The cost is $30 per hour for the boat and guide. The boat will take up to six people. Anglers should also contact the guides at the Fiesta.

ADVENTURES IN NATURE

The **mangrove swamp** in this area is being studied by Earthwatch. The mangroves here play a role in preventing erosion and damage to the coral reefs. They provide housing for fish and crocodiles and migratory and residential birds. Especially important in this region is the boat-billed heron. The delicate environment of the mangrove is being threatened by tourism due to the demand for more luxurious hotels.

DOING GOOD

If you are interested in preserving the area, learning about it, or if you would like to join a study group coordinated and led by university professors, visit www.earthwatch.org. If you are observing on your own, be sensitive to the environment. Don't litter, stay on the trails and use muscle-powered vehicles.

ADVENTURES ON HORSEBACK

Horseback riding is possible along the beach for $10 an hour. Daniel Hallas, ☎ *315-351-5059,* is the owner of the horses and he can be e-mailed at dlh3648@yahoo.com. He also offers a ride to the waterfall (see previous page) for the same price.

OUTFITTER/TOUR OPERATOR

Immersion Adventures, *at La Manzanilla (third house on the right),* ☎ *315-351-5341, or at the Campamento Ecologico on the beach walking toward Boca de Iguanas,* has tours for all skill levels. A very active itinerary includes four or more hours of paddling and an hour of snorkeling. Duration can be adjusted to suit your energy level. Birding is also offered. Trips cost about $115 per person, per day, and includes all kayaking gear. If you want to tour without a guide, you can rent kayaks by the hour. Organized trips run to Tenacatita Bay, where there is good snorkeling over the fringe coral reef. From the bay they enter La Vena mangrove estuary, where birding is big.

Tenacatita Bay.

This trip from La Manzanilla takes about 10 hours and costs $37. The **Careyes Bay** trip is good for strong paddlers who can hold their own for a few hours. Parts of the bay have high cliffs and rugged landscape. Good kayak control is required. They stop at a tiny beach called Esmeralda, where the group snorkels. This nine-hour trip costs $100 per person, per day.

SHOPPING

La Manzanilla is developing into an artistic community with numerous ex-pats. I was surprised at the number of artists working here. If you want to take home something unique, a piece of original art may be just the thing. The talent here is amazing. There are numerous art shops in the village where you can browse.

ARTISTS TO LOOK FOR

Sylvain Voyer is a Canadian landscape artist who has been active in Canada for years. He has worked with the Canadian Artists Representation, Alberta Art Foundation and Medici Art Foundation. He also taught art at the University of Alberta. Sylvain went to Mexico to paint in 1988 and had a major exhibition in 1992 of his work that portrayed Maya ruins of the Yucatán as the subject. He later started painting scenes of the west coast of Mexico. His list of commissioned paintings is long.

German **Sara Henze** was influenced by her father, an abstract artist. She studied at the School for Visual Art and Design in Cologne. After a few distractions (school and kids) she returned to painting. She does a mix of abstract and realistic portraits in bold and muted colors. You can find her works in La Manzanilla.

I know little about **Stephanie Doucette**, but she does a lot of Mexican portraits, some of which incorporate mystical figures.

Ron Stock does faux-naif style paintings that have tremendous detail in simple scenes.

Carlos Kieling offers an assortment of designs featuring everything from Van Gogh to Shakespeare and abstract t-shirt designs. He also likes to paint wildlife.

Jack Rutherford, an American painter and writer, paints pieces that are influenced by Picasso's style. His work is varied and his exhibitions numerous.

PLACES TO STAY

One-star **Posada del Cazador**, *Maria Asuncion #183*, ☎ *315-351-5000, $,* is at the north end of town. It has basic rooms with fan and private bathroom.

HOTEL PRICE SCALE	
Room price, in US $	
$	up to $20
$$	$21-$50
$$$	$51-100
$$$$	$101-$150
$$$$$	$151-200

Hotel Puesta del Sol, *Calle Playa Blanca #94*, ☎ *315-351-5033, $$,* has basic but clean rooms with private bathrooms and fans. The rooms are located around a central patio. There is a porch with a fridge, sink and gas stove for guests to use. There is also a pool. The hotel is just one block from the beach at the south end of town.

Posada Tonala, *Av Maria Asuncion #75*, ☎ *315-351-5474, www.posadatonala.com, $$,* is a tiny hotel with rooms on two floors built around a common sitting area. Each room has a double bed, TV, fan or air conditioning, tiled floor, bed lamp, desk and private bathroom with hot water. Run by a German couple, the place is sparkling

clean and right on the beach. There are also three spacious bungalows for rent that are just as clean and cozy as the rooms. They cost between $25 and $60, depending on the number of guests. Monthly rates are available.

Eileen's, ☎ *315-351-5383, eizack1@yahoo.com, $$,* has two nicely decorated rooms with private bathrooms and double beds. The rooms open onto a garden patio furnished with deck chairs. Full kitchen facilities are available for guest use. The house is decorated with artistic tiles, the halls are dotted with potted plants and the building is spotless. This is a unique guesthouse with exceptionally low rates. Guests get the luxury of eating meals cooked at the owner's cooking school.

Calypso Hotel, *Calle Anden de la Calechosa # 10,* ☎ *315-351-5124, $$,* is a neat and tidy little place with eight rooms and three bungalows. The rooms have private bathrooms, desks, fans and tiled floors. The décor is plain but clean.

Hotel Fiesta Mexicana, *Km 8.5 on highway to Melaque/ Barra de Navidad,* ☎ *314-333-2181, $$$,* has 194 rooms in a Mediterranean-style hotel. Each room has air conditioning, private balcony, TV, private shower, iron and board, and telephone. There is a restaurant, a bar, a coffee shop, a gift shop, private parking and a money exchange. The food in the restaurant is acceptable.

Casa Maguey*, ☎ *315-351-5012, www.casamaguey.com, $$$,* has three bungalows fully equipped and ready to move into. Just bring food and drink. There is tile on the floors and rattan furniture throughout. Each bungalow has a private bathroom and a separate living room and is surrounded by gardens. There are no pets allowed.

La Casa Maria, *Calle Los Angeles Locos and Concha Molida,* ☎ *315-351-5044, www.lacasamaria.com, $$$$$,* has camping ($5 per person) and a number of little cozy cabins that can sleep up to six people. They have kitchens with small fridges, microwaves and all needed cooking utensils. The bedrooms are large. This funky place is just five minutes from the beach.

El Tamarindo Golf Course and Resort, *Km 7.5 on the road to Melaque/ Barra de Navidad, www.eltamarindoresort.*

com, ☎ *800-397-0877, $$$$$,* has one of the nicest pools in the area. There are thatched-roof villas with wooden floors and private plunge pools on the decks. The rooms were remodeled in 2001 and each has a telephone, data port, air condition-ing, and wardrobe, as well as a covered terrace, dining area and private garden. Villa rates run be-tween $235 and $670 for two people, per night. This in-cludes the use of all non-motorized sports equipment, the fitness room and the tennis courts. The big draw is the golf course. You will

The interior of a "Jungle" Villa.

be offered a welcoming drink when you arrive and break-fast is included in the price. Despite the luxury, you may find the service a bit lacking. The staff seems disinter-ested in the welfare of their guests when things go wrong.

PLACES TO EAT

Eileen's, ☎ *315-351-5383,* serves a choice of two meals each day at 6:30 pm. Reservations are required. The eat-ing area is on the rooftop of Eileen's house. The day I was here, she served pecan-covered dorado (fish) with pump-kin-seed green sauce and vegetables and rice. The other choice was chicken breasts with lentils and green beans. All meals come with a salad and homemade dressing. The cost for my meal was $12.50, and the cheesecake with mango sauce was an extra $3. The food was excel-lent.

Martin's, *center of town,* is open daily from 8 am-11 pm, but closed on Thursday. This large palapa-hut restau-rant serves things like homemade soup for $2.50 and a Caesar salad big enough for two for $8. The enchiladas, also very good, cost between $5 and $6. The view of the ocean is as good as the food.

Martha's, *near the garden in the center of town,* has the best tacos in Mexico. They are like sandwiches, only you get to put a hundred times more flavors into them. This is a family-run establishment and the owners are friendly. The food is excellent.

Jolandas, *Playa Blanca #43,* ☎ *315-351-5449,* is open Thursday to Monday, 3-10 pm. The bar is open an extra hour at night. This is the funkiest place along the Costalegre (Happy Coast) and also the most popular for dinners with the young surfers.

El Quetzal, *one block from the beach*, is open 8 am-11 pm. Meals such as roast duck or rabbit are highly recommended. The good thing about this café is that it is open for breakfast – with coffee and *huevos rancheros* for about $3.

Palapa Joe's, *Calle Maria Asuncion on the beach*, is open 8 am-9 pm. It's a good place to eat. The food is mainly fish, but the fish is exceptional. Just sitting here and having a beer with the in crowd is fun too.

Barra de Navidad/ Melaque

As is common in Mexico, these two towns are so close together, they are considered the same place. Barra is located on a sand spit that forms the southern end off the bay and separates the bay from the Laguna de Navidad. At the south end of the bay and across from the tip of the spit is the entrance to the lake. Just offshore are Isla de Navidad and San Patricio de Melaque, called simply Melaque. These two islands are good for birding. Isla de Navidad is also a destination for those who love golf and luxury and have lots of cash to fulfill their needs. The island has 1,235 acres of developed land that includes the golf course, two marinas, a tennis ranch, a spa, a night club and a number of private villas and condominiums.

HISTORY

Cortez wrote to Charles V of Spain describing a port along the coast that was strategically well situated. Some believe the port he referred to was Navidad. However, historically, **Francisco de Hijar** is given credit with finding the bay in 1535. He named it Puerto Xalisco.

According to historian Tony Burton, in his book *Western Mexico – A Traveler's Treasury*, the bay was of interest to the Spanish long before Hijar arrived because they had heard rumors that Isla de Navidad was inhabited only by women who had a cache of pearls. Naturally, the Spanish sailors thought they could save the women from their man-less fate by coming to the rescue. When Hijar arrived, he and his men were sadly disappointed. All they found were rebellious locals, most of whom were men.

On December 25, 1540, **Viceroy Don Antonio de Mendoza** arrived to put down Indian uprisings. Because of his arrival date, he renamed the place Navidad, which means "Christmas" in Spanish.

The port became a good naval base for the Spanish. In 1564 they sent an expedition from here to the Philippines under the leadership of Miguel Lopez de Legazpi and Friar Andres de Urdaneta. The expedition was successful and led to the Spanish conquering the Philippine Islands.

Today, the Spanish/Mexicans are still trying to entice men to the area, although they are no longer using the lure of stranded women laden with pearls. They have developed a 27-hole golf course and a luxurious hotel.

SERVICES

Post office, *Calle Nueva Espana, Monday to Friday, 8:30 am-4:30 pm, and Saturday until 1 pm.*

ADVENTURES ON WATER

BEACHES

Playa Principal is the main beach in Barra. It is a bit steep and at the south end near the lagoon, surfers are able to catch a few strong waves. Body surfers and paddlers should be careful here as there is an undertow. Windsurfing is a good sport for this area. Surfboards can be rented in Melaque from the tour office next door to La Paloma Art Studio.

Playa Laguna is the beach beside the jetty. It is small with gentle waves and is good for kayak paddlers. The lake is not good for swimming because the water is stagnant.

SURF TURF

Surfing in the area requires some social etiquette. Some locals are territorial about their place on the beach, so it has become customary to go first with either a tour operator or a local so that you can be introduced to the Mexican surfers. When they see that you are not a threat to their waves, you will be left to surf solo.

Playa Melaque is the beach near the town of the same name. The beach has a steep slope so the waves break close to shore. This area is not good for snorkeling except for a tiny spot at the west end of town that has some calm water.

BUGS BUG OFF!

Mosquito repellent is essential while you travel the Pacific coast. The mangrove swamps that border some beaches and separate them from the mountains are a great breeding place for insects. If you have not brought your own (I recommend Deep Woods Off that is 95% DEET, available in Canada and the US), then **Autan Classic**, manufactured by Bayer de Mexico, is good alternative. It can be purchased at most department stores. Mosquito coils, called **Raid-O-Litos** in Mexico, will also help when sitting at a palapa-hut restaurant or in your room at night. Malaria and dengue fever, spread by mosquitoes, are a problem usually after rainy season only. The incidence of these diseases in Mexico is low. For the *jejenes* (sand fleas), use an oil; **Skin-So-Soft** by Avon is a good one.

ADVENTURES OF THE BRAIN

Amiga's Spanish Lessons in Paradise, *Calle Michoacan #58, between Mazatlan and Veracruz, www.easyspanish. net,* teaches conversational Spanish in private and semi-private classes. Field excursions are included. Their method of teaching has students speaking while doing practical tourist things like bargaining in the market or looking for a room. They also teach slang, a useful part of any language. Lessons are available from November to April and cost $15 an hour for private lessons, $12 an hour for semi-private and $7.50 an hour for group lessons with three to six students.

OUTFITTERS/TOUR OPERATORS

Sea to Sierra Outdoor Adventures, *Ejidatarios #4, Barra de Navidad,* ☎ *315-355-7140, www.seatosierra. com,* offers bike tours to places like Tenacatita, El Tecuan, Boca de Iguanas, Las Joyas, Colimilla on Isla Navidad and Cihuatlan. Their bikes have front-end suspension and are in good shape and the beers served after a ride are cold. Sea to Sierra specializes in safe, off-road biking and tours from two to six hours a day. Most tours are vehicle-assisted (if you conk out, you can ride in a car). Helmets, water and bikes are included in the price of about $100 per day. Beer is a little extra. The company also runs horseback riding trips that cost between $20 and $25 per hour, depending on how many people ride. The minimum is two people for two hours.

South Swell Surf Shop, *16A Benito Juarez, Melaque,* ☎ *314-872-2457 (cell), is open 8 am-7 pm daily.* South Swell rents snorkeling and surfing equipment and also offers surfing lessons in English or Spanish. They run $10 per hour, plus the cost of the board. To rent the boards without lessons costs $12.50-$20 a day or $8-$10 for a half-day, depending on the type of board you use. Snorkeling sets rent for $9-$10 per day and boogie boards are the same price. They run guided trips to other beaches for $50 a day, plus the cost of gasoline. This shop keeps up to date on water and wave conditions for surfers.

Fishing guide **Alfredo Molinas**, ☎ *315-355-6049,* is good. Call him and make an appointment. He knows where the fish are located.

PLACES TO STAY

There are hundreds of places between Barra and Melaque. Some are basic; others, like the one on the island, are beyond the financial reach of most of us.

■ IN BARRA

Hotel Caribe, *Calle Sonora,* ☎ *315-355-5952, $,* has very basic clean rooms and a nice sitting area on the porch as well as a rooftop patio.

The Sands, *Morelos #24,* ☎ *315-355-5018, $$,* has been a popular spot with travelers for years because of its nice

HOTEL PRICE SCALE	
Room price, in US $	
$ . . . . up to $20	
$$ . . . . $21-$50	
$$$ $51-100	
$$$$ . . . . $101-$150	
$$$$$ $151-200	

pool and well-kept gardens that feature caged monkeys. The rooms all have private bathrooms, fans, tiled floors, wooden-framed windows and tasteful furnishings. Breakfast is included in the rate. The hotel has the lagoon on one side, the ocean on the other and a pool with a bar at one end. The disco, which at one time kept guests awake, has now closed.

Hotel Delfin, *Morelos #23, http://hoteldelfinmx.com,* ☎ *315-355-5068, $$,* is on the lakeside of the spit and across from the Sands Hotel. This is a fairly large place with arched open hallways overlooking the street. It is clean and the big rooms each have a private bathroom. The disco down the street that at one time was a bother has been closed due to popular demand.

Posada Pacifico, *Mazatlan #136,* ☎ *315-355-5359, $$,* is a motel-style place with rooms on two floors located around a central courtyard. Each large room has a private bathroom and ceiling fan.

Casa de Don Ramon, *Del Galeon,* ☎ *315-355-6114, www.pathcom.com/~msclarke, $$,* is next to the harbor master's office and is recognized by its yellow and red wall surrounded by red bougainvilleas. If you like flowers, this is a good place. Each of the five rooms has a screened window, a fan and air conditioning, and a private bathroom. Guests have access to a communal patio and a kitchen equipped for light meals.

Casa de Marco, *Miguel Lopez de Legazpi #60,* ☎ *315-355-6091, www.casademarco.com, $$$,* has one- and two-bedroom apartments for rent by the week; one is wheelchair-accessible. Located close to the beach, the hotel also has a pool. The kitchens have a fridge, a microwave, a toaster, a blender, a coffee maker, an iron and pots, pans and dishes. There is also cable TV, a stereo CD player and an in-wall safe. There is a balcony for each suite. This clean spot is an excellent choice for those who want to stay in Barra for awhile.

Bungalows Mar Vida, *Mazatlan # 168,* ☎ *315-355-5911, $$$,* has five air-conditioned bungalows with kitchenettes, private bathrooms and hot water. There is a pool on site. The hotel is very clean and safe.

Casa Chips, *198 Miguel Lopes de la Gaspi,* ☎ *315-355-5555, www.casachips.com, $$$/$$$$,* is a beachfront hotel that has been operating for more than 10 years. It has seven rooms, each with ceiling fan, two queen-sized beds, small fridge, private bathroom and arched windows facing the street or the ocean. There is also a full apartment, a studio and a sunset suite for rent. Some suites have a balcony. The comfort level and tasteful décor of these places is commendable. The hotel's beachside café offers barbequed ribs for $8 per serving on Tuesday. It's open 9 am-9 pm.

Hotel Cabo Blanco, *Bahia de las Navidades #3,* ☎ *315-355-5170, $$$$,* has 83 rooms and is the most luxurious hotel in town (excluding the Grand Bay Isla Navidad hotel). It is set on the canal and is a bit of a walk from the beach. The rooms are small, but there is a pool with a bar, and a children's playground. This hotel, because of its location, likes to offer an all-inclusive package. Most people who have stayed here are happy with what they got.

■ IN MELAQUE

Although most people stay in Barra, Melaque is just two miles up the road.

Hotel de la Costa, *Calle Ignacio Vallarta # 19,* ☎ *315-355-5126, $$,* has 20 rooms in a clean place without frills.

El Palmar Beach and Tennis Resort, *Calle Esmeralda and Zafiro, across from the Bungalows Pacifico in the Obregón section of town,* ☎ *315-355-6263, $$$,* has a nice pool and garden, plus tennis courts where you can meet and challenge other players. The rooms have two beds, purified water, very large bathrooms, tiled floors and apartment-size fridges. One- and two-bedroom apartments are available, too.

Attractive **Hotel Club Nautico**, *Gomez Farias # 315*, ☎ *315-355-5770, $$$,* has 56 rooms with air conditioning, fan, balcony, cable TV and telephone. There's a small pool and a restaurant, El Dorado. English is spoken.

Hotel Monterrey, *Calle Gomez Farias # 27,* ☎ *315-355-5004, $$$,* is near the bus station and a good choice if you have arrived by bus and don't want to search too far for a place to stay. It is an attractive hotel with an enclosed courtyard. The 22 rooms are moderate in size and have private bathrooms and fans. There is a restaurant, bar, off-street parking and a pool. Two bungalows with kitchenettes are available. The hotel is near the beach.

■ ISLA DE NAVIDAD

The Grand Bay Isla Navidad Hotel, ☎ *315-331-0500, www.wyndhamvacations.com*, costs between $520 and $600 a night for a golf/room package. This includes your room, your game and breakfast for two people. You can also stay for a mere $380 a night without the golf game. There is no extra charge for up to two children under the age of 10. Visit their website to learn about other package vacations.

The hotel has 200 rooms with private balconies overlooking the bay or out to the mountains. They feature tasteful décor, air conditioning and ceiling fans, tiled floors and muted fabrics. The bathrooms are all marble and there are in-room safes. Bathrobes are supplied and hypo-allergenic bedding is available. Each room has cable TV, coffee maker, fridge, hair dryer and iron. A plate of fresh fruit and bottled water is delivered daily. The place is gargantuan and oozes sexuality.

There are three tennis courts, a workout room, putting green, private marina, three swimming pools, a bar, a restaurant and a private beach. The childcare facilities have skilled workers who are able to entertain the kids for hours. Travel around the island is complimentary, as are daily newspapers. You are welcomed by a doorman, and photo ID and a credit card are required upon check-in for any extras. The lobby bar has a view of the beach and lake, and live music most nights.

All your food needs will be fulfilled. The Grand Café is a casual restaurant that serves meals either inside or on the terrace. There is a swim-up bar in the main pool, a sandwich and beer restaurant beside the pool and Antonio's, a formal dining room featuring Continental cuisine and Mexican seafood dishes. Take your pick from over 200 brands of tequila. The décor includes original paintings by well-known artists.

If the hotel is not upscale enough for you, there are some villas available. The smallest, called the **Albatros**, undoubtedly named because of its size, just 8,600 square feet/800 square meters. There are three bedrooms, a kitchen, living room, a palapa-roofed hut beside the small pool and a two-car garage. The other villas go up to 13,450 square feet/1,250 meters in size. Inquire for rates.

The Meson Doña Paz is a tri-level mansion where guests can stay in rooms if they don't want a villa or the expanse of the large hotel. It has a restaurant, two cocktail bars, a pool with bar, a whirlpool, an exercise room and a tennis court.

The **golf course** is a par 72, 27-hole course designed by Robert Von Hagge. It offers views of the ocean, the mountains and the lagoon and is tucked between the hill on the island called Cerro del Caracol and the marina. The huge clubhouse has a bar, a restaurant and a pro shop that offers instruction for a fee. It is built in colonial style, with terra cotta tiles to contrast the polished marble. The bathrooms are segregated and include showers, sauna and a Jacuzzi. Guests can have Turkish baths and massages, or work out in the gym. Non-guests pay $260 each to play a round. Rental clubs are $50, gloves are $20, and a caddy is mandatory.

If you are interested in staying on the island, contact Hotel Operator and Reservations, *Ruben Dario 1262, Colonia Providencia, 44630 Guadalajara, Jalisco, Mexico,*

☎ *333-641-5326 or 800-849-2373 in Mexico City*, for general information.

PLACES TO EAT

IN BARRA

Casa Chips, *Miguel # 198*, ☎ *315-355-5555,* is open 9 am-9 pm daily. This is a beachside café that has snacks and drinks all day. On Tuesdays it offers barbequed ribs for $8 per serving. This is a popular meal; if you want to be guaranteed a dish, make reservations.

Cenadura Esperanza, *Av Veracrus, no phone*, has Chinese food that is always such a treat after a steady diet of rice and beans or chicken. The stir-fried vegetables are highly recommended. The cost is under $5 per serving.

Mar y Tierra, *Av Lopez de Legazpi, no phone,* at the east end of town is where to go when you want a Mexican meal or a hamburger served with a special flare. Meals cost under $8.

Restaurant Ambar, *Av Veracruz # 101A,* is open 5 pm-midnight. The upstairs restaurant serves French cuisine and crêpes. Even if you don't want to do a whole delicious meal here, come for an after-dinner drink and a crêpe.

Popeye's Restaurant, *Av Miguel Lopez de Legazpi #44, no phone,* is on the beach at the point where the *malecón* starts. Their specialty is seafood, and they offer a fantastic avocado and shrimp salad. Shrimp wrapped in bacon and stuffed with cheese is another favorite. Prices are high, $10+ for a meal.

Panchoz Restaurant, *Av Miguel Lopez de Legazpi # 53,* ☎ *315-355-5176,* has some long-resident parrots to entertain you while you eat. Panchoz' specialty is ceviche, a pickled fish dish that is super as an appetizer or as a main meal. The fish is "cooked" in lime juice and the tartness is especially good if you are thirsty. The cost is $5-$10 for a dish.

Mr Crocodile Lucky, *Calle Morelos #26,* ☎ *315-355-8205,* open Tuesday to Sunday noon – midnight, is the place to go for Italian dishes. Pizza, spaghetti and lasagna are all recommended along with a cool beer. Meals cost less than $10.

Café and Jugos Manhattan, *Calle Lopez de Legazpi,* opens every day at 7:30 am and closes at 3 pm. It is inside the Alondra Hotel, which was still not open when I was there. However, some shops inside were doing business. Breakfast coffee is a specialty of the Manhattan, but the carrot cake for under $3 a slice is also worth your time.

■ IN MELAQUE

It is often nice to walk to this village for a meal. You get a change of scenery and can share your presence (and dollars).

The Alcatraz, *Av. Lopez Mateos (upstairs) near the trailer park at the east end of the street, no phone.* Try their Chicken Alcatraz – onions, green peppers and chicken served in a hot-pot. This is one of the most popular restaurants in Melaque.

Highly recommended **Pedro's Fish and Chips**, *Alejandrina # 38,* has garlic and Cajun shrimp, both hot and delicious. They are open only for supper, 5-9 pm every day except Sunday. Meals cost about $8.

NIGHTLIFE

Terraza Bar Capri, *Av Miguel Lopez de Legazpi # 119, Barra de Navidad*, is open 2pm-2 am. Their happy hour runs from 6-9 pm daily. There are pool tables, a nice dance floor and recorded music.

Club Felix, *Calle Jalisco #48, Barre de Navidad,* has tables inside and outside on the street. This is a popular meeting place where you can have a peaceful drink and talk. However, the benches don't have backs, so you may want to sit inside where there are chairs.

Appendix

RECOMMENDED READING

NATURE

Where to Find Birds in San Blas, by Soalind Novick and Lan Sing Wu, is available by mail (178 Myrtle Court Arcata, CA 95521, US $4.50).

Where to Watch Birds in Mexico, Steve Howell, A&C Black Publishers, 1999. Covers 100 sites and about 1,000 species.

Guide to the Birds of Mexico and Northern Central America, Steve Howell, Oxford Press, 1995. Describes 1,070 species and covers Mexico and Central America down to northern Nicaragua. The guide features 71 color plates, plus maps.

Chasing Monarchs: Migrating with the Butterflies of Passage, Dr. Robert Michael Pyle, Houghton-Mifflin, 2001.

HISTORY

Heroic Defense of Mezcala Island, by Alberto Santoscoy is available as an e-book at www.epmassoc.com/catalog/175php?sp=3. If this link is broken, type in the book title in your search engine to find another link. The book is an account of the fight between the people living on Mezcala Island and the Spanish.

GLOSSARY

■ THE CALENDAR

dia . . . . day
semana . . . . week
mes . . . . month
año . . . . year
domingo . . . . Sunday
lunes . . . . Monday
martes . . . . Tuesday
miercoles . . . . Wednesday
jueves . . . . Thursday
viernes . . . . Friday
sabado . . . . Saturday
enero . . . . January
febrero . . . . February
marzo . . . . March
abril . . . . April
mayo . . . . May
junio . . . . June
julio . . . . July
agosto . . . . August
septiembre . . . . September
octubre . . . . October
noviembre . . . . November
diciembre . . . . December

■ NUMBERS

uno . . . . one
dos . . . . two
tres . . . . three
cuatro . . . . four
cinco . . . . five
seis . . . . six
siete . . . . seven
ocho . . . . eight
nueve . . . . nine
diez . . . . ten
once . . . . eleven
doce . . . . twelve
trece . . . . thirteen
catorce . . . . fourteen

quince . . . . fifteen
dieciséis . . . . sixteen
diecisiete. . . . . seventeen
dieciocho. . . . . eighteen
diecinueve . . . . nineteen
veinte. . . . . twenty
veintiuno. twenty-one
veintidós . . . . twenty-two
treinta . . . . thirty
cuarenta . . . . forty
cincuenta . . . . fifty
sesenta . . . . sixty
setenta . . . . seventy
ochenta. . . . . eighty
noventa . . . . ninety
cien. . . . . hundred
ciento uno. . . . . one hundred one
doscientos . . . . two hundred
quinientos. . . . . five hundred
mil . . . . one thousand
mil uno . . . . one thousand one
dos mil . . . . two thousand
millón . . . . one million
primero . . . . first
segundo . . . . second
tercero . . . . third
último. . . . . last

■ CONVERSATION

¿Como esta?. . . . . How are you?
¿Bien, gracias, y usted? . . . . . Well, thanks, and you?
¿Que pasa? . . . . What's happening?
Buenas dias. . . . . Good morning.
Buenas tardes.. . . . . Good afternoon.
Buenas noches.. . . . . Good evening/night.
Nos vemos. . . . . See you again.
¡Buena suerte! . . . . Good luck!
Adios. . . . . Goodbye.
Que la vaya bien . . . . . Goodbye (for someone special)
Mucho gusto. . . . . Glad to meet you.
Felicidades. . . . . Congratulations.
Feliz compleaños. . . . . Happy birthday.
Feliz Navidad. . . . . Merry Christmas.

Feliz Año Nuevo. . . . . Happy New Year.
Gracias. . . . . Thank you.
Por favor. . . . . Please.
De nada/con mucho gusto. . . . . You're welcome.
Perdoneme. . . . . Pardon me (bumping into someone).
Permitame . Pardon me (passing in front of someone).
Desculpe . . . . Excuse me (interrupting conversation).
¿Como se dice esto? . . . . What do you call this?
Lo siento. . . . . I'm sorry.
Quiero... . . . . I want/I like...
Adelante. . . . . Come in.
Permitame presentarle... . . . . May I introduce...
¿Como se nombre? . . . . What is your name?
Me nombre es... . . . . My name is...
No se. . . . . I don't know.
Tengo sed. . . . . I am thirsty.
Tengo hambre. . . . . I am hungry.
Soy gringa/gringo . . I am an American (female/male).
¿Donde hay...? . . . . Where is there/are there...?
Hay... . . . . There is/are
No hay . . . . There is none
¿Que es esto? . . . . What is this?
¿Habla ingles? . . . . Do you speak English?
¿Hablan ingles? . . . Does anyone here speak English?
Hablo/entiendo un poco . . . . . . I speak/understand
  Español . . . . a little Spanish.
Le entiendo.. . . . . I understand you.
No entiendo. . . . . I don't understand.
Hable mas despacio por favor. . . Please speak slowly.
Repita por favor. . . . . Please repeat.
¿Tiene...?. . . . . Do you have...?
Tengo... . . . . I have...
Hecho... . . . . I make/made
¿Puedo? . . . . Can I?
¿Permite me? . . . . May I?
La cuenta por favor . . . . The bill, please.
bolsa. . . . . bag
muchila. . . . . backpack

■ TIME

¿Que hora es? . . . . What time is it?
Son las... . . . . It is...
... cinco. . . . . five o'clock.

... ocho y diez. . . . . ten past eight.
... seis y cuarto. . . . . quarter past six.
... cinco y media. . . . . half past five.
... siete y menos cinco. . . . . five of seven.
antes de ayer. . . . . the day before yesterday.
anoche. . . . . yesterday evening.
esta mañana. . . . . this morning.
a mediodia. . . . . at noon.
en la noche. . . . . in the evening.
de noche. . . . . at night.
mañana en la mañana. . . . . tomorrow morning.
mañana en la noche. . . . . tomorrow evening.

■ DIRECTIONS

Llevame alla ... por favor. . . . . . Take me there please.
¿Cual es el mejor camino para...? . . Which is the best
. . . . road to...?
Derecha. . . . . Right.
Izquierda. . . . . Left.
Derecho/directo. . . . . Straight ahead.
¿A que distancia estamos de...? . . . How far is it to...?
¿Es este el camino a...?. . . . . Is this the road to...?
¿Es cerca? . . . . Is it near?
¿Es largo? . . . . Is it a long way?
¿Donde hay...? . . . . Where is... ?
... el telefono. . . . . the telephone.
... el baño. . . . . the bathroom.
... el correos. . . . . the post office.
... el banco. the bank.
...casa de cambio. . . . . the money exchange office.
... estacion del policia. . . . . the police station.

■ ACCOMMODATIONS

¿Que quiere? . . . . What do you want?
Quiero un hotel... . . . . I want a hotel that's...
... buena. . . . . good.
... barato. . . . . cheap.
... limpio. . . . . clean.
¿Dónde hay un hotel buena? . . Where is a good hotel?
¿Hay habitaciones libres? . . . . . . Do you have rooms?
¿Dónde están los baños/servicios?. . . . Where are the
. . . . bathrooms?
Quiero un habitacion . . . . I would like a room.
habitacion sencillo. . . . . single room.

habitacion con baño privado. . . . room with a private
. . . . bath.
habitacion doble. . . . . double room.
baño comun . . . . without a private bath / shared bath
ducha . . . . shower
¿Esta incluido? . . . . Is that included?
¿Puedo verlo? . . . . May I see it?
cama . . . . bed
cama matrimonial . . . . double bed
¿Algo mas? . . . . Anything more?
¿Cuanto cuesta?. . . . . How much?
¡Es muy caro! . . . . It's too expensive!

■ FOOD

comer . . . . to eat
pan . . . . bread
carne . . . . meat
papas . . . . potatoes
leche . . . . milk
frutas . . . . fruit
jugo . . . . juice
huevos. . . . . eggs
mantequilla . . . . butter
queso. . . . . cheese
agua mineral . . . . mineral water
cerveza . . . . beer
pescado . . . . fish
helado . . . . ice cream
arroz. . . . . rice
ensalada . . . . salad
jamon . . . . ham
pollo. . . . . chicken
toronja . . . . grapefruit
naranja. . . . . orange (the fruit)
mariscos. . . . . seafood
sopa . . . . soup
vino tinto . . . . red wine
vino blanco. . . . . white wine

CONSULATES

■ AMERICAN

Acapulco, Hotel Continental Plaza, ☎ 744-484-0300 or 485-7207. Call only for specific emergencies.

Hermosillo, Edificio Sonora, Planta Baja, ☎ 662-217-2375, Monday to Friday, 9 am-5 pm.

Mazatlan, Playa Gaviotas #202, across from Hotel Playa Mazatlan, ☎ 669-916-5889, Monday to Friday, 8 am-4 pm.

Nogales, Calle Campillo, Edificio del Estado, 2nd Piso, ☎ 631-913-4820, Monday to Friday, 8 am-4:30 pm.

Puerto Vallarta, Zaragoza #160, Vallarta Plaza, ☎ 322-222-0069, Monday to Friday, 10 am-2 pm.

■ AUSTRIAN

Acapulco, Calle de Juan R. Escudero #1, 1st floor, ☎ 744-482-5551, Monday to Friday, 9 am-noon.

■ AUSTRALIAN

Mexico City, Ruben Dario #55, Col. Polanco, ☎ 555-101-2200, Monday-Thursday, 8:30 am to 5:15 pm; Friday, 8:30 am-2:15 pm.

■ BRITISH

Acapulco, Costera Miguel Aleman, ☎ 744-484-1735. This is an honorary consulate, so calling to make an appointment is necessary.

Mexico City, Lerma 71, Col. Cuauhtemoc, ☎ 555-242-8500, Monday-Thursday, 8 am-4 pm; Friday, 8 am-1:30 pm.

■ CANADIAN

Acapulco, Centro Comercial Marbella, ☎ 744-484-1306, Monday to Friday, 9 am-5 pm.

Mazatlan, Playa Gaviotas, # 202, ☎ 669-913-7320, Monday to Friday, 9 am-1 pm.

Appendix

Puerto Vallarta, Zaragoza #160, Vallarta Plaza, ☎ 322-222-5398, Monday to Friday, 1-4 pm.

FINNISH

Mexico City, Monte Pelvoux 111, 4th floor, Lomas de Chapultepec, ☎ 555-540-6036. Call for hours.

FRENCH

Mexico City, Lafontaine 32, Col. Polanco, ☎ 555-171-9840, Monday to Friday, 9 am-noon and 3:30-6:30 pm.

GERMAN

Mexico City, Lord Byron #737, Col. Polanco, ☎ 555-283-2200, Monday to Thursday, 7:30 am-3:30 pm; Friday, 7:30 am-3 pm.

ITALIAN

Acapulco, Gran Via Tropical #615-B, ☎ 744-481-2533. Call for hours.

Mexico City, Paseo de las Palmas, ☎ 555-596-3655. Call for hours.

JAPANESE

Mexico City, Paseo de la Reforma #295, 3rd floor, Col. Cuauhtemoc, ☎ 555-202-7900. Call for hours.

NEW ZEALAND

Mexico City, José Luis Lagrange #103, 10th floor, Col. Los Morales, ☎ 555-283-9460, Monday to Thursday, 8 am-4 pm; Friday, 8 am-1:30 pm.

SWISS

Mexico City, Torre Optima, Av. De las Palamas #405, Col. Lomas de Chapultepec, ☎ 555-853-5520, Monday to Friday, 9 am-noon.

Index